Leisure and Tourism
for Intermediate GNVQ

second edition

Tony Outhart
Lindsey Taylor

Series editor: Tony Outhart

D0452646

Published by HarperCollins *Publishers* Limited
77–85 Fulham Palace Road
Hammersmith
London
W6 8JB

www.**Collins**Education.com
On-line support for schools and colleges

First published 2000
Reprinted 2000 (twice)

ISBN 0 00 329111 1

Tony Outhart and Lindsey Taylor assert the moral right to be identified as the authors of this work.

British Cataloguing in Publication Data
A cataloguing record for this publication is available from the British Library

Almost all the case studies in this book are factual. The accompanying images are for aesthetic purposes only and are not intended to represent or identify any existing person, location or subject. The publishers cannot accept any responsibility for any consequences resulting from this use, except as expressly provided by law.

Series commissioned by Charis Evans
Edited and typeset by DSM Partnership
Cover designed by Patricia Briggs
Cover picture by Tony Stone
Pictures by Helen Evans
Project managed by Kay Wright
Production by Emma Lloyd-Jones
Printed and bound by Scotprint

www.**fire**and**water**.co.uk
The book lover's website

Contents

Acknowledgements

We would like to thank Charis and Kay for their invaluable advice and Peter Carr for reading the draft manuscripts and giving his support and guidance in the development of the text.

Tony Outhart and Lindsey Taylor

Thanks to Gill, Katy and Megan for their support.

Tony Outhart

My grateful thanks to Nick, Lucy and Alice for their patience and support and to Sharon for her morale-boosting e-mails.

Lindsey Taylor

Introduction

Leisure and Tourism for Intermediate GNVQ is specially written for everyone starting a GNVQ Leisure and Tourism course from September 2000. The popular first edition was published in 1995. This second edition book builds upon its strengths with a wealth of up-to-date content, new activities and a fresh, accessible design for GNVQ 2000. Like the first edition, we hope you find this book, and its approach to GNVQ, a strong basis for success.

This activity-centred book includes a general introduction to GNVQ, with full coverage of the three compulsory units, structured activities, case studies and summary sections to reinforce your learning. We've added a listing of some of the most useful websites for Intermediate GNVQ Leisure and Tourism students to help you with the information-seeking aspects of the course.

Before you begin your course, it is worth thinking about what makes GNVQ different from GCSE courses, and the type of things that you will learn through doing it.

What is GNVQ?

The letters GNVQ stand for General National Vocational Qualification.

- **General** because GNVQ courses provide a broad-based vocational education focused on a particular area of work, such as the leisure and tourism industries.
- **National** because the GNVQ is based on national standards. These were introduced in 1992 and revised in 1995 and 2000. GNVQs are nationally available in schools and colleges.
- **Vocational Qualification** because GNVQ relates directly to the world of work. This is one of the biggest differences between GNVQ and GCSE. GCSEs are based on knowledge and understanding of academic subjects; GNVQs are based on the knowledge, skills and understanding that are needed in a particular industry or area of work.

What will I learn on this course?

Through practical investigation, Intermediate GNVQ Leisure and Tourism gives you the opportunity to develop your skills, knowledge and understanding of the ways in which the leisure and tourism industries work to meet people's demands for using their leisure time. It will help you to explore the importance of marketing and customer service within the industry. This GNVQ can be the basis for further education or for entering a job in the field of leisure and tourism.

Much of what you will learn about leisure and tourism for your GNVQ course will be through your own practical investigations. You will plan and carry out your own enquiries, often in connection with assignments agreed with your teacher. These investigations may include:

- visiting workplaces and talking to the people who work there
- hearing about the experience of local employers and business people during interviews and arranged visits and from speakers coming to your school or college
- carrying out research in libraries
- conducting surveys into people's activities, preferences and opinions
- using case studies and undertaking role plays to gain more insight into leisure and tourism
- studying company brochures and published reports in the press
- work experience with a local employer.

Overall, you will actively investigate the world of leisure and tourism. You will present your findings in various ways, including giving talks and presentations – two skills that will be essential in your working life.

What do I need to do to complete an Intermediate GNVQ?

To gain your Intermediate GNVQ Leisure and Tourism you will need to complete the three compulsory units covered in this book. Unless you are a Part One student, you will also need to complete three optional units. Your teacher will advise you about the optional units available to you. These optional units are not covered in this book, although you will find the information contained in the compulsory units a useful foundation for your optional unit work.

What is Part One GNVQ?

Part One is the name given to the Foundation and Intermediate GNVQs that pupils aged 14–16 can study at school. Part One GNVQ students study only the three compulsory units covered in this book, and not the three optional units needed to complete the full six-unit Intermediate GNVQ award in Leisure and Tourism.

What is the portfolio?

Part of your GNVQ assessment (see page ix) will be based on the portfolio of evidence that you will collect. The portfolio will be an important part of your assessment for the course as it shows that you have developed the skills and acquired the knowledge required to pass the GNVQ. Your portfolio has to be carefully planned, maintained, organised and indexed, so it requires your special and regular attention. The evidence that you collect for your portfolio can take many forms, including:

- **written work** – for example, notes that you have taken from a book, lecture or interview, a brief report, a detailed plan of a campaign or an example of a service provided
- **witness statements** – for example, written evidence of your skills and understanding provided by your teacher or some other person (perhaps an employer) who has watched you taking part in a discussion, dealing with a customer, or making a presentation
- **presentations, group discussions and role plays** – suggestions for discussions and scenarios for role plays are given throughout the book
- **other evidence** – for example, letters, photographs, certificates or video or audio recordings which demonstrate that you have done other, relevant work.

How will this book help me with my GNVQ course?

The content, structure and features of *Leisure and Tourism for Intermediate GNVQ* are designed to help you to get the most out of your course. The content directly matches all the underpinning knowledge that you will need to understand the compulsory units. The units in this book are organised into sections to make them easier to follow. Each section is packed with information, questions and activities to help you learn in an active and stimulating way. You can identify each section by looking at the top corner of every right hand page.

The special features include activities, case studies, webstracts and questions which will help you to develop your understanding of what you have been reading and to apply it to your own experience. You will be able to complete many of the activities in class, sometimes by working with other people.

Some activities involve investigations outside the classroom. Some activities will ask you to analyse case studies, figures and documents that you will find in this book. Whatever the type of activity, you will be given clear instructions on what to do.

The special features in the book are indicated by individual icons, as shown here.

Build your learning

Each section throughout the book ends with a brief summary that highlights the key points, words and phrases that you have covered. Key words and phrases are also highlighted in the index at the back of this book. For example, look up 'target markets' in the index.

Summary activity

As you complete a section within each unit there is a summary activity. These are bigger than the activities and case studies that appear throughout the section and can include some useful opportunities for you to generate evidence for your portfolio assessments. As you work through the course, your teacher will tell you when you can use the summary activities to work towards your final assessment.

Unit assessment

You will find assessments on pages 86 and 232 for two of the three compulsory units. These are based on the assessment criteria that you are required to meet in order to pass your GNVQ course. You are also given tips and suggestions on where to find information that will help you complete these assessments. Check with your teacher before starting any assessment work that will contribute to your portfolio of evidence. There is no portfolio assessment for unit 2 as this will be provided by the awarding body.

PORTFOLIO ASSESSMENT

Key skills

You may also gain credit for key skills through doing your GNVQ course. Your teacher will advise you about the key skills available and how to achieve them. Opportunities to cover key skills are signposted in the unit assessment.

Jobs in leisure and tourism

This additional section provides you with useful information about careers and jobs in the leisure and tourism industries, and how to apply for them.

Internet directory

There is a massive amount of information about leisure and tourism available on the internet. This section provides you with a mini-directory of useful internet websites, listed in alphabetical order, to help you with your research.

Good luck with your course!

Credits

The authors and publisher would like to thank the following for permission to reproduce photographs and other material:

Action Images (p. 131)
adidas (p. 109)
Allsport, Gray Mortimore (p. 121)
Alton Towers (p. 97)
Barclays Bank plc (p. 162)
Barking Dog Art (p. 18)
Bethan Matthews (p. 205)
Britannia Airways (pp. 218, 219)
British Airways (p. 63)
British Tourist Authority (p. 111)
Center Parcs (p. 57)
Daniel Betts (pp. 191, 215)
Design Storm (p. 79)
easyJet (pp. 64, 65)
English Tourism Council (p. 53)
Essex County Council tourism section© (p. 60)
Eurostar (p. 63)
Forte Hotels (p. 54)
Going Places (p. 48)
Guide Friday (pp. 52, 109)
John Birdsall (pp. 128, 209, 234–5 lower)
Jorvik Viking Centre (p. 113)
Lunn Poly (p. 48)
Madame Tussaud's (p. 96)
McDonald's (p. 139)
Merlin Entertainments (pp. 97, 98)
Merseyside Tourist Board (p. 62)
Mike Williams Photo Library (p. 34)
National Express (p. 63)
National Space Science Centre (p. 109)
Natural History Museum (p. 42)
O_2 (p. 80)
P&O (p. 63)
PGL Travel Ltd (pp. 39, 177)
Pizza Hut (p. 58)
Planet Hollywood (p. 109)
Rank Group (p. 73)

Sally & Richard Greenhill Photo Library (pp. 189, 197, 234–5 upper)
Telegraph Colour Library (pp. 88–9, 102, 149, 170–1, 174, 197, 198, 211, 234, 235)
TGI Fridays (p. 58)
The Countryside Agency (p. 35)
The Dome, Doncaster (pp. 2–3, 20, 21)
The Guild of Registered Tourist Guides (p. 176)
The National Trust (pp. 158, 160)
The National Trust Photographic Library (pp. 158–9)
The National Trust, Killerton House (p. 163)
Thomas Cook (p. 48)
Travel Training Company (p. 238)
United Cinemas International (UK) Ltd (p. 26)
Virgin Enterprises Ltd (p. 63)
Virgin Group (p. 187)
Warner Village Cinemas (pp. 25, 26)
West Country Tourist Board (p. 41)
Woking Leisure (p. 83)
Yellow Pages (p. 22)

Every effort has been made to contact copyright holders, but if any have been inadvertently overlooked, the publishers will be pleased to make the necessary arrangements at the first opportunity.

Investigating leisure and tourism 1

This unit helps you understand the important part that leisure and tourism plays in today's society.

You will learn that the leisure and tourism industries are made up of many different facilities and organisations, from leisure centres and theatres to travel agents and airlines. You will consider how the leisure and tourism industries are linked and how businesses work together to offer visitors a good service. After completing the unit, you should have a good overview of the components of the industries, the products and services they offer, the role of the public, private and voluntary sectors, and the links between them.

You will also investigate the leisure and tourism industries in a chosen area. You will gather information on facilities in the area and match them to the key components of the leisure and tourism industries.

This unit provides a solid basis for the more detailed study of the leisure and tourism industries that you will carry out through other parts of your GNVQ.

Introduction to the leisure and tourism industries

The leisure and tourism industries are very large and varied, and nearly everybody makes use of them at some time. They include a wide range of activities, organisations, facilities and events in a large number of places. In order to begin to understand this variety, it is helpful to understand some of the terms that are used.

Leisure

Leisure can be defined as:

> the opportunity available to an individual after completing the immediate necessities of life, when he or she has the freedom to choose, and engage in, an experience which is expected to be personally satisfying.

The meaning of leisure

What do you think are the key words and phrases in the definition of leisure? With a classmate, identify and discuss each of them. For example, what are 'the immediate necessities of life'?

Each individual decides his or her own leisure needs, so leisure activities vary according to personal preferences. What one person may enjoy, another may loathe! Leisure activities may be active (such as taking part in sports) or passive (such as reading) or a combination of both. They may take place in the home (for example, watching television, listening to music) or elsewhere (for example, eating out, going to the pub). The list of things that people do in their free time is almost endless.

Many factors influence people's leisure needs and choice of activities, including their age, sex, family situation, where they live, their friends, income, job, traditions, culture and religion; and because there is such a variety of preferences and types of customer, the leisure and tourism industries provide a very broad range of products to their customers.

These **products** may be goods or services or a combination of both. **Goods** are things which can be seen, touched, and perhaps taken away. They are objects such as souvenirs, exercise bikes or computer games. **Services** cannot be seen or touched but are the skills or information which can be provided by trained people, such as sports coaches, travel agents, concert organisers and caterers.

Many leisure services are provided in what is called a **facility**. This might be a building with specialised equipment, such as a cinema, a leisure centre or a heritage centre. It might, on the other hand, be a natural feature of the landscape, such as a lake which provides the opportunity for wind-surfing, or a Scottish mountain suitable for skiing.

Goods and services are made available by many providers, from individuals and small local companies to local councils and the government and international corporations.

Taking all these terms together, we can say, for example, that a football club (the provider) offers its supporters (the customers) a seat (a service) at a match (an event) in a stadium (a facility) and sells them a souvenir programme (a good).

> What are the differences between goods and services?

ACTIVITY

Word search

Look at the word search box. There are 12 types of leisure activity, pastime or facility hidden in the box. Find each one and make a list of them.

We have highlighted one answer in red to get you started. (The answers are on page 262.)

V	J	E	A	T	N	G	O	T	T	R	E	L	P	W	L
L	R	O	S	T	E	N	I	N	G	E	A	E	M	A	I
E	I	R	E	S	T	A	U	R	A	N	T	I	E	T	T
I	L	S	H	C	P	B	R	C	R	D	I	S	E	C	C
S	G	C	T	A	I	U	A	E	E	L	N	U	T	H	O
U	L	E	I	E	S	N	D	N	S	S	G	R	I	I	M
R	E	A	D	I	N	G	G	T	T	G	O	T	N	N	P
E	D	I	Q	E	S	I	T	R	A	P	U	W	G	G	U
C	Q	P	L	B	L	O	N	M	S	U	T	A	F	T	T
E	V	O	U	U	N	I	N	G	I	N	G	T	R	E	E
N	P	U	X	B	V	R	N	Z	T	M	A	C	I	L	R
T	C	E	N	T	R	I	H	P	X	O	M	H	E	E	G
R	L	I	S	T	Y	L	C	I	N	E	M	A	N	V	A
E	K	H	M	A	L	T	C	H	I	N	T	U	D	I	M
P	F	N	L	I	B	R	A	R	Y	O	Y	C	S	S	E
U	O	P	C	I	N	E	L	A	R	Y	Y	E	E	I	S
E	P	D	X	L	Y	J	T	I	O	L	E	V	V	O	C
G	R	E	G	A	M	E	V	S	I	N	G	E	A	N	O

ACTIVITY

Leisure time activities

Draw up a table (like the one below) to illustrate your leisure time activities. First, list all your interests, hobbies, pastimes and sports undertaken in your 'free time'. Some will occur more often than others and you should identify whether they are:

- regular (for example, once a week)
- occasional (for example, once a month)
- rare (for example, a few times a year).

Also, state which activities are active or passive, and whether they take place in or away from home. (The table below gives two examples; your table should list all your leisure activities.)

Leisure activity	Frequent, occasional or rare	Active or passive	Home or away
watching television	frequent	passive	home
skiing	rare	active	away

Draw up similar tables listing the types of activities these kinds of people might like:

- a retired person aged 50 or over
- an unmarried working man in his thirties
- a mother of two children in her twenties.

You may be able to base your tables on someone you know, such as a friend or a relative.

Travel and tourism

Travel and tourism is also a broad area to define, but it usually involves travelling away from home, whether for leisure or business purposes. **Tourism** is about the temporary, short-term movement of people to destinations outside the places where they normally live and work, and about their activities during their stay at these destinations. It includes travel for all purposes as well as day visits or excursions. An essential part of tourism is the intention of the traveller to return, whether this is from a day trip, a holiday or a short business trip.

Most tourist activities take place during people's leisure time. Going on holiday, visiting relatives and day trips can all be classified under the general heading of **leisure travel**. If the reason for travel is business, then we class this as **business travel**.

Leisure travellers are sometimes divided into tourists and day visitors. If people stay one or more nights away from home they are classed as **tourists**; if they travel and return home, or pass through an area, without staying overnight, they are classed as **day visitors**. The distinction is not always important, but you may come across it when you are reading or doing research.

ACTIVITY

Defining tourism

What do you think are the key words and phrases in the definition of tourism? With a classmate, identify and discuss each of them. For example, why does the definition include the phrase 'the intention of the traveller to return'?

Travel is to do with how people get to their chosen destination and how they travel around the area they are visiting. There are many methods of travel, including:

- air
- rail
- ferry
- bus
- taxi
- car hire
- coach.

In this book, we will use the term travel and tourism to cover the whole phenomenon of people travelling away from home (whether for business or leisure), and the industry that supports this activity.

Tourists can also be grouped according to where they come from. Overseas visitors to the United Kingdom are often referred to as **incoming tourists**, while British residents travelling abroad are regarded as **outgoing tourists**. Another commonly used term is **domestic tourist**, which describes British residents visiting places inside the United Kingdom.

ACTIVITY

Types of tourist

Using the descriptions of different types of tourist (on page 7), complete the table by filling in the boxes.

Description of visitor	Business or leisure	Day visitor or tourist	Domestic, incoming or outgoing
Françoise Villeneuve from Lille attends a business meeting in London. She will return the same day.			
Jack and Doris Brooks from Durham go on a day trip to London.			
The Jones from Bargoed in Wales take their annual two-week holiday in Ibiza.			
Bartholomew Tapp from Brussels visits relatives in Norwich for five days.			
The Platt family from Northampton spends a long weekend at Center Parcs in Nottingham.			
Jim Bowen from Glasgow flies to a sales conference in Berlin. He returns the same day.			

Tourists have a range of reasons for travelling. The purpose of travelling could be:

- going on a holiday
- sightseeing
- visiting an attraction
- attending a business meeting
- visiting relatives and friends
- going to a sports event.

As Figure 1.1 shows, the most popular reason for travel by domestic and incoming tourists is holidays. Visits to friends and relatives also account for a large number of trips by domestic tourists.

Figure 1.1: Reasons for travel to and within the United Kingdom

	Domestic	Incoming
Holiday	65.1	10.5
Business	13.7	6.9
Visit friends or relatives	38.4	5.4
Other	5.1	2.9
Total	122.3	25.7

Note: Figures in millions of trips
Source: British Tourist Authority

Components of the leisure and tourism industries

The **leisure and tourism industries** are made up of a diverse range of organisations, facilities, products, services and events which provide opportunities for people to pursue their leisure interests and activities. Since these industries cover such an enormous range of activities in a wide variety of situations, it is useful to divide them into a number of key components. These **key components** are shown in Figure 1.2, and each will be described in detail later in this unit.

The **leisure industry** consists of seven key components:

- sport and physical recreation – sports and leisure centres, running tracks, stadiums, gymnasiums, fitness centres, swimming pools
- arts and entertainment – theatres, concert halls, galleries, art centres, museums, bingo halls, race tracks
- countryside recreation – land-based, water-based, air-based activities and activity centres
- home-based leisure – television, computers, the internet, gardening, DIY
- visitor attractions – theme parks, museums and stately homes
- children's play activities – playing fields, playgrounds, play schemes
- catering – pubs, restaurants, fast food takeaways.

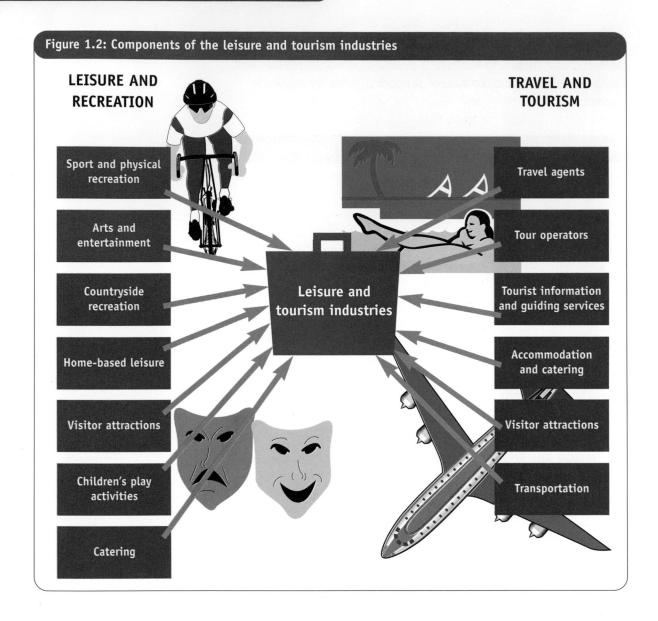

Figure 1.2: Components of the leisure and tourism industries

LEISURE AND RECREATION

- Sport and physical recreation
- Arts and entertainment
- Countryside recreation
- Home-based leisure
- Visitor attractions
- Children's play activities
- Catering

Leisure and tourism industries

TRAVEL AND TOURISM

- Travel agents
- Tour operators
- Tourist information and guiding services
- Accommodation and catering
- Visitor attractions
- Transportation

The **travel and tourism industry** consists of six key components:

- travel agents – for example, Thomas Cook, Going Places, Lunn Poly
- tour operators – for example, Thomson, First Choice, Airtours
- tourist information and guiding services – for example, tourist information centres, Guide Friday
- accommodation and catering – for example, Forte Hotels, Butlins, Macdonald's
- attractions – for example, Alton Towers, Madame Tussaud's, Edinburgh Castle
- transportation – for example, British Airways, Virgin Trains, P&O Ferries.

It is important to understand that although the leisure and tourism industries are considered separately, many of the components are interrelated. For example, horse riding can be classed both as a sport and as a countryside recreation activity. If the horse riding were to be undertaken during a holiday, then there would also be links with components of the travel and tourism industry, such as transportation and accommodation.

We have now identified the two parts of the leisure and tourism industries, namely leisure and recreation, and travel and tourism, and their main components. Before investigating these in detail it is useful to identify three different types of organisation or **sectors** which can be found in the industries.

Sectors of the UK leisure and tourism industries

Public sector

Public sector organisations are largely funded by central or local government and this influences their strategies and policies. Public sector organisations include many leisure centres, tourist boards and art centres.

Public sector services are provided for the public and paid for, collectively, through government. Their operation is usually ultimately accountable to elected bodies, including local councils and Parliament. Commercially-operated public services are frequently subsidised. Most public services are non-profit-making.

Local authorities are by far the largest providers of local public leisure facilities and services. These include community recreation facilities, such as sports centres and swimming pools, tourist information centres, libraries, museums and education services (such as hobby classes for adults, summer play schemes, youth centres).

Some government departments, including the Department of Environment, Transport and the Regions and the Department for Culture, Media and Sport, are involved in the leisure and tourism industries, although they do not directly provide or operate facilities and services at a local level. Their role is to oversee national developments and to create a framework within which services can operate. Government departments fund, and sometimes supervise, the work of many agencies and public bodies, such as the national tourist boards, the Countryside Agency, English Heritage and Historic Scotland.

Private sector

> Private sector organisations are directly or indirectly in private ownership. They are normally profit making. Examples include hotels, tourist attractions, coach companies, health and fitness clubs.

The **private sector** comprises a variety of commercial operations owned by individuals or companies, whose main aim is to generate profits from the services and other products they sell to their customers. The sector has a very large number of sole traders and small businesses; and, in 1998, there were approximately 200,000 self-employed people in the leisure and tourism industries. However, in terms of income, the private sector is dominated by large national and international leisure corporations, such as the Rank Organisation, Time Warner, Mecca and Thomson. Examples of private sector facilities include theme parks, hotels, health clubs, public houses, social clubs, restaurants, cinemas and theatres.

Voluntary sector

> Voluntary sector organisations are managed and operated largely by volunteers. They are often non-profit-making or charitable, such as local sports clubs and travel clubs.

In many cases, **voluntary sector** organisations are simply small groups formed to further a common interest or cater for a need in the local community. Examples include church youth clubs and the YMCA/ YWCA, uniformed organisations such as the Guides and Boys' Brigade, sports associations and amateur dramatic societies. Voluntary sector organisations are usually funded by membership subscriptions, grants and donations, fund-raising and sales of goods and/or services.

This introduction to the leisure and tourism industries has provided a series of definitions of key terms used in your GNVQ studies. You should understand that the leisure and tourism industries encompass an enormous range of organisations, facilities, products, goods and services. The breadth of these industries can be fully appreciated if you look at a copy of your local Yellow Pages directory, which will include many categories of leisure and tourism providers and facilities, goods and services. Figure 1.3 shows an A–Z of leisure and tourism providers and facilities which was taken from a local Yellow Pages for 1998–9. The list contains 120 entries.

Figure 1.3: A–Z of leisure and tourism providers, facilities and products

amusement parks and arcades
airlines
airports
aquariums
art and craft shops
art galleries

ballet schools
balloons, hot air
bands (music)
banqueting function rooms
bars
betting shops
bingo halls
boat hire companies
bookshops
bouncing castles and inflatables
bowling centres
bus and coach services

cafés
car hire
caravan holiday parks
castles
caterers
cinemas
coach hire
community associations
computer games shops
conference facilities
cruises
cultural associations and groups
currency exchange bureaux
cycle hire and shops

dance bands
dance companies and schools
disco and dance halls
discos (mobile)
DIY stores
drama schools

entertainers
evening classes
exhibition and show organisers

ferry services
fitness equipment suppliers

golf courses
greyhound racing tracks
gymnasiums

hang-gliding clubs
health and fitness centres
historic buildings/stately homes
holiday accommodation
holiday centres
horse riding centres and schools
hostels
hotel booking agents
hotels and inns

leisure centres
libraries

marinas
motels
motorsport circuits
museums
music sound systems

nature and wildlife parks
nightclubs

outdoor pursuit centres

parish halls
parks and gardens
pizza delivery
playgroups
playing fields
public houses

racecourses
railway services
railway stations and offices
record shops and companies
restaurants
rifle and pistol ranges

safari parks
sailing clubs and schools
satellite television suppliers
saunas and solariums
shooting and fishing agents
showgrounds
skating rinks
ski centres
snooker and pool centres
social clubs
sports centres
sports clubs and associations
sports coaching
sports goods shops
sports grounds and stadiums
squash courts
swimming pools

take away food outlets
taxis and private hire vehicles
television, video and radio shops
television broadcasting services
tennis clubs and courts
theatres and concert halls
theatre ticket agencies
theatrical companies
theme and leisure parks
timeshare holidays
tour operators
tourist attractions
tourist information centres
tours and sightseeing
toy and games shops
travel agents

video tape rental

watersports
wildlife parks
wine bars

yacht clubs
youth clubs and organisations
youth hostels
zoos

Build your learning

Summary points

- The leisure and tourism industries in the UK provide activities for people to enjoy their leisure time.

- The leisure and tourism industries encompass an enormous range of organisations, facilities, products, goods and services.

- The leisure and tourism industries can be divided into a number of key components.

- Leisure and tourism organisations operate in one of three sectors: public, private or voluntary.

Key words and phrases

You should know the meaning of the words and phrases listed below as they relate to the organisation and components of the leisure and tourism industries. Go back through the last 10 pages to refresh your understanding if necessary.

- Leisure
- Product
- Goods
- Services
- Facility
- Tourism
- Travel
- Leisure travel

- Business travel
- Tourist
- Day visitor
- Incoming tourist
- Outgoing tourist
- Domestic tourist
- Component

- Leisure and tourism industries
- Leisure industry
- Travel and tourism industry
- Sector
- Public sector
- Private sector
- Voluntary sector

SUMMARY ACTIVITY

These activities will help you to understand the leisure and tourism industries and will also help you complete your unit assignment on pages 86 to 87.

1 Copy and complete the following description of the leisure and tourism industries. You may find it useful to refer to pages 4 to 12.

Leisure activities are undertaken by people during their _____ time. These activities may take place in the home, such as _____, or away from the home, such as _____.

There are many factors which influence people's leisure needs and choice of leisure activity, such as age, _____, _____ and _____.

The industries which cater for these activities are referred to as the _____ and _____ industries. These industries provide a _____ range of products, services and facilities and can be divided into two industry groups. These are known as the _____ and _____ industry and the _____ and _____ industry. Each industry contains a number of _____ which are often interrelated. A component may consist of a group of activities (for example, sports and physical recreation), facilities (for example, travel agencies) or products and services (for example, catering). The leisure and recreation industry contains seven main components. These are: _____, _____, _____, _____, _____, _____ and _____. The travel and tourism industry contains six main components. These are: _____, _____, _____, _____, _____ and _____.

There are three main organisational _____ within the leisure and tourism industries. The _____ sector is largely funded by central or local government. Most _____ sector organisations such as _____ are profit making. Voluntary organisations are managed and operated largely by _____ , and examples include _____ and _____.

2 Using the list of your own leisure activities from the activity on page 6, place each entry into one of the industry groups using the table below.

Travel and tourism industry	Leisure and recreation industry

Did you find any leisure activities difficult to place into only one of the industry categories?

3 Study a copy of the Yellow Pages directory for your area. Identify at least 30 leisure and/or tourism organisations, facilities, products and services. Your examples should cover both main industry groups (leisure and recreation, and travel and tourism) and the three sectors (public, private and voluntary). You should also identify the location and component of each example. Present your information in a table like the one below. You may also find it useful to mark each facility and provider on a map, with a key to indicate differences by industry and other characteristics.

Facility/provider	Location and map reference	Type of organisation	Industry	Main component	Product or service (example)
Sports centre	Housing estate	Public (local council)	Leisure and recreation	Sports and physical recreation	Keep-fit classes
Travel agent	Main street	Private (Thomas Cook)	Travel and tourism	Travel agents	Holiday booking service

You could also work with colleagues to carry out a more detailed investigation and produce a report. The team could produce a full A–Z guide of leisure and tourism facilities and providers in a particular locality, including lists, maps, posters and other displays. You will be able to use this work when you complete your assignment for this unit.

Components of the UK leisure industry

We will now look at the seven key components of the leisure industry, giving examples of facilities, products and services. These components are shown in Figure 1.2 (see page 10). These components are all **interrelated**. For example, a public park may provide opportunities for sports and physical recreation, children's play activities and countryside recreation, and tourists use products and services from the leisure industry when they eat out and visit places of entertainment. It is also important to remember that the components all have one main thing in common – they provide opportunities for individuals to spend their leisure time.

Sports and physical recreation

There is an enormous range of **sport and physical recreation** activities available to individuals and groups. Sport UK estimates that around two-thirds of the British population take part in sport or physical recreation at least once a month. Millions more watch or follow sport at the local and national levels. Sport is part of our culture and heritage – many of the world's great sports were invented in Britain – and it gives immense value to our national prestige. In 1992, the GB Sports Council (now Sport UK) published *Sport in the Nineties*, which outlined the importance and future development of sport and physical activities. The report highlighted that sport:

- contributes to greater fitness, better health and a sense of personal well-being
- plays a vital part in a rounded education for children
- offers opportunities for varied experiences and new fellowship in the community
- generates nearly £10 billion of expenditure in the economy
- provides 470,000 jobs
- promotes and enhances Britain's standing in the world.

Growing interest in healthy lifestyles, and the link with fitness and exercise, has been a major influence on sports participation since the mid-1980s. Figure 1.4 shows the ten most popular participation sports and physical activities in Great Britain, as indicated by the *General Household Survey 1998*. As you can see, walking was by far the most popular activity in the survey.

Why do you think that taking part in sport and physical activity is so popular?

Figure 1.4: Top sports, games and physical activities for men and women

Men	%	Women	%
walking	49	walking	41
snooker/pool/billiards	20	keep fit/yoga	17
cycling	15	swimming	17
swimming	13	cycling	8
soccer	10	snooker/pool/billiards	4
weight training	9	weight training	3
golf	8	tenpin bowling	3
running	7	running	2
keep fit/yoga	7	badminton	2
tenpin bowling	4	tennis	2

Note: Adults aged 16, participation rates in four weeks before interview.
Source: Office of National Statistics, *Living in Britain: General Household Survey, 1998*

As people become increasingly aware of the link between fitness and health it seems likely that walking, jogging, keep-fit and aerobics will continue to be popular activities. Consumer spending on fitness classes, facilities and products has boomed since the 1980s, and the value of the market has continued to flourish in the 1990s (see Figure 1.5).

Figure 1.5: Spending on aerobics and exercise classes

| £220m | £255m | £290m | £330m | £345m | £355m | £372m |
| 1992 | 1993 | 1994 | 1995 | 1996 | 1997 | 1998 |

ACTIVITY

S	R	U	N	N	R	B	S	S	Q	A	B	F
O	E	A	S	H	U	F	H	W	K	S	A	E
O	E	L	T	E	N	O	S	I	E	O	L	N
P	T	I	E	S	N	O	O	M	E	E	H	S
K	E	E	P	F	I	T	T	M	F	T	K	Q
C	K	H	A	O	N	B	E	I	G	T	B	N
Y	K	E	E	O	G	A	Q	N	I	N	O	G
C	D	A	R	T	S	L	I	G	N	K	W	O
A	S	H	O	S	S	L	E	E	W	I	L	O
N	H	C	B	C	C	K	S	Q	U	A	S	H
N	C	Y	I	Y	S	N	O	O	K	E	R	L
G	N	I	C	A	N	O	E	I	N	G	N	L
S	O	L	S	I	N	G	S	S	L	A	W	B

Word search

In the box there are 11 hidden sport and recreation activities. Identify each one.

We have highlighted one answer in red to get you started. (All the answers are on page 262.)

Sports facilities

There are many facilities used for sport and physical activities including sports centres, leisure centres, ice rinks, squash courts and fitness centres. In addition, there are specially constructed outdoor facilities such as athletic tracks, golf courses, natural and artificial playing pitches and sports stadiums. There are also natural resources such as rivers, lakes (and reservoirs), beaches, hills, mountains and caves which provide suitable sites for a range of sports and physical activities. Most localities now have swimming pools, sports centres, health and fitness centres, playing fields and sports pitches.

Swimming pools

Most recreational swimming takes place in indoor pools, which are nearly all run by the public sector. In 1999, it was estimated that there were 1,400 public indoor swimming pools in the United Kingdom and a further 3,500 pools in primary and secondary schools. These are mainly conventional 25-metre pools. However, in recent years a number of new-style leisure pools with flumes, chutes and wave machines, islands and water rapids have been developed.

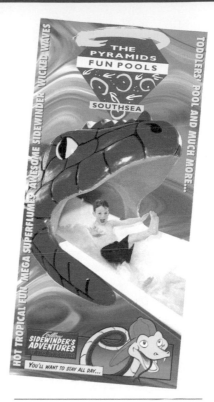

▲ Swimming pools offer a wide range of activities

Sports centres

In 1960, there was only one purpose-built public sports facility in the United Kingdom; now there are over 2,500 centres. Like swimming provision, this area is dominated by the public sector, including local authorities and schools.

Sports centres vary in the size, facilities and the range of services they offer. They usually contain a main sports hall with changing and reception facilities. Sometimes there are also specialist facilities such as squash courts, weights room, a climbing wall and social areas, including cafés, bars and function rooms. A sports centre will provide a range of products and services. For example, a sports centre might provide:

- sports activities
- lessons and classes for different groups of people
- facilities for parties, wedding receptions, etc.
- food and drink
- purchase and hire of equipment.

Health and fitness centres

Growing awareness of the health benefits of an active lifestyle has created a demand for health and fitness products and services. This demand is partly met by private health and fitness centres. These typically have weights and exercise

▲ The Kensington Sports Centre in London is a local authority sports facility

Shaping up...
...winding down

Our wide range of leisure clubs are gradually becoming fully-fledged health and fitness clubs in their own right. Known as 'Spirit' they offer membership and the facilities and ambience to match any other private club. As a Posthouse guest, of course, you are entitled to enjoy them free of charge.

Spirit

Each **Spirit** will have a full-size swimming pool and fully equipped gym as well as a wide range of beauty and relaxation treatments on offer, from conventional facials, massages and manicures to 'alternative' therapies like reflexology and aromatherapy.

▲ Spirit leisure clubs can be found in many Posthouse hotels

rooms with equipment, such as exercise bikes, treadmills and rowing machines, designed to improve heart and lung (cardiovascular) fitness. Some also provide swimming pools, saunas, Jacuzzis, steam rooms and other health-related services such as massage, aromatherapy and beauty therapy. It is estimated that there are now around 2,200 private health and fitness clubs in the UK.

Many of the larger hotel chains, including Forte and Thistle Hotels, have established health and fitness suites as part of the services they provide free to guests. Specialist health farms and country clubs have also been developed to cater for the needs of an increasingly health-conscious society.

Leisure complexes

Some leisure complexes provide a combination of facilities under one roof; for example, the Dome, in Doncaster, is one of Europe's largest indoor leisure complexes, offering more than 50 activities (see case study opposite).

ACTIVITY

What's on offer

Make a list of the facilities and activities provided at a sports centre in your locality. You may need to visit the facility, or obtain details of its programme to complete this activity. You will be able to use this information to complete the unit assignment on page 86.

When you have completed your list, compare the range of facilities and activities provided at the Dome (see the case study opposite) with those at your chosen sports centre.

CASE STUDY

The Dome, Doncaster

The Dome is the UK's largest indoor leisure facility, with spectacular sports facilities, first class dining and entertainment, luxurious fitness studios and state-of-the art conference halls all under one roof.

- The Lagoons area is a tropical waterworld, featuring six leisure pools, water geysers, two Jacuzzis, outdoor rapids and slides.

- Ice Caps is a two-tier ice skating rink offering temperature-controlled comfort all year round. Staff are more than happy to assist customers with specific needs and will take wheelchairs onto the ice.

- The Main Hall seats 2,000. It regularly features top international stars in concert and hosts major sporting events. The hall is an ideal venue for business conferences and exhibitions.

- The Fitness Village is one of the key attractions at the Dome. It has over 170 pieces of fitness equipment under one roof.

- The Oasis Suite allows you to relax and feel revitalised in specially themed surroundings which include two Finnish sauna cabins, a large circular Roman steam bath, a giant Jacuzzi, needle showers and a sun terrace with spectacular views.

- The Sundeck Studio classes cater for all levels of fitness, offering step, aerobics, total body workout, stretch and tone, and much more.

- The Sunbeds Suite allows you to relax while tanning. You can then take advantage of a free swim after every tanning session.

- The Treatment Village offers massage therapy and physiotherapy by qualified therapists.

- Primetimers is a leisure day every Thursday for the over 50s, offering a wide range of leisure activities such as old time dancing, aquafit, table tennis, short tennis, squash, bowls and much more.

- School holiday activities include the prestigious Dome camps and a full range of activities for 8–13 year olds.

- A selection of catering is on offer in the Icebreaker Lounge, the Sports Bar and the Mall Diner. All eating areas have a relaxed and friendly environment, a wide range of food and the Sports Bar additionally offers three large screen televisions to watch all all important fixtures.

Sports clubs and associations

There are estimated to be 150,000 voluntary sports clubs in Britain that are affiliated to the 400 or so national governing bodies of sport. These clubs and associations provide a wide range of sport and recreational activities both for their members and for visitors. If you look in the sports section of any local newspaper (or the Yellow Pages) you will find many examples of these sports clubs.

Sometimes a community forms a sports association that provides a range of activities. For example, a village sports association might provide facilities for football, cricket, hockey, tennis and bowls. Many will also provide social facilities, such as a bar, function room and meeting room. As the vast majority of these clubs and associations operate on a 'not-for-profit' basis, they are classified as voluntary sector organisations.

ACTIVITY

Sports clubs and associations

Obtain a copy of the Yellow Pages for a region of your choice. Go to the section labelled 'sports clubs and associations'. (You may also find it useful to look in other linked sections, such as clubs and associations.)

Make a list of the sports clubs and associations in one locality covered by the Yellow Pages directory. You will probably find that there are many clubs listed in the directory, so remember to limit your list to a specific locality within the region.

Find out more information about one of the sports clubs or associations on your list. You may need to visit the organisation or interview someone who is a member. Find out the following information:

● what sports and other activities does the club provide?

● who does it provide it for?

● what facilities does it have (include social facilities as well as sports facilities)?

● who pays for them?

● who runs the club?

You will be able to use this information to complete the unit assignment on page 86.

Playing pitches

It is impossible to obtain an accurate estimate of the total number of playing pitches in the United Kingdom. Sport England (formerly the English Sports Council) calculates that there are 70,000 pitches in England alone. Football accounts for about half of all pitch provision and cricket one quarter. The remainder are mainly rugby and hockey pitches. In addition, there are now around 300 artificial grass pitches in England.

Figure 1.6 shows the national distribution of five other major groups of sports participation facilities in the United Kingdom. Bowls centres and athletics tracks are usually provided by the public sector, while the majority of ice rinks, ski slopes and golf courses are privately owned.

Figure 1.6: Provision of selected sports facilities

	England	Scotland	Wales	Total
Indoor bowls	300	50	15	365
Ice rinks	40	34	2	76
Athletics tracks	412	49	24	485
18-hole golf courses	1,270	385	121	1,776
Dry ski slopes				99

Source: Sport England website

Sports spectating

Popular national sports such as football, rugby league, rugby union, cricket, golf, motor racing and horse racing can draw large crowds of spectators. In recent years, many facilities have been redeveloped to provide better services for both participants and spectators. Indeed, sports stadiums are now often multipurpose leisure facilities. Old Trafford, for example, home of Manchester United Football Club, is not only a venue for football matches but has also hosted rugby league matches and pop concerts. The stadium has been developed by increasing its capacity, improving parking facilities and making it an all-seater facility, with a range of spectator services from family enclosures to executive boxes costing several thousand pounds per game. The club also offers guided tours of the stadium, has a football museum and operates as a venue for conferences, exhibitions and private functions such as weddings and parties.

ACTIVITY

Sports stadiums

1 Match each well-known facility in the table with the spectator sport it caters for. Some facilities may provide a venue for more than one sport. (The answers are on page 262.)

Facility	Spectator sport(s)
1 Lords	A Rugby union
2 Vicarage Road	B Horse racing
3 The Crucible	C Motor racing
4 Murrayfield	D Football
5 Epsom	E Football and rugby union
6 Silverstone	F Snooker
7 Wimbledon	G Cricket
8 Wentworth	H Rowing
9 Aintree	I Football and rugby league
10 Henley	J Tennis
11 Elland Road	K Golf
12 Stadium of Light	L Horse racing

2 Select one of the venues listed and identify the range of facilities, products and services it offers its customers. Alternatively, you could investigate a sports spectator facility in your area with which you are familiar.

Sports retail

The popularity of sporting and physical recreational activities has created huge consumer demand for a wide range of sports clothing and equipment. In 1998, consumers spent an estimated £3,500 million on sportswear and equipment and manufacturers such as Nike, adidas, Puma and Reebok have all become household names. Chains of sports retailers such as Olympus, Sports Division and JJB Sports have emerged alongside the many independent sports shops, to ensure that sports retail outlets are commonplace in the high street. Sports manufacturers and retailers are all private sector organisations.

Arts and entertainment

It is useful in thinking of **arts and entertainment** to distinguish between those activities which occur in the home and those which take place in public. The development of the home as a 'leisure centre' has made it harder for 'live' entertainment to compete. Attendances at sporting events are often lower when there is live television coverage, and the resulting loss of income has to be made up from fees from television companies, sponsorship and advertising sales. Nevertheless, there are more public venues providing arts and entertainment than ever before, ranging from classical ballet to modern dance, Shakespeare plays to pub theatre, and symphonic music to hip hop.

Cinema

The popularity of the cinema reached its peak in 1946, when 1,600 million tickets were sold. By 1984, this number had fallen drastically, due largely to the development of television, with only 53 million visits to the cinema. However, since the mid-1980s there has been an increase in attendances with about 145 million visits to cinemas in the United Kingdom in 1999.

◀ The foyer of a new multiplex cinema

One of the main reasons for the recent growth in cinema going has been the development of large multi-screen cinemas (sometimes known as multiplex cinemas) which can show several films at the same time, thereby catering for a wide range of customer tastes. There were only 11 multiplexes in the United Kingdom in 1988, but by 1998 this figure had risen to over 100. Major commercial operators such as Warner, Odeon, UCI and Virgin have developed chains of multiplex cinemas and it is likely that the numbers will continue to grow. Multiplex cinemas are often located in out-of-town developments or in shopping malls where there is a range of retail and leisure facilities to attract customers.

ACTIVITY

Multiplex cinemas

Find out what films are showing at a multiplex in your region. Work out which film is intended to appeal to what kind of audience and consider whether the manager has provided a sufficient range to attract a wide variety of customers.

▲ Imax screens are a new cinema attraction

Maximising audiences is vital for the film industry. Hollywood films currently cost on average around £30 million to make, and over half of all films lose money. However, successful films, such as the 1999 Star Wars movie, *Episode 1: The Phantom Menace*, make huge profits from box office takings worldwide. Because of the amount of money that has to be invested, and the high risk involved, this part of the leisure and recreation industry is dominated by the private sector.

Theatres, concert halls and light entertainment venues

Theatres, concert halls and other facilities for live performance range from temporary venues and those adapted for one-off events (such as an outdoor stage or a school hall) to national venues with resident companies, such as the Barbican in London, home to the Royal Shakespeare Company.

The range of live performances and shows is enormous, with most of the larger productions located in major cities. The greatest concentration of theatres is in London's West End,

where there are almost 50 privately-owned theatres. There are around 500 theatres outside London, presenting performances from companies as diverse as national touring companies and local amateur theatre groups. In addition, schools, colleges, leisure centres, village halls, pubs, social clubs, community centres and other temporary venues can also be adapted for single performances. As well as regular programmes, there are many theatre and entertainment festivals, ranging from small local ones, such as Scout fairs, to internationally known events like the Edinburgh Military Tattoo.

Theatres and other venues for live performances and shows are often heavily subsidised by public authorities. The main national companies – the Royal National Theatre on London's South Bank, the Royal Shakespeare Company and the Royal Opera and Ballet, Covent Garden – all receive funding from the Arts Council of Great Britain. The Arts Council also supports many regional and local organisations including dance, opera and theatre companies. Usually, these organisations also fund their work through donations and sponsorship and by generating advertising revenue.

The voluntary sector is well represented in this area with numerous amateur music and drama groups, operatic societies and other groups of performing clubs and societies. However, most of the well-known venues for live performances are in the private sector. Major theatres such as the London Palladium and concert venues such as Wembley and Earl's Court are owned by private companies.

Museums and art galleries

Millions of people visit museums and art galleries in the United Kingdom every year for a variety of recreational, educational and cultural reasons. Recent research by MORI shows that the popularity of museums is growing (see the press article below).

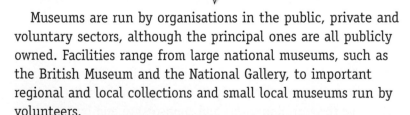

Museums more popular than live soccer

New research by MORI on behalf of the Museums and Galleries Commission (MGC) and the Campaign for Museums shows that the popularity of museums is growing, and has overtaken theatre-going and sports events.

The survey shows that in 12 months 35 per cent of British adults had been to a museum or art gallery, compared with 33 per cent going to a zoo or wildlife park, 32 per cent to a stately home and 30 per cent to performances of drama, opera or ballet. Only 26 per cent went to live sporting events, and theme parks, seen as main competition for museums, attracted only 28 per cent.

And the traditional reason for putting people off museums, that they 'don't make people feel welcome' has all but disappeared. Only one in a hundred said they were intimidated by museums.

Loyd Grossman, chairman of the Campaign for Museums and MGC commissioner, said: 'This research proves a key message of the Campaign for Museums – that this country's museums and galleries are exciting and popular places to visit. I believe that more and more people will learn that the United Kingdom has museums for everyone.'

Campaign for Museums
7 June 1999

Museums are run by organisations in the public, private and voluntary sectors, although the principal ones are all publicly owned. Facilities range from large national museums, such as the British Museum and the National Gallery, to important regional and local collections and small local museums run by volunteers.

The Museums Association defines a museum as:

> an institution which collects, preserves, exhibits and interprets material evidence and associated information for the public benefit.

This definition encompasses general municipal museums and those which specialise, for example, in social history, natural history, transport, science, military artefacts, past industrial processes, and agriculture. The Campaign for Museums organisation has developed the 24 Hour Museum, which provides extensive information about museums on the internet. The campaign's website (**www.24hourmuseum.org.uk**) includes a museum finder. The museum collections are placed in a number of categories:

- archaeology
- art and design
- transport
- maritime
- personalities
- weapons and war
- natural history
- science and technology
- social history
- national collections
- costume
- archives
- world cultures
- coins and medals
- music.

The English Tourism Council lists about 950 museums in the United Kingdom, each attracting at least 5,000 visitors a year. London is the major centre for museums of all kinds, containing 47 public museums and galleries attracting 50,000 or more visits a year. London is also home to the five most popular national museums (see Figure 1.7). Outside the capital, the largest museums are located in major cities, such as the Glasgow Art Gallery and Museum which attracted almost 1.3 million visitors in 1998.

Figure 1.7: Most popular national museums

Museums	Estimated attendance in 1999 (in millions)
British Museum	5.5
National Gallery	4.8
Tate Gallery	3.0
Natural History Museum	1.9
Science Museum	1.6

Source: English Tourism Council

@ WEBSTRACT

24 Hour Museum

Thomas Cook

Center Parcs

easyJet

The Rank Group

The 24 Hour Museum officially went live on the 13 May 1999 in the presence of Chris Smith MP at the Imperial War Museum in London. The museum exists only in cyberspace and is an exciting development for the United Kingdom's cultural heritage.

At the opening, the Secretary of State for Culture, Media and Sport announced that the 24 Hour Museum had been awarded National Collection status, giving it the same status as only 12 other world famous institutions. The museum will receive funding to maintain and develop the site further, providing access to artistic masterpieces and historic artefacts and allowing it to remain on the cutting edge of internet technology.

About the 24 Hour Museum

The 24 Hour Museum is the United Kingdom's gateway to museums, galleries and heritage attractions. It is quality controlled, which means that only museums and galleries registered with the Museums and Galleries Commission, and non-profit-making galleries, historic houses and heritage attractions are included on the site.

The 24 Hour Museum's primary objective is to provide public access to non-profit-making museums, galleries and heritage attractions in the United Kingdom. The 24 Hour Museum is open for registered museums, museums that are in the process of registering, children's museums and discovery centres, historic sites with collections and other institutions whose primary purpose is the display of art, specimens or artefacts for the public benefit.

Source: **http://www.24hourmuseum.org.uk**

Finding out about museums in your area

If you have access to the internet go to the 24 Hour Museum site (**www.24hourmuseum.org.uk**).

Undertake a detailed search to find out information on museums in a chosen locality. Find out information about the facility and complete the table below.

If you do not have access to the internet you can complete this activity by gathering information from visitor guides, or by visiting museums in your locality.

Opening times	Shop	Library	Food	Baby rooms	Disabled access	Study area	Parking	Collection details
British Museum Mon–Sat 10.00–17.00 Sun 12.00–18.00	✓	✓	✓	✓	✓	✓	✗	Archaeology, archives, world cultures, weapons and war, costume, coins and medals, art and design, social history, national collection

You will be able to use this information to complete the unit assignment on page 86.

Libraries

In spite of competition from television, radio, music and home computers, reading remains a major leisure pursuit. Publishing and bookselling are big business, with 80,000 new book titles published each year. Libraries play an important part in leisure and, in recent years, they have diversified to offer records, cassettes, compact discs and videos. The library service is generally regarded as an essential element of public sector provision and there are currently over 4,000 libraries in Britain that are run by local authorities.

Pubs and clubs

Like libraries, public houses and social clubs are an important part of British social life. The local pub or social club is a central feature of many communities and provides valued leisure and recreational opportunities for customers. A wide variety of social clubs and associations has evolved to cater for the needs of all types of people, including working men's clubs and institutes, ex-armed forces associations and political clubs. In addition, there are national chains of privately owned social clubs, such as those of Mecca Leisure and the Rank Organisation. These provide bingo and other entertainments, as well as nightclubs and discos.

Figure 1.8: The bar facts

- There are 61,000 pubs in the United Kingdom.
- They employ more than 600,000 people.
- Eight out of ten people who go to a pub once a week regard themselves as happy.
- Pubs raise £60 million a year for good causes.
- Two in five adults in England and Wales eat in a pub at least once a month.
- Pubs are the top choice for eating out, serving 25 million meals a week.
- Pub grub is now a £4.8 billion-a-year market.
- More than 36,700,000 barrels of beer are drunk in pubs each year.
- Britons spend more than £15 million a year on beer.
- The busiest day of the year is Mother's Day followed by Valentine's Day.
- The trade is worth £22 billion a year, growing by 10 per cent a year.
- More than £12 million a week is spent refurbishing and extending pubs.
- The average pub injects at least £64,000 a year into the local economy before business taxes.

Source: *Financial Mail on Sunday*, 12 April 1998

ACTIVITY

What's on in your area

Look at the 'what's on' sections of your local newspaper. Make a list of the events/entertainments available. For each one, find out what organisation provides it and identify which sector the organisation belongs to (public, private or voluntary). Present your findings in a table.

Event/entertainment	Organisation	Sector

You will be able to use this information to complete the unit assignment on page 86.

Countryside recreation

The term **countryside recreation** covers a broad range of leisure and recreational activities which can be classified as land-based (such as walking, potholing), water-based (such as sailing, water skiing) or air-based (such as hang-gliding, hot air ballooning). Obviously, many leisure activities in the countryside are sports, or require particular physical effort, but there are many other activities which need not be, for example those associated with parks, gardens and the countryside.

The countryside provides significant opportunities for millions of people to enjoy a variety of leisure pastimes and activities, including outings, drives, picnics, walks and visits to parks, monuments and historic properties. For many, the countryside is a place to enjoy scenery, wildlife and tranquillity.

Countryside parks

▶ Mam Tor, which lies within the Peak District national park

Perhaps the best known areas of the countryside providing recreational opportunities are the national parks, which were initially created by an Act of Parliament in 1949. There are now 11 national parks in England and Wales, with a twelfth, the New Forest, in planning (see Figure 1.9). In 1995, the Environment Act established independent national park authorities (NPAs) to:

- conserve and enhance the natural beauty, wildlife and cultural heritage of the national parks
- promote opportunities for the public to understand and enjoy the national parks' special qualities.

NPAs also try to foster the economic and social well-being of local communities within the parks.

In addition to the national parks there are other designated areas of the countryside which provide recreational opportunities. These include:

- areas of outstanding natural beauty (for example, Kent Downs, North Pennines)
- heritage coasts (for example, South West coast, Norfolk coast)
- national trails and long distance paths (for example, Cleveland Way, Thames Path)
- country parks (for example, Strathclyde Park, Motherwell, Crawfordsburn Park, Belfast).

There have also been a number of projects to create parks out of derelict industrial areas (for example, Lee Valley and Colne Valley regional parks).

Figure 1.9: National parks in England and Wales

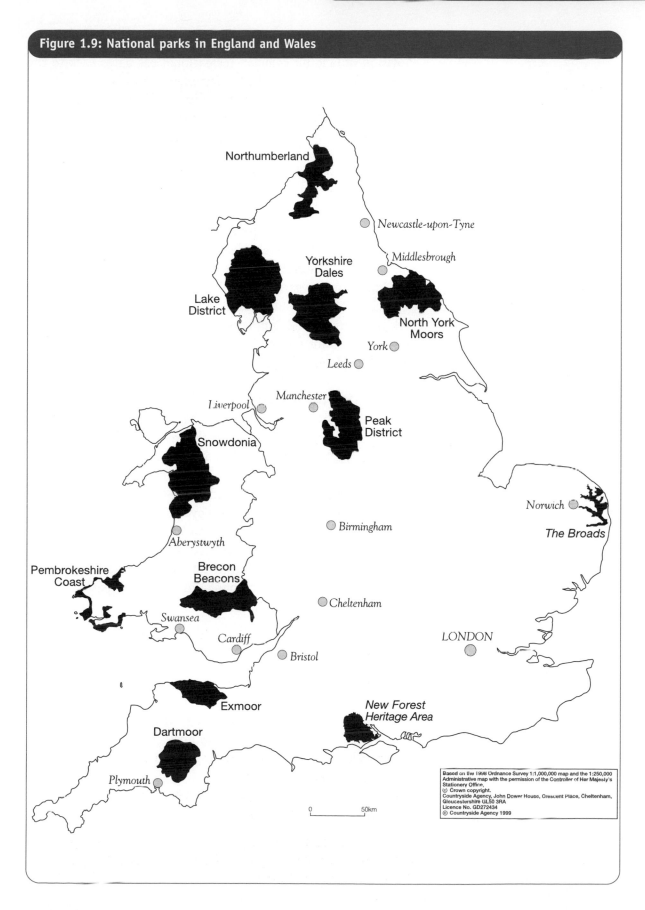

Northumberland

Newcastle-upon-Tyne

Middlesbrough

Yorkshire Dales

Lake District

North York Moors

York

Leeds

Manchester

Liverpool

Peak District

Snowdonia

Norwich

The Broads

Aberystwyth

Birmingham

Pembrokeshire Coast

Brecon Beacons

Swansea

Cheltenham

Cardiff

LONDON

Bristol

Exmoor

New Forest Heritage Area

Dartmoor

Plymouth

0   50km

Based on the 1998 Ordnance Survey 1:1,000,000 map and the 1:250,000
Administrative map with the permission of the Controller of Her Majesty's
Stationery Office.
© Crown copyright.
Countryside Agency, John Dower House, Crescent Place, Cheltenham,
Gloucestershire GL50 3RA
Licence No. GD272434
© Countryside Agency 1999

Urban parks, gardens and amenities

Provision of land for common recreational use dates back to the Middle Ages. The loss of these commons, due to their 'enclosure' by local landlords in the first half of the last century, led Parliament to make specific provision for open spaces and playgrounds (although not until 1926). It was, however, following the creation of local town and city councils a hundred years ago that public gardens and parks were set up in any number. Today most local authorities have a parks department.

Many areas have urban parks, gardens and allotments in addition to the more recent development of amenities such as children's play areas, walking trails and cycleways. Some of the best known urban parks include Hyde Park, Regent's Park and St James's Park in London, Kelvingrove Park in Glasgow, Sefton Park in Liverpool and Sophia Gardens in Cardiff. The London area also contains two of the most visited gardens in the United Kingdom: Kew Gardens and Hampton Court.

Home-based leisure

The industry catering for the home-based leisure market is huge. The vast majority of households have television, radio and music systems. In 1998, digital television was launched and the internet continues to expand, providing opportunities for both business and leisure use.

> What impact do you think digital TV and the internet will have on home-based leisure?

The term **home-based leisure** covers a wide range of activities. The Leisure Industries Research Centre (LIRC) identifies 13 key types of home-based leisure activity, based on consumer spending totals. Figure 1.10 shows these activities, and identifies the projected change in consumer spending for each one between 1997 and 2002.

LIRC predicts that spending on home leisure will continue to expand well, with some areas such as computers and television seeing growth of over 20 per cent between 1997 and 2002. The digital revolution will increase spending on new television products and services, as well as on computers, but video may suffer from this competition. Demand for do-it-yourself (DIY) and gardening products will remain buoyant, but some traditional activities such as reading books and newspapers are forecast to decline.

LIRC forecasts that, overall, consumer spending on home leisure up to 2002 will grow faster than away from home leisure activities. However, as the internet becomes more widely used, shopping for leisure on the internet is likely to greatly increase spending on home-based leisure up to and beyond

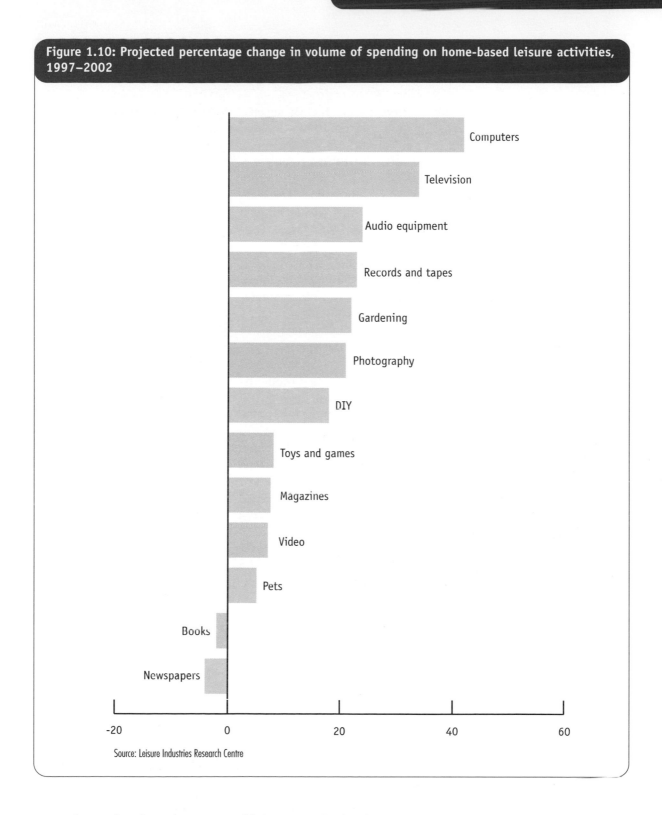

Figure 1.10: Projected percentage change in volume of spending on home-based leisure activities, 1997–2002

Computers
Television
Audio equipment
Records and tapes
Gardening
Photography
DIY
Toys and games
Magazines
Video
Pets
Books
Newspapers

-20 0 20 40 60

Source: Leisure Industries Research Centre

2002. Currently, the prime areas of leisure purchasing by internet users in the United Kingdom are books (such as **amazon.com**), music compact discs (such as **hmv.co.uk**), travel tickets and holidays as shown in the article overleaf.

Surf the net for holiday bargains

There are thunderstorms and torrential downpours across Britain, so it must be summer again. And it is time to book that last-minute jaunt to sunnier climes. If you want to save time, effort and money, start with the web.

Researching and booking holidays is one of the most popular internet activities. According to Fletcher Research, an internet consultancy, 1.4 million people have bought travel tickets online. And it believes internet bookings will be worth £275 million by 2002.

Flights are ideally suited to web distribution because they are simple. And the later you are prepared to book, the greater the bargain because the airline is desperate to fill the plane. But don't be too fussy about when and how you go.

You can either go direct to the airline or via an online travel agent. EasyJet (**www. easyjet.co.uk**) the discount airline, has had great success online and now sells about a third of all tickets over the net. It offers £1 off every one-way flight and £2 off every return flight bought online. There are no tickets involved – all you need to take with you is your confirmation number and passport. Go (**www.go-fly. com**) the low-cost arm of British Airways, has a similar service on its simple website.

For a wider selection of flights and destinations you need to go to a broker, such as Cheap Flights (**www.cheap-flights.co.uk**), which gives you a round-up of all the best travel agents' deals and links users to their websites. Flightbookers (**www.flightbookers.com**) is also useful. Last Minute (**www. lastminute.com**) will refund the difference if you find a cheaper flight.

Of course, the big travel websites, such as Expedia (**www.expedia.co.uk**), Travel-ocity (**www.travelocity.com**) and a2btravel.com (**www .a2btravel.com**) also offer flight booking, but include weekend breaks, package holidays, hotel reservations and car hire booking. For last minute packages, Bargain Holidays.com (**www.bargain-holidays.com**), is a good bet. Even Bob Geldof has jumped on board with his own site, **www.deckchair.com**. Virgin Net offers a well-designed all-round travel service. There are even websites, such as QXL (**www.qxl.com**) and Last Minute, that allow you to bid at auction for tickets and holidays. Be prepared to hunt for the best bargain and make sure that the travel sites you book through are accredited by a recognised body.

Sunday Times
6 June 1999

Children's play activities

In its broadest definition, **play** can involve any spontaneous activity undertaken for enjoyment during a person's free time. For the purpose of the GNVQ study of the leisure and tourism industry, we shall confine our investigation to the provision of play areas and play schemes for children.

A supervised adventure playground

Playgrounds

Outdoor playgrounds for children are usually provided by public authorities. They often contain a combination of swings, climbing frames and roundabouts and are located in or near residential areas so that children have easy access. In terms of design, some have remained fairly unchanged since the 1950s and are now outdated, with equipment that doesn't meet today's safety standards. Nevertheless, many have been provided with varied, colourful and safe equipment, often protected by low fences to keep dogs away, and some have added equipment and areas for newer activities, such as skateboarding. Most playgrounds are not supervised by full-time staff and this has led to the development of a number of alternatives in recent years.

Play areas and schemes

Some adventure playgrounds, play centres and activity centres are open all year round and provide modern equipment in a safe environment with a full-time supervisor. They usually have indoor and outdoor facilities, and offer a range of play opportunities. Many 'family-friendly' pubs also provide play areas for children. If you have access to the internet you can identify facilities that provide play areas for children by searching the Families site (**www.families.co.uk**).

Some play areas and schemes are only supervised part time. These include holiday play schemes, after school clubs, junior youth clubs and play sessions in community facilities such as sports halls. By far the most popular of these are the summer holiday play schemes provided by most local authorities. Sometimes, local authorities provide play schemes in conjunction with local voluntary groups and associations. Holiday play schemes vary widely in the type of play

A colourful climbing frame for children

opportunities they offer, from arts and crafts to sports and outdoor pursuits.

Voluntary organisations such as Scouts, Guides, kids clubs and a range of community youth clubs offer play opportunities for children of all ages.

ACTIVITY

Children's play activities

Using the Families internet site (**www.families. co.uk**), or your own knowledge of your local area, list five facilities or venues that provide children's play activities. For each facility or venue provide the following information:

- location
- provider/owner
- the sector the facility belongs to
- facilities, products and services.

You will be able to use this information to complete the unit assignment on page 86.

Visitor attractions

This component of the leisure industry ranges from historic sites which are centuries old, such as Stonehenge and Scara Brae, to the latest technology-enhanced attractions such as Alton Towers theme park and Sega Mega World.

Historic buildings and sites

There are around 450,000 listed historic buildings and sites in the United Kingdom, but not all are open to visitors. They include:

- stately homes, palaces and manors (for example, Blenheim Palace, Castle Howard)
- castles and forts (for example, Edinburgh, Caernarfon, Dover)
- cathedrals, churches and abbeys (for example, Westminster Abbey, Coventry Cathedral, Rievaulx Abbey)
- monuments and ruins (for example, Hadrian's Wall, Glastonbury Tor)
- battlefields (for example, Naseby, Towton)
- historic ships (for example, Cutty Sark, HMS Victory).

Apart from their historic significance, these properties and sites have facilities and services for visitors including souvenir shops, restaurants, cafés, visitor centres and guide services. Many, including Westminster Abbey and York Minster, are owned and run by religious organisations. Both Westminster Abbey and York Minster attract more than two million visitors every year. Local authorities, the National Trust and English Heritage are also involved in preserving and maintaining historic buildings for the public to visit, while the five historic palaces – the Tower of London, Hampton Court, Kensington Palace, Kew Palace and the Banqueting House, Whitehall – are run by the government agency Historic Royal Palaces. About one third of the historic properties in the United Kingdom open to the public are owned and managed by the private or voluntary sector, including the National Trust.

Some towns and cities promote their areas as heritage centres. Bath, Chester, Edinburgh, Stratford-upon-Avon and York are examples.

CASE STUDY

Bath

Bath has a 2,000-year-old tradition of welcoming visitors to the city.

The unique character of this world heritage city is created by magnificent architecture set in beautiful landscapes. Choice and quality are celebrated in the city's shopping, entertainment and cuisine.

The museum collections are unrivalled in the West of England. Beyond Bath visitors can sample a range of famous attractions including stately homes, gardens, wildlife parks, caves and more.

A short break in the city is a good opportunity to enjoy the rich variety of activities both in and around Bath.

Heritage experience attractions

These are a relatively new group of attractions. They offer a simulated experience through technology-based techniques such as interactive displays, rides, animation, sounds and even smells. These facilities often contain museum collections and exhibits, although they are secondary to the 'experience' aspect. Such attractions are expensive to develop and build, so they are usually run by the private sector and charge admission fees.

The Jorvik Viking Centre in York, which opened in 1984, is an early example of a heritage experience attraction. Visitors are taken in a 'time car' back through the centuries to Viking Britain. A bustling market, dark smoky houses and a busy wharf have all been recreated in accurate detail so that visitors experience in sight, sound and smell what it was like to live and work in the Viking city of Jorvik.

As technology advances, it is likely that more of these attractions will be developed in the future. For example, the company that runs the Jorvik centre also has 'experiences' in Canterbury (The Canterbury Tales) and Oxford (The Oxford Story). The Natural History Museum, in London, has redeveloped its Earth Gallery in a £12 million facelift; visitors can now descend into a volcano to witness a simulated lava flow while a platform rocks in a mock earthquake.

▶ The new Earth Gallery at the Natural History Museum

Theme and leisure parks

Theme park is the term used to describe an action packed, family-centred leisure and entertainment complex. Parks may include high-technology versions of traditional funfair rides and roller coasters (sometimes referred to as white-knuckle rides), as well as amusement arcades, adventure playgrounds, computer simulations and laser games. They often also include a variety of sports facilities, heritage activities, zoos and wildlife areas.

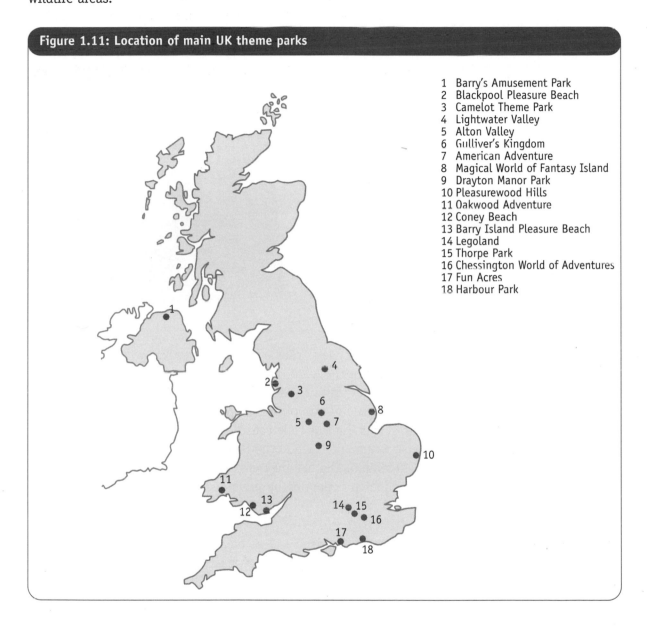

Figure 1.11: Location of main UK theme parks

1 Barry's Amusement Park
2 Blackpool Pleasure Beach
3 Camelot Theme Park
4 Lightwater Valley
5 Alton Valley
6 Gulliver's Kingdom
7 American Adventure
8 Magical World of Fantasy Island
9 Drayton Manor Park
10 Pleasurewood Hills
11 Oakwood Adventure
12 Coney Beach
13 Barry Island Pleasure Beach
14 Legoland
15 Thorpe Park
16 Chessington World of Adventures
17 Fun Acres
18 Harbour Park

The parks usually charge a daily admission, covering the cost of all rides, shows and entertainments. Alton Towers, in Staffordshire, is the largest admission-charging theme park in the United Kingdom, attracting over 2.6 million visitors in 1999. Figure 1.12 shows the leisure parks in England which attracted at least one million visitors in 1999.

Some theme and leisure parks do not charge admission fees, so it is possible only to estimate the total number of visitors each year. The English Tourist Board (now the English Tourism Council) estimates that up to 7.8 million people visit Blackpool Pleasure Beach each year. Other free parks attracting more than a million visitors each year include the Palace Pier, Brighton, the Pleasure Beach at Great Yarmouth, Pleasureland at Southport and Frontierland at Morecambe.

Figure 1.12: Leisure parks attracting more than one million annual visitors

Park	Operator
Alton Towers	Tussauds Group
Chessington, Surrey	Tussauds Group
Thorpe Park, Surrey	Leisure Sports Ltd
Flamingoland, North Yorkshire	Flamingoland Ltd
Drayton Manor Park	Drayton Manor Park Ltd
Legoland, Windsor	The Lego Group

We can see that theme and leisure parks in the United Kingdom in the 1990s are big business, attracting huge numbers of visitors. This has involved major financial investment, running into millions of pounds. For example, the Pepsi Max Big One rollercoaster at Blackpool Pleasure Beach cost £12 million, while the Nemesis ride at Alton Towers cost £10 million. The majority of theme parks in the United Kingdom are operated by private sector organisations.

Catering

Hospitality, catering and accommodation is an industry in its own right, but one which is closely linked to the leisure and tourism industries. Many leisure facilities include some form of **catering services**, ranging from vending machines to full service restaurants. Examples of catering and services that can be found in leisure facilities include:

- sports centres (bars, cafés, meeting rooms)
- cinemas (bars, snack and confectionery shops)
- theme parks (restaurants, bars)
- swimming pools (vending machines, cafés)
- sports stadiums (conference and reception facilities, restaurants)
- social clubs (bars, restaurants, reception facilities).

Build your learning

Summary points

- The term leisure covers an enormous range of activities and pastimes in a wide range of situations.

- The leisure industry can be divided into seven key components:
  - sports and physical recreation
  - arts and entertainment
  - countryside recreation
  - home-based leisure
  - children's play activities
  - visitor attractions
  - catering.

- These components are often interrelated.

- Leisure organisations and facilities provide a wide range of products and services.

Key words and phrases

You should know the meaning of the words and phrases listed below as they relate to the separate components of the leisure and recreation industries. Go back through the last 29 pages to refresh your understanding if necessary.

- **Key components**
- **Facilities**
- **Products**
- **Services**

- **Interrelated components**
- **Sports and physical recreation**
- **Arts and entertainment**
- **Countryside recreation**

- **Home-based leisure**
- **Play activities**
- **Visitor attractions**
- **Catering services**
- **Theme parks**

SUMMARY ACTIVITY

1 Describe the components of the leisure industry in an area of your choice. For each of the components listed below, give examples of the organisations and facilities and identify their main activities:

- sport and physical recreation
- arts and entertainment
- countryside recreation
- home-based leisure
- children's play activities
- visitor attractions
- catering.

You may wish to present your findings in a table (see below). If you add a fourth column and identify which sector each facility belongs to, you will not need to do task 1 of the summary activity on page 76.

Component	Organisation/facility	Activities(products and servicies)

2 Select two facilities from your chosen area and describe the products and services provided to local people and/or visitors.

3 Compare and contrast the products and services offered by the two facilities studied in task 2.

4 Identify any gaps in leisure provision in your area, explaining how they can be addressed by the facilities.

Components of the travel and tourism industry

Travel and tourism is one of the United Kingdom's largest industries. According to the government's 1995 White Paper *Competitiveness: Forging Ahead*, the industry provides about 1.5 million jobs (one in 13 of all jobs). Employment in travel and tourism has increased by about 25 per cent in the last decade. Tourism revenues amounted to £61 billion in 1998, making the industry the fourth largest earner of foreign exchange. It is estimated that this £61 billion of consumer expenditure comprised:

◄ How does tourism benefit the UK economy?

- £31 billion spent on domestic tourism day visits
- £14 billion spent on domestic holidays of one night or more
- £13 billion spent by overseas visitors whilst in the UK
- £3 billion paid by overseas passengers to UK international carriers.

The industry continues to grow as towns, cities and resorts increase their efforts to attract visitors from overseas (known as incoming tourists) and from other parts of the UK (known as domestic tourists). The industry also caters for British residents who travel overseas for leisure or business purposes (known as outgoing tourists). United Kingdom residents took 29 million overseas tourism trips in 1998.

The industry, which supports domestic, incoming and outgoing tourism, contains a number of separate, yet interrelated components. If you look back at Figure 1.2 (see page 10) you will see that the travel and tourism industry can be divided into six key components:

- travel agents
- tour operators
- tourist information and guiding services
- accommodation and catering
- attractions
- transportation.

This section describes each of these components, giving examples of the facilities, products and services available. The private sector dominates provision in all the components except information and guiding services, which are often provided by the public and voluntary sectors.

Travel agents

Travel agents serve people's leisure and business travel requirements. They include high street travel agents who sell a range of leisure and business travel products and services to outgoing, incoming and domestic tourists.

About 7,000 travel agencies in the United Kingdom are members of the Association of British Travel Agents (ABTA). They range from independent outlets with one or two offices to national chains with branches in almost every town and city. National chains include Thomas Cook, Lunn Poly, Going Places, AT Mays, Co-operative Travel and American Express.

Travel agents act as the link between customers and tour operators. They advise customers, suggest possible holidays or resorts and answer questions, and make bookings with tour operators by computer link or telephone. If you go into a travel agent's office you will see dozens of holiday brochures promoting all types of holiday, from cruises to skiing, children's activity weeks to holidays for the retired. It is the job of the travel agent to make sure customers select the holiday package which best suits their needs. Many travel agents also make coach, flight, rail or ferry bookings for clients who want independent travel arrangements, and many provide specialist services for business travellers, including travel, car hire and accommodation. Travel agents may also provide a range of ancillary products and services which include travel insurance, foreign currency and traveller's cheques, arranging for passports and visas, booking airport parking and advice on health requirements.

ACTIVITY

Travel agencies in your area

Make a list of all the travel agencies in a locality of your choice. You will be able to obtain this information from a telephone directory, the Yellow Pages or by visiting the locality yourself.

From your list, select one of the travel agencies and describe the range of products and services it provides for its customers. You may need to visit the agency to complete this part of the activity.

You will be able to use this information to complete the unit assignment on page 86.

@ WEBSTRACT

24 Hour Museum

Thomas Cook

Center Parcs

easyJet

The Rank Group

Thomas Cook is one of the most widely recognised and respected brands in the world. With a history dating back to 1841, Thomas Cook is today a leading international travel and financial services group.

Thomas Cook's customers have access to services at more than 3,000 locations in over 100 countries. In 1996, the company achieved gross sales of more than £20 billion.

More than 14,000 people are employed by Thomas Cook around the world. Every year, they serve over 20 million customers, ranging from leisure travellers seeking the ideal vacation, to major international corporations looking for better ways to do business with the world.

In addition to its worldwide network of locations, Thomas Cook also offers leisure travellers the convenience of planning and purchasing vacations from home through Thomas Cook Direct in the United Kingdom, Canada and Australia. This website offers residents of the United Kingdom the opportunity to plan their holidays and flights as well as order foreign money online.

Throughout all aspects of its business, Thomas Cook has a clear mission – to provide 'exceptional service from exceptional people'. The company prides itself on its reputation in seeking to fulfil that mission.

The breadth of its network enables Thomas Cook to offer its leisure travel customers access to the Worldwide Customer Promise. Customers who buy their travel arrangements from any Thomas Cook location around the world are entitled, free of charge, to airline ticket revalidation or rerouting, hotel reservations, car rental reservations, changes to hotel arrangements, travel planning and emergency assistance.

Source: **http://www.thomascook.co.uk**

THE ONE STOP **HOLIDAY SHOP**

AT THOMAS COOK

HOLIDAY MONEY
All major currencies and
Travellers Cheques available instantly*

TRAVEL INSURANCE
Excellent cover at competitive prices

AIRPORT HOTELS
FREE accommodation for children
under 16

AIRPORT CAR PARKING
Secure parking at competitive rates and
exclusive discounts

HOLIDAY CAR HIRE
Low cost hire option, in association
with Hertz

SEE OVER FOR MORE DETAILS

Thomas
Cook

Subject to availability

▼ Some well-known tour operators

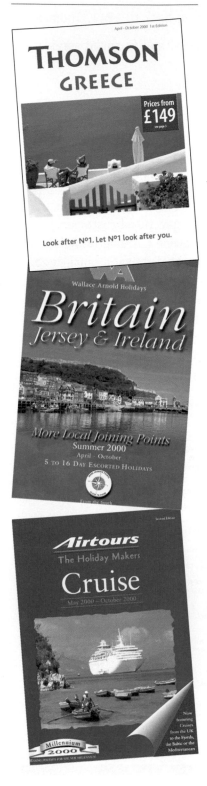

Currency exchange

Most overseas visitors carry cash in their own currency or traveller's cheques (a much safer way of carrying large sums of money), which they exchange for pounds sterling. This can be done at high street banks, some travel agencies and at currency exchange bureaux (bureaux de change). The exchange is made at the advertised rate for the day, minus a commission to the bank or agency. Some large hotels also exchange traveller's cheques, although usually with a larger commission. More and more people simply use cash cards or credit cards to obtain money from an automatic teller, settling accounts when they get home.

Tour operators

Tour operators arrange the transport, accommodation and leisure activities which make up the holiday package. These packages are usually sold to clients through travel agents who receive a commission for acting as the link between the customer and the supplier. Alternatively, tour operators may sell their holidays direct to the public, by telephone, via computer link or through the mail. The best known tour operators are those who provide packages for British tourists going abroad, although there are many others which deal with holidays in Britain, particularly those offering coach holidays and tours. Most of the market in outgoing tours is shared between a few major commercial companies, such as Thomsons, First Choice and Airtours. These companies have a variety of well-known tour operating brands including Horizon, Skytours, Portland (all Thomson). These companies often also own travel agencies and charter airlines: Thomson owns Lunn Poly and Britannia Airways, for example.

It is estimated that there are 700 tour operators currently providing around 20 million holiday packages for United Kingdom residents travelling abroad. If we also take into account the many small and medium-sized tour operators which cater for domestic, outgoing and incoming tourists, it is obvious that tour operations is a major component of the travel and tourism industry.

The main role of tour operators is to make arrangements for the various elements that comprise holiday packages by contracting with transport carriers (airlines, ferry and coach companies) and accommodation providers (hotels, self-catering venues and caravan and camping sites).

Advertised holidays often include entertainments and visits to local attractions, so the operator must also contract with a variety of organisations to produce the full holiday package. Their role does not end once the package has been put together and advertised in glossy holiday brochures: they have to ensure that holidays are run properly and deal with any problems and emergencies which may arise. Tour operators employ representatives at airports and resorts to look after customers, give advice and make arrangements so that holidays run smoothly.

Tour operators

Look at the travel pages of a national newspaper (Sunday editions may be the most useful) and find examples of tour operators that offer holiday packages:

- direct to the public

- through travel agents

- for outgoing tourists

- for domestic visitors.

Tourist information and guiding services

This component of the industry includes tourist and visitor information centres and guiding services. National and regional tourist boards, together with local authorities, play a key role in promoting tourism to bring employment and business to their areas. They support the development of tourism through marketing, publicity, research, education and information services. Part of this involves the provision of specially designated tourist information centres.

Tourist information centres

There are around 700 **tourist information centres** (TICs) in the United Kingdom, mostly funded and operated by local authorities and the regional tourist boards. They aim to provide accurate information for visitors to their area, and sell guidebooks, maps and souvenirs. They also operate booking services for accommodation, sightseeing tours, theatres and special events. For many visitors the tourist information centre is the first port of call on arrival in a locality, and the larger

▲ Tourist information centres have distinctive signs and logos

TICs often handle tens of thousands of enquiries, in person or over the telephone, every year. For example, 167,000 people visited the TICs in York in 1998. Although York City Council owns the premises of the TIC, the service is managed and provided by a private company, Guide Friday, and this is a practice which is becoming more common.

Tourist guides

Tourist guides are often self-employed and work is largely seasonal. **Guiding services** usually provide specialist knowledge of an area, a tourist attraction or a historic building. Many services are operated through the national and regional tourist boards 'blue badge' guides scheme (green in Wales). Some guide services are operated by commercial firms, of which Guide Friday is the largest. It caters for more than a million visitors a year and its distinctive green and cream open-top buses are a familiar sight in some of Britain's most popular heritage centres.

Many people work as voluntary guides, notably in historic buildings and churches. Indeed, in some buildings only volunteers demonstrating a required level of knowledge can give guided tours. Volunteers often belong to voluntary guide associations, which provide free tours and also provide training and support for their members.

▼ One of Guide Friday's distinctive tour buses

Accommodation and catering

In terms of jobs, accommodation and catering is by far the largest component of the UK travel and tourism industry. About one million people are employed in tourism-related accommodation and catering services, with 50,000 new jobs being created every year. The range of facilities varies enormously, from the owner-managed guest house, café or restaurant to national hotel groups and restaurant chains.

Accommodation

Accommodation can either be full service, which includes meals and housekeeping, or self-catering. Several classification schemes group providers according to the range of facilities and services they provide. For example, the national tourist boards for England, Scotland and Wales have developed the Crown and Key classification system for serviced and self-catering accommodation. They inspect over 20,000 hotels and similar establishments and 11,000 self-catering facilities a year, using a national grading and classification system (see Figure 1.13).

Figure 1.13: English Tourism Council's national grading and classification system

ACTIVITY

The English Tourism Council's grading system

Study the national grading and classification system for hotels and guest accommodation set out in Figure 1.13. In a locality of your choice, try to find an example of a facility in each category. So, for example, identify a five-star hotel, a four-star hotel, etc., and similarly a five-diamond self catering facilty, a four-diamond facility, etc.

You may find it useful to obtain an accommodation guide for your chosen locality. These are usually available from tourist information centres.

You will be able to use this information to complete the unit assignment on page 86.

Serviced accommodation

Hotels, guest houses and other serviced accommodation can be divided into three broad categories according to size:

- small (ten rooms or fewer)
- medium-sized (11–50 rooms)
- large (more than 50 rooms).

There are around 50,000 places of accommodation in the United Kingdom, of which 40,000 belong to the small category of ten rooms or fewer; the traditional bed and breakfast guest house is an example. There are only about 1,500 large hotels in the United Kingdom, most operated by hotel groups including Forte, Hilton and Thistle. These hotels provide many facilities and services, extending to baby minding, hair salons, fitness clubs, shops, currency exchange and conference and meeting rooms. Some of these groups operate a range of hotel types, to meet the needs of different customers. For example, Forte offers accommodation from budget standard at its Travelodges to 4-star or 5-star hotels under the Forte Grand banner. Figure 1.14 lists the top hotel groups in the United Kingdom by the number of hotels and bedrooms.

▲ Forte is one of the UK's largest hotel groups

Figure 1.14: Largest hotel groups in the United Kingdom

	Hotels	Bedrooms
Whitbread Hotel Company	206	12,458
Forte	161	22,203
Granada Travelodge	155	6,621
Regal Hotel Group	102	5,568
Thistle	97	13,329
Jarvis Hotels	64	5,447
Stakis Hotels	55	8,302
Queen's Moat Houses (UK)	51	7,103
Holiday Hospitality	46	6,399
Hilton (UK)	40	8,536

Source: *The Caterer and Hotelkeeper*, April 1998

ACTIVITY

Where to stay?

Suggest suitable accommodation in your locality for the following customers.

- A company director attending a midweek business conference and who receives daily expenses of £150 to cover accommodation and meals.

- A self-employed sales representative with a maximum accommodation budget of £75 a night and who requires photocopying facilities.

- A retired couple wishing to spend a weekend visiting friends in the area. They require bed and half board (breakfast or evening meal) and can afford £50 a night.

- A family of four, comprising two adults and two young children. They require six nights' accommodation, bed and breakfast only, for £150.

- A couple wishing to celebrate their first wedding anniversary in style. They require one night's accommodation and have £350 to spend.

You may find it useful to obtain a copy of a local 'Where to Stay' or the accommodation guide from your nearest tourist information centre

▼ The Caravan Club operates a number of sites

Self-catering accommodation

This is usually cheaper than serviced accommodation because less is provided. Examples include holiday cottages and homes, chalets, camp sites, caravan parks and timeshare properties. Many people prefer self-catering as it gives them more scope to plan their days as they please. Holiday centres that combine self-catering accommodation with activities and entertainments on a single site are also popular. Butlins, Center Parcs, Pontin's and Haven Warner are examples of companies which have invested large sums in creating purpose-built holiday and entertainment complexes.

@ WEBSTRACT

24 Hour Museum

Thomas Cook

Center Parcs

easyJet

The Rank Group

Center Parcs is the European market leader in the provision of short break holidays, operating in the Netherlands, Belgium, Britain, France and Germany.

Center Parcs has been in existence for 30 years, its first venture being a small complex of 40 holiday villas and limited sporting facilities in Holland. It has grown to become an international group of 13 major holiday villages: five of these are located in Holland, three in Great Britain, two in Belgium, two in France and one in Germany. Centre Parcs is part of Scottish & Newcastle plc, the UK publicly quoted brewing and leisure company.

The Center Parcs village

The average size of each European village is around 100 hectares; the sites are combinations of woodland and water, always located inland, with high quality accommodation in individual villas and an extensive range of indoor and outdoor sport and leisure facilities. The focus of each village is the Center Parcs subtropical swimming paradise, a transparent covered dome-shaped construction which houses a selection of water activities, including a wave pool, river slides and rides, children's pools, Jacuzzis and saunas. The temperature is a constant 28°C, and the setting is landscaped with specially quarried and polished natural rocks, luxuriant tropical trees, plants and flowers.

Center Parcs is targeted primarily at the family market, and caters for all ages with ample facilities for babies and children. Its location in relation to significant population centres is extremely important to ensure that the villages are easily accessible for the short stay periods which comprise its main business.

There is an average of 650 villas in each village, with a choice from one to four double bedrooms, spacious living areas, well equipped kitchens and full central heating. Each villa also has its own furnished patio.

The range of sports and leisure facilities, both indoor and outdoor, is extensive, and includes pursuits such as tennis, squash, riding, sailing, windsurfing and golf with fitness, health and beauty spas. There is a selection of themed restaurants and each village's own supermarket and themed shops cater for a range of purchases from sportswear to food for cooking in the villa.

Care for the environment

The company's criteria for site selection, during the planning and the construction of a village ensure that the minimum amount of disruption is caused to the indigenous surroundings. The layout of the central features and the villas, which are built in small groups, harmonise with the surroundings, the minimum number of trees are removed, with extensive planting and landscaping implemented as an essential element of the construction phase. It is not unusual for 500,000 new trees and comparable quantities of plants and bushes to be planted as part of the environmental programme for a village. Herds of deer, ducks, swans, wild birds, rabbits and squirrels are permanent residents of the villages.

The strength of Center Parcs' environmental policies and its continuing regard for ecological matters are recognised by leading specialists and organisations throughout Europe, and a number of prestigious awards have been won by the company and its villages.

Bicycles are used in the villages to transport guests to and from their villas and the sports and leisure facilities. These can be hired on arrival for the duration of the stay, provide a healthy travel alternative and ensure safety on the village roads for children. Guests use their cars to deliver and collect their luggage at their villas on arrival and departure, then leave them in specially landscaped parking areas in the villages.

The Center Parcs formula

In creating a mixture of sports, leisure and environmental facilities, using a blend of sophisticated technology, detailed attention to the enjoyment of its guests and its focus on nature and wildlife, Center Parcs has ensured that the weather will not affect its guests' enjoyment with indoor facilities, such as covered plazas housing the sports, shopping and eating areas.

Center Parcs offers primarily short break stays, of weekends, Friday to Monday, and midweeks, Monday to Friday. The option of longer stays at prime holiday times is also offered. The success of the Center Parcs formula is demonstrated in its booking figures which show occupancy levels of over 90 per cent throughout the year; in 1997, the company had over three million guests staying in its villages.

Source: **http://www.centerparcs.co.uk**

ACTIVITY

Center Parcs

Read the information about Center Parcs on this page.

- What company owns Center Parcs?
- What sector does it operate in – public, private or voluntary?
- At what market is Center Parcs mainly targeted?
- How does the company care for the environment?
- What facilities, products and services are offered to visitors at Center Parcs?

To answer the last question you may also find it useful to obtain a Center Parcs brochure or visit its website.

▲ These two large catering chains have restaurants throughout the country

Catering

The list of **catering** establishments serving food and drink to meet the needs of individuals is seemingly endless, from expensive à la carte restaurants and self-service cafeterias to burger bars, pizza houses and takeaways. The following is a list of only a few examples of catering facilities which can be found in most towns and cities in the United Kingdom:

- restaurants
- cafés
- bistros and wine bars
- fast food and takeaway outlets
- pizza houses
- pubs
- snack bars
- mobile snack bars.

ACTIVITY

Catering outlets in your area

From your knowledge of a locality, give examples of catering facilities for each of the categories above. You may find it useful to refer to a copy of the Yellow Pages or a local newspaper.

Visitor attractions

Any facility or event which draws visitors to a particular place can be called a **visitor attraction**. There are many such attractions in the United Kingdom, ranging from small local heritage sites and buildings to major leisure and theme parks visited by millions every year. Figure 1.15 shows some of the most popular admission-charging visitor attractions in the country.

Earlier, we identified many of the leisure facilities that can be regarded as visitor attractions, including theatres, museums, heritage sites, theme parks and countryside parks. Touche Ross, a firm of management consultants, estimated that, in 1994, there were over 1,100 visitor attractions in the United Kingdom which each receive at least 100,000 visitors a year. Few, if any, localities do not have some form of visitor attraction. A good idea of the range of attractions in a particular area can be gained by studying a road touring map, which uses different key symbols to denote various types of attraction. Alternatively, you can obtain information from the Yellow Pages or from visitor guides for a particular locality. If you have access to the internet you can obtain information about most attractions. Some useful websites are provided in the internet directory (see page 253).

▼ Two well-known visitor attractions

Figure 1.15: Top twenty visitor attractions charging admission, 1999

Attraction	Visitors
Alton Towers, Staffordshire	2,650,000
Madame Tussaud's, London	2,640,000
Tower of London	2,422,181
Natural History Museum, London	1,739,591
Legoland, Windsor	1,620,000
Chessington World of Adventures, Surrey	1,550,000
Science Museum, London	1,480,000
Royal Academy, London	1,390,000
Canterbury Cathedral	1,350,000
Windsor Castle, Berkshire	1,280,000
Westminster Abbey, London	1,268,215
Edinburgh Castle	1,219,720
Flamingo Land Theme Park, Yorkshire	1,197,000
Drayton Manor Park, Staffordshire	1,174,448
Windermere Lake Cruises, Cumbria	1,140,207
St. Paul's Cathedral, London	1,076,222
London Zoo	1,067,917
Chester Zoo	965,721
Victoria and Albert Museum, London	945,677
Thorpe Park, Surrey	926,000

Source: www.staruk.org, ETC and BTA figures

ACTIVITY

Visitor attractions

Using the key and symbols, identify and list all of the visitor attractions on the map.

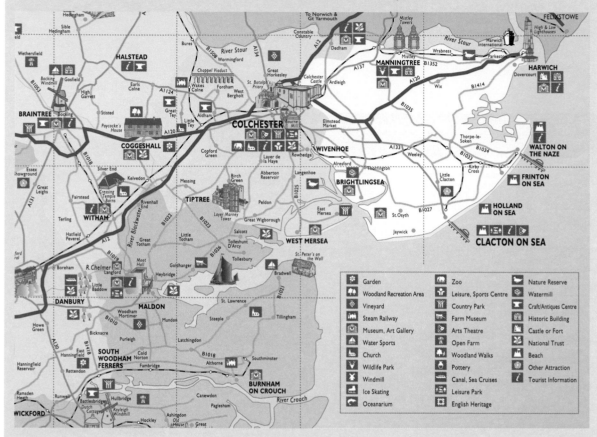

List five visitor attractions in your area and describe, briefly, why you think people visit these places. For one of the attractions in your list, describe the facilities, products and services it offers visitors.

You will be able to use this information for your unit assignment on page 86.

Tourist destinations

Often, visitor attractions are clustered in particular **tourist destinations**. Sometimes, an attraction is the main purpose for a visit (for example, Stonehenge) but usually visitors travel to a locality with the intention of seeing several things, ranging from natural features (beaches, lakes, hills) to purpose-built facilities such as shops, museums, theatres and heritage sites. Some areas contain both natural and purpose-built attractions.

Popular seaside holiday resorts

Copy or trace the outline map and identify the location of these popular seaside resorts by matching the correct number to the resorts listed below.

- Great Yarmouth
- Southend-on-Sea
- Brighton
- Torbay
- Newquay
- Pwllheli
- Blackpool
- Ullapool
- Scarborough
- Skegness
- Torquay
- Tenby
- Douglas
- Anglesey
- Eastbourne
- Cowes
- Bognor Regis
- Weymouth

Select one of these seaside resorts and make a list of the natural features and purpose-built facilities that combine to make it a popular tourist destination.

In addition to the established centres and holiday resorts, a number of other locations are seeking to increase their tourism potential. One is Liverpool, which attracts over 30 million day visitors and tourists a year. Tourism is now a major force in the city's economy. The city has successfully changed its image, so that people now see Liverpool as an interesting place to visit. Tourism promotion has been backed by large investment in new attractions, notably the refurbished Albert Dock.

CASE STUDY

Liverpool

Liverpool is a vibrant and exciting place to visit and a warm welcome is always guaranteed. The centre is alive with theatres, clubs, restaurants and attractions that are able to provide something for everyone.

Liverpool is one of the world's most famous and historic cities and its distinguished life as a centre for world trade and commerce is clearly reflected in its rich culture and architectural heritage, a fact reinforced by being shortlisted for the City of Architecture and Design 1989. Liverpool is host to many major sporting and spectator events throughout the year.

Over 2,500 listed buildings are located within the area and many are built to classical designs. William Brown Street is home to a number of the city's finest buildings, including the Walker Art Gallery, Liverpool Museum and Central Libraries. Nearby St George's Hall, constructed in an age when size and grandeur were of paramount importance, is widely regarded as the finest neo-classical building in Europe. The Town Hall is the jewel of Liverpool's historic buildings with its golden Minerva sitting proudly atop the golden dome. Both are being refurbished with a view to opening them up to the public, to see their splendour.

The city can also boast of being one of the greenest cities in Britain. Relax and enjoy the pleasant surroundings of the 2,400 acres of parkland and open spaces. Croxteth Hall and Country Park Estate is set in 500 acres of woodland with a collection of working farm animals, miniature railway and adventure

playground. The historic mansion contains period rooms and character figures and provides a welcome throughout the summer.

So whether it is to be the Beatles or Beethoven; museums to musicals; theatre to tall ships; cathedrals to caverns; soccer to shopping; galleries to gardens; discos to drama; eating to entertainment – Liverpool has got what it takes.

Source: Liverpool and Merseyside
Visitor Guide

Urban attractions

Read the case study about Liverpool. Make notes for a similar article about a town or city you know and which is not usually thought of as a place for tourists to visit.

If you can, obtain a map or guide to identify the range of natural and purpose-built attractions in the area.

Transportation

A variety of operations in the transport sector are supported by the travel and tourism industry. The type of transport required usually depends on the distance to be travelled, how much the traveller can afford to spend, the time available, the purpose of the visit and the relative ease of access to departure points.

Transportation can be divided into three categories, namely, land-based, air-based and water-based. The most common modes of transport within each are:

- land (car, coach, taxi, bus, bicycle, train, etc.)
- air (charter flights, scheduled flights, helicopter trips, etc.)
- water (ferries, cruise ships, hovercraft, canal barges, etc.).

Transport carriers form a significant part of the travel and tourism industry. In the United Kingdom they are now mainly private companies. They include organisations such as British Airways, Virgin Atlantic Airways, P&O European Ferries, Stena Sealink, Eurostar and National Express.

These travel carriers use a well-developed transport network comprising roads, railways, inland waterways, shipping lanes and airways. It contains many terminals which people use at the beginning and end of their journeys. Thus, bus and rail stations and ports and airports can also be regarded as important facilities within the travel and tourism industry. The map within the activity on page 66 shows the location of the principal air and sea ports in the UK.

Heathrow is the United Kingdom's largest and busiest airport, handling 59 million passengers in 1998. Most airports and seaports provide a wide range of facilities to keep travellers occupied. Many have developed into large shopping centres. Heathrow's Terminal 4, for example, contains 22 stores, and seven bars and restaurants.

▲ Some of the UK's well-known transport providers

ACTIVITY

Transport providers

For a chosen locality, identify at least one transport provider for each category in the table below. If there is no provider for any of the categories, select the nearest from outside your locality. An example is provided to help you get started.

Transport category	Name of company	Location/Terminal
Car hire		
Bicycle hire		
Coach		
Taxi		
Train		
Airline	easyJet	Liverpool Airport
Helicopter		
Ferry		
Cruise ships		
River boats/canal barges		

Select one transport provider from your list and describe the range of services it offers to customers.

ACTIVITY

easyJet's cheap flights

Read the extract from the easyJet website (opposite).

- How does easyJet justify its claim that it can provide lower cost air tickets than most airlines?

- What is the nearest airport to you from which easyJet operates its low cost service?

- Compare the cost of an easyJet flight with that of another airline for a selected date/route.

- Describe reasons why there is a difference in price between the two services selected above.

Use the internet, look at newspapers or visit a travel agent to find information about flight dates, routes and fares.

@ WEBSTRACT

24 Hour Museum

Thomas Cook

Center Parcs

easyJet

The Rank Group

easyJet offers a simple, no frills service at rock bottom fares. Its European destinations include Amsterdam, Barcelona, Geneva, Madrid, Malaga, Nice, Palma and Zurich.

Mission statement

To provide our customers with safe, low cost, good value, point to point air services. To offer a consistent and reliable product at fares appealing to leisure and business markets from our bases to a range of domestic and European destinations. To achieve this we will develop our people and establish lasting partnerships with our suppliers.

How can we offer these great fares?

Fares can be offered at such good value for four main reasons.

- **No travel agents ...** easyJet is the only airline which has never paid a penny in commission to a travel agent. All bookings are made direct with easyJet reservations centre or booked direct on the internet. Cutting out the middleman saves the commission fee paid to a travel agent.

- easyJet is a **ticketless airline**. All you need to fly is your passport and your confirmation number. This is less hassle for the customer who does not have to worry about collecting tickets before travelling, and cost effective for easyJet.

- **No Heathrow ...** easyJet uses uncongested, inexpensive airports with the cost advantages being passed on to travellers. Using uncongested airports also allows easyJet to get much better use out of its aircraft rather than wasting time waiting for slots at a busy airports.

- **There's no such thing as a free lunch ...** So easyJet does not offer one. Plastic trays of airline food only mean more expensive flights. easyJet passengers are given the choice as to whether they wish to buy themselves drinks or snacks from the in-flight easykiosk. Our customer feedback illustrates that passengers do not want a meal on board a short-haul flight. They prefer to pay less for the flight and have a choice to purchase snacks on board if desired.

Source: **http://www.easyjet.com**

ACTIVITY

Major airports and sea ports

Copy the map and match the airports and seaports to the appropriate location reference on the map.

Seaports

- Dover
- Felixstowe
- Folkestone
- Harwich
- Holyhead
- Hull
- Newcastle upon Tyne
- Newhaven
- Plymouth
- Poole
- Portsmouth
- Stranraer
- Swansea
- Weymouth

Airports

- Birmingham
- Bristol
- East Midlands
- Edinburgh
- Gatwick
- Glasgow
- Heathrow
- Humberside
- Leeds Bradford
- London City
- Luton
- Manchester
- Teesside

Both

- Aberdeen
- Belfast
- Cardiff
- Liverpool
- Southampton

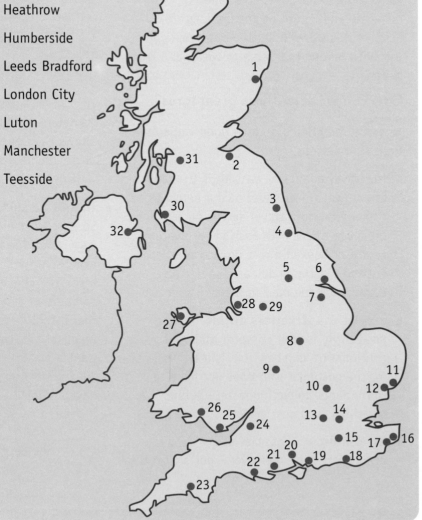

Build your learning

Summary points

- The travel and tourism industry covers an enormous range of activities in a wide variety of situations.

- The industry can be divided in to six key components:
  - travel agents
  - tour operators
  - tourist information and guiding services
  - accommodation and catering
  - visitor attractions
  - transportation.

- These components are often interrelated.

- Travel and tourism organisations and facilities provide a wide range of products and services to customers.

Key words and phrases

You should know the meaning of the words and phrases listed below as they relate to the organisation and components of the travel and tourism industries. Go back through the last 20 pages to refresh your understanding if necessary.

- **Key components**
- **Facilities**
- **Products**
- **Services**
- **Interrelated components**

- **Travel agents**
- **Tour operators**
- **Tourist information centres**
- **Guiding services**
- **Accommodation**

- **Catering**
- **Visitor attractions**
- **Tourist destinations**
- **Transportation**

SUMMARY ACTIVITY

1 Describe the main components of the travel and tourism industry in an area of your choice. For each of the components listed below, give examples of organisations and facilities and identify their main activities:

- travel agents
- tour operators
- tourist information and guiding services
- accommodation and catering
- visitor attractions
- transportation.

You may wish to present your findings in a table (see below). If you add a fourth column and identify which sector each facility belongs to, you will not need to do task 1 of the summary activity on page 76.

Component	Organisation/facility	Activities (products and services)

2 Select two facilities from your chosen area and describe the products and services provided to local people and/or visitors.

3 Compare and contrast the products and services offered by the two facilities studied in task 2 above.

You may be able to combine your investigation of the travel and tourism industry in your locality with the earlier activity on the leisure industry (see page 46).

Public, private and voluntary sectors

We have identified the structure of the leisure and tourism industries in the United Kingdom and the range of products and services they provide. This section identifies the different types of organisation which can be found in the leisure and tourism industries and examines their roles.

Broadly speaking, we can divide leisure and tourism organisations into two groups: those which are publicly owned and those which are privately owned. We can further divide the latter into privately owned organisations operating with the aim of making a **profit** (the private sector) and organisations which are **not operating for profit** (the voluntary sector). See pages 11–12 for definitions of the public, private and voluntary sectors.

These sectors provide a basis for comparison. For each organisation this involves identifying and describing, among other things:

- **the scale of the operation** – international, national, regional or local
- **who does the work** (its personnel) – and whether they are paid employees, volunteers or a combination of both
- **how they are funded** – by government grants, private capital, membership subscriptions or a combination of these
- **the financial basis of the operation** – to make profits, to cover costs, to break even with a subsidy.

The public sector

Local authorities are by far the largest providers of local public leisure and tourism facilities and services. Most provide a wide range of facilities and services such as:

- museums and art galleries
- leisure centres and swimming pools
- youth and community centres
- parks, gardens and allotments
- playing fields and sports pitches
- public halls and conference centres
- tourist information centres
- catering services
- children's playschemes and summer playschemes
- libraries.

Most local authority leisure and tourism facilities and services are subsidised by local taxes, including council tax and business rates. Local authorities also generate income by charging for the facilities, products and services they provide. Charging for admission is the most common example of revenue. Public sector organisations sometimes make profits but do not have profitability as their main objective. This is why a public sector facility may offer certain groups of people, such as the unemployed or those on low incomes, free or subsidised admission.

ACTIVITY

A–Z of leisure and tourism facilities

Find out what leisure and tourism facilities and services are provided by your local authority. Put together an A–Z of facilities. You may find this information useful when completing the assignment for this unit (see page 86).

> What is the main aim of private sector organisations?

The private sector

The private sector is made up of a variety of commercial operators owned by individuals or companies, whose main aim is to generate profits from the services and products which they provide for their customers. The main activities of the private sector in the leisure and tourism industries are in the fields of:

- retail sales
- catering and accommodation
- entertainment
- travel services
- tourism.

Figure 1.16 identifies some of the United Kingdom's largest leisure companies, and gives a brief explanation of their interests and areas of activity.

Many private sector leisure organisations such as Rank, Granada, Ladbrokes, Thomas Cook, Thomson and Virgin are household names and make a major contribution to the wealth of the United Kingdom. Leisure and tourism facilities commonly provided by the private sector include golf courses, theme parks, health and fitness clubs, travel agencies restaurants and hotels.

Many private sector organisations are now also involved in the management of public facilities on behalf of public sector organisations. However, in general, private sector companies are unlikely to get involved in the non-profit-making areas of the leisure and tourism industries. It is unusual to find private sector companies willing to open a facility unless they are confident that they can achieve an appropriate financial return on their investment.

Figure 1.16: Major leisure companies

Company	Activities and interests
Airtours	Tour operators
Bass plc	Hotels, bingo clubs, betting shops, bowling centres, gaming machines
David Lloyd Leisure plc	Sports and leisure facilities
First Leisure Corporation plc	Bowling, discos, piers, leisure centres, hotels, snooker clubs and theatres
Granada Group plc	Interests in the leisure, television, communications and service industries
Ladbroke Group plc	Retail and credit betting, property, DIY retail, hotels
Pearson plc	Newspaper publication, magazines, books, family entertainment attractions
Rank Leisure Ltd	Leisure and entertainment services
Scottish & Newcastle plc	Interests include holiday villages
Stanley Leisure plc	Operation of licensed betting offices and casinos
Thomas Cook	Travel agents, tour operators
Thomson Holidays	Tour operators
Tussauds Group plc	Daytime family entertainment
Whitbread plc	Brewing, pubs, hotels, restaurants and off-licences
Vardon plc	Operators of visitor attractions and bingo facilities

Private sector leisure companies

Look at the share price section in any broadsheet national newspaper, such as *The Times*, the *Daily Telegraph* or *The Guardian*. Find and make a list of the companies that appear under the heading 'leisure'.

In groups, discuss the types of organisation listed and the products and services they provide. Which components of the leisure and tourism industries are best represented?

@WEBSTRACT

24 Hour Museum

Thomas Cook

Center Parcs

easyJet

The Rank Group

The Rank Group is a leader in leisure and entertainment and operates two business streams: it provides services to the film industry and entertains consumers directly through its portfolio of strong leisure and entertainment brands.

Rank aims is to become one of the leading leisure and entertainment companies in the world. Already one of the UK's leading leisure companies, Rank employs over 40,000 people based mainly in the UK, North America and mainland Europe. It owns some of Britain's best known brands, as well as the globally recognised Hard Rock. Since the 1930s Rank has been synonymous with entertainment.

Over the last two years, the company has undertaken extensive reorganisation, rationalising its operation to concentrate on key businesses and markets, exploiting the power of its brands and developing a dynamic and entrepreneurial management culture throughout the group.

Butlins

Butlins is the brand leader in the UK holiday market selling some 1.8 million holidays each year. In 1997, Rank announced plans to invest £139 million in Butlins over the next two years to revitalise the Butlins brand.

Minehead, Bognor Regis and Skegness were relaunched as family entertainment resorts for the 1999 season, while Ayr and Pwllheli have become Haven All Action Parks.

The three relaunched resorts now boast new accommodation, Splash Water Worlds, bars, restaurants and entertainment venues such as Pinewood Studios themed cafés, Jaks live music venues and West End style shows performed by the Redcoats.

At the centre of each resort is a massive Skyline Pavilion which now allows Butlins to offer year round weatherproof holidays for the first time.

Source: **http://www.rank.com**

Deluxe	Leisure	Holidays	Hard Rock	Universal
Film laboratories	Mecca bingo	Haven	Cafe	Universal escape
Video services	Grosvenor casinos	Butlins	Live!tv	Universal Japan
Pinewood studios	Odeon cinemas	Warner	Records	
	Rank entertainment	Oasis	Live! music	
	Tom Cobleigh	Resorts USA	Hotels	
	Machine services	Leisure services	Beer	
			NBA alliance	

ACTIVITY

The Rank Group

Read the extract from the Rank Group website. Find out information about the facilities, products and services provided by one of the Rank Group's brands, such as Butlins. You will find it useful to search the website (**www.rank.com**) to gather information. It may be possible to obtain information from a Rank operation in your area, or you could obtain a brochure from a travel agent.

Rank Group

You will be able to use this information to complete the unit assignment on page 86.

The voluntary sector

It is estimated that there are more than 200 national voluntary leisure and tourism groups in the UK, with a combined membership of over eight million people. These include:

- youth and community groups
- sports clubs and associations
- conservation and heritage groups
- touring groups
- social clubs
- animal welfare and wildlife conservation groups.

If you add all the thousands of small local clubs, societies, associations and other groups which can be found throughout the United Kingdom, it becomes clear that the voluntary sector is a major provider of leisure and tourism opportunities.

Most amateur sport in the United Kingdom, for example, is managed by local voluntary clubs and associations which are supported by their members, local businesses and members of the community. In the field of art and entertainment, there are thousands of arts clubs and societies which are run by volunteers and which receive support from the Arts Council through its regional offices. Access to the countryside for recreation is promoted through voluntary organisations like the National Trust, the Ramblers Association and the Youth Hostel Association which have been established for more than a century. In the countryside, environmental protection is promoted by organisations that provide many volunteers who give up their time to restore the natural environment. And in the field of tourism, museums and art galleries frequently rely upon volunteers to act as guides, whilst many smaller tourist

◀ Is the main aim of voluntary sector organisations to make a profit?

attractions are run entirely on a voluntary basis.

The voluntary sector is funded in a number of different ways. Large organisations like the National Trust may operate along similar lines to private sector organisations and run retail outlets but, like all voluntary sector organisations, it relies on subscriptions from members, donations, gifts and legacies, government grants, sponsorship and fundraising events.

Many voluntary organisations have **charitable status**. This gives them some financial advantages that may include rate and VAT relief, relief from income tax on investments, bank deposits and covenants. Voluntary sector organisations that register as charities have to satisfy certain conditions. Their objectives must be charitable, non-profit-making, for the advancement of education or for other purposes beneficial to the community.

ACTIVITY

Voluntary organisations in your area

Give examples of the following types of voluntary organisations in an area of your choice:

- a uniformed group which provides recreational opportunities for teenagers

- a youth organisation affiliated to a religious group

- a conservation group

- a sports group or association

- an art or drama group

- a registered charitable organisation.

Compare your findings with others in your group. Using these findings, compile a list of all of the voluntary organisations in your area. For each organisation identify which industry component it belongs to. For this activity you may be able to use some of the information you gathered on sports clubs and associations, when you did the activity on page 22.

Select one organisation from your list and investigate the products and services it provides for its members.

You will be able to use this information to complete the unit assignment on page 86.

CASE STUDY

The National Trust

The National Trust is a registered charity. It is the largest voluntary organisation in the UK. It was founded in 1895 to protect the countryside and properties.

The trust uses its income to preserve the properties which it already owns and to buy others which are at risk from development or which have been allowed to decline. The National Trust receives income from over 2.5 million members. In 1998, 35,000 volunteers worked over 2 million hours for the trust.

The National Trust owns 27 national nature reserves, 207 historic houses, 162 gardens, 25 industrial monuments and 51 religious buildings. It cares for over 240,000 hectares of countryside in England, Wales and Northern Ireland, plus 575 miles of outstanding coastline.

Build your learning

Summary points

- Leisure and tourism organisations operate in one of three sectors: the private sector, the public sector or the voluntary sector.

- Private sector organisations aim to make a profit.

- Public sector organisations do not usually have profit making as a main objective. They aim to offer facilities and services to benefit local people and visitors.

- Voluntary sector organisations are not run to make a profit, but to provide facilities and services for their members or to promote good causes.

Key words and phrases

You should know the meaning of these phrases as they relate to the organisation of leisure and tourism businesses.

- **Public sector**
- **Private sector**
- **Voluntary sector**
- **Profit**
- **Not-for-profit**
- **Comparison**
- **Scale of operation**
- **Who does the work**
- **How they are funded**
- **Financial basis of operation**
- **Local authorities**
- **Charitable status**

SUMMARY ACTIVITY

1 Go back to the end of section activities on pages 46 and 68. Identify the sector of each of the leisure or travel and tourism organisations and facilities that you listed in your chosen area. You may wish to add a fourth column to the tables you completed for these activities to show this information.

2 Study the following description of six leisure and tourism facilities. Match each facility listed in the table opposite with the descriptions and identify the sector which relates to each description.

Owner	Facility	Personnel	Financial basis
1 Local council	Facility attracts 20,000 visitors a year, mainly from the local community.	Workers employed by the council, including a manager, curator and guides.	Funded by the council, with free admission. Visitors may make donations if they wish.
2 Regional tourist board	Facility attracts over 100,000 visitors a year and handles around 200,000 telephone and postal enquiries.	Workers employed by the tourist board, including information clerks and guides.	Funded by grants from local councils and tourist board, with income from the sale of maps, guides and booking fees.
3 Major commercial organisation	Part of a national chain of 25 facilities, the facility attracts 500,000 customers annually.	Employees, including a manager, box office staff, catering and technical staff.	Aims to make a profit (25% gross a year); income from admission charges, sales of food, drink and souvenirs.
4 Privately owned organisation	Only open between May and September, it can accommodate a maximum of ten adults and ten children a night.	The owner does most of the work. At busy periods some temporary part timers are employed.	Generates sufficient income to meet expenses and provide an income for the owner. Customers pay for the service.
5 Sports association	Features a football pitch and a cricket pitch and a small clubhouse with a bar (the club has 85 members).	Volunteers, except a part-time groundsman and bar staff on match days.	Grant from the council, income from membership and match fees, bar sales, local sponsorship. The club aims to break even.
6 National organisation	One of 230 houses and 130 sites, including coastal and wild sites, collectively attracting around seven million visitors a year.	Paid workers and volunteers.	Registered as a charity, non-profit-making. Income from donations, admission charges, membership fees and government grants.

Facility	Description number	Sector
Seaside resort guesthouse		
Village sports club		
Multiplex cinema		
National Trust property		
Museum		
Tourist information centre		

Links between leisure and tourism

Although the leisure and tourism industries have been investigated separately, there are many links between the two. Both industries are dependent upon each other for customers. For example:

- a family day out at a visitor attraction is a leisure activity but also involves travel and tourism
- travelling to a major sporting event could be considered as both leisure and tourism
- going on holiday and many activities undertaken while on holiday could be considered as both leisure and tourism
- going to the theatre and staying in a hotel overnight is both leisure and tourism
- the local tourist information centre provides details of both leisure and tourism facilities and activities available in the area
- transport providers operate services to places of interest for both the leisure market and tourists.

These are just a few examples of the many links between leisure and tourism. The next activities provide specific examples of how the industries are linked. For your unit assignment you will need to find examples of links within the locality you chose to investigate. The type of links may vary from locality to locality. To give you an idea of links, look at Figure 1.17 which identifies typical links between leisure and tourism facilities and organisations.

Figure 1.17: Examples of links between leisure and tourism facilities

Facility	Examples of links
Tourist Information Centre	• Accommodation providers • Transportation providers • Visitor attractions in the area • Sports centres/leisure facilities • Guiding services • Arts and entertainments in the area • Catering services/restaurants • Children's play activities • Outdoor pursuits centres
Visitor attraction	• Accommodation providers in the area • Transportation providers (rail, coach, taxi,etc.) • Catering services/facilities • Tour operators (coach parties, tour groups, etc.) • Guiding services • Tourist information services • Other visitor attractions in the area
Airport/ferry port or train station	• Travel agents • Tour operators • Accommodation providers • Transportation providers • Children's play activities (crèche, play areas, etc.) • Tourist information services • Visitor attractions in the locality
Sports centre	• Transportation providers • Catering services and facilities • Children's play activities • Visitor attraction (used by tourists and locals) • Tourist information centres • Outdoor pursuits centres • Arts entertainments
Travel agent	• Tour operators • Transportation providers • Tour guiding services • Visitor attractions • Countryside recreation • Accommodation providers • Catering services • Major sports events

Euro '96

Research by the Leisure Industries Research Centre reveals that in total over 280,000 visiting spectators and media came to England to attend Euro '96 matches, spending approximately £120 million (see Figure 1.18).

Like any major event, the European football championships involved many leisure and tourism providers from several of the key industry components. In small groups, discuss the types of leisure and tourism providers that you think were involved in providing products and services to the Euro '96 fans. Make a list of the main types of providers and describe how they were linked.

When you have completed the task, look ahead to the possibility of England staging another major sporting event such as the 2006 football World Cup. What components of the UK leisure and tourism industry do you think would most benefit from staging this event?

Figure 1.18: The economic impact of Euro '96

	Additional expenditure (£m)	Expenditure per game (£m)	Expenditure per visitor (£)
Total economic impact	120	3.88	77.00
London	34	3.10	67.09
Birmingham	11	2.73	56.72
Manchester	10.3	2.05	60.90
Liverpool	7	1.68	55.00
Leeds	4	1.34	59.37
Newcastle	5	1.65	55.54
Sheffield	5	1.65	55.25
Nottingham	7	2.38	60.87
Outside host cities	37	1.20	75.00

Source: Leisure Industries Research Centre

ACTIVITY

The O$_2$ complex

Retail/leisure complexes such as the O$_2$ development in London have become commonplace in the UK. These complexes contain a range of retail and leisure facilities that attract large numbers of customers. Other well-known examples include Lakeside in Thurrock, the Metro Centre in Gateshead and Meadowhall in Sheffield.

Located adjacent to Finchley Road tube station, the O$_2$ complex contains an eight-screen Warner Village cinema, Esporta health club, the largest Sainsbury's in London and a number of restaurants. It is being billed by the developers as 'the new centre of North London life, an unmissable venue for relaxing in the capital'.

Describe how the leisure and tourism organisations and facilities in the O$_2$ complex are linked. What, do you think, is the most popular type of leisure and tourism facility on the site?

Links between leisure and tourism organisations

Although the public, private and voluntary sectors have differing objectives, they have become increasingly linked in recent years. The principle underlying this development is that joint ventures between two or more sectors can lead to outcomes which could not otherwise result. There are many examples of such joint ventures, two of the most common being:

- dual use and joint provision
- partnership and sponsorship ventures.

Dual use and joint provision

Dual use and **joint provision** are both types of shared provision. Dual use has been defined as:

> the longer-term, regular use on an organised basis of facilities, particularly those financed from public funds, by the general public, either as members of groups or clubs or as individuals, for whom the facility was not primarily intended.

The most common form of dual use is where schools and the public use the same leisure facilities. This may involve a school allowing use of its sports hall or swimming pool by the public outside school hours and during holiday periods. This type of provision usually involves liaison between the local education authority, the local authority and local voluntary organisations.

If leisure facilities are shared between the school and the public during the day, and used by the public at all other times, then this is referred to as joint provision. Joint provision facilities are usually funded primarily by local authorities, with assistance from local education authorities.

Dual use and joint provision schemes are not confined to partnerships within the public sector (that is, between education authorities and local authorities). Many large private sector organisations provide leisure facilities for their employees. These organisations often have agreements with public and voluntary sector organisations to encourage multiple use of their facilities.

Dual use of sports and leisure facilities

Survey a selection of schools in your area which have sports and/or leisure facilities. Find out if their facilities are open to the public and if so, when and how often.

You may be able to base part of your investigation on your own school or college if it has leisure facilities that are open to the public at certain times.

Partnership and sponsorship ventures

Partnership and **sponsorship** ventures between public, private and voluntary organisations are becoming increasingly common in the provision of leisure and tourism facilities and services, particularly where significant financial investment is required. Investment in the leisure and tourism industries is, like any business, a gamble. Leisure and tourism organisations invest millions of pounds in risky ventures in order to capitalise on market opportunities.

Perhaps the biggest leisure investment in recent years was the building of the Channel Tunnel, which involved many millions of pounds of investment. As with any risk venture, there is a danger that Eurotunnel will not be able to provide its owners (the shareholders) with any return (dividends) on their investment. Indeed, if the company goes bankrupt, then shareholders will lose all of their investment and the financial backers of the project (the banks) will not recoup the huge sums they have loaned Eurotunnel.

Now imagine that there is a major leisure and tourism development proposal in your area for a leisure complex. There is undoubtedly a need for the development, but who is going to finance it? The local authority does not have sufficient money and no single private sector organisation is prepared to take the risk. One possible solution would be for the local authority to reduce the amount of risk by ensuring that planning permission is granted and by offering various incentives for private sector investors, such as low rents and reduced business rates. The private sector would be more likely to invest in such a project, as the risks are spread. Examples of cooperation between local authorities and private sector organisations like this are becoming commonplace.

There are several common types of partnership and cooperative ventures which take place between the three sectors.

- **Sponsorship and patronage** – large private sector organisations often provide financial backing to the public and voluntary sectors to provide facilities and services and to run events.
- **Grants** – central government can provide public, private and voluntary sector organisations with grants to support new developments. Organisations can also access grants from European Commission development funds and urban regeneration schemes.
- **Planning gain** – local authorities can lift planning restrictions on private sector developments in return for public leisure facilities. For example, planning permission for many large shopping complexes (or malls) funded by the private sector has been granted in return for provision of community leisure facilities.

There are hundreds of partnership ventures which have led to the development and improvement of leisure facilities. Perhaps the best way of demonstrating the nature and extent of cooperation between the sectors is by looking at some examples.

◄ How may an organisation benefit from sponsorship ventures?

McLaren makes more vroom in the pool

Themed around the thrills and spills of Grand Prix racing, the Team McLaren Vroom Flume Water slide game ride has opened at the Pool in the Park in Woking. The ride has been developed through a partnership between Woking Borough Council, Woking Leisure, and the Formula One racing team McLaren. The aim of the game is to score points by descending the slide as fast as possible and touching illuminated targets along the flume walls. The ride is completely blacked out and contains laser beams. An IT package computes points won and time taken into a race score which appears on a large exterior monitor, seconds after riders crash through the chequered flag finish.

Sport Management, July 1999

Cricket club development

Warwickshire County Cricket Club is building an indoor cricket facility at its ground in Edgbaston, which will provide top facilities for players to be coached and to practice. The centre has been backed by lottery cash, the Warwickshire Supporters' Association, and Birmingham City Council.

Leisure Opportunities
20 July 1999

Skint time ahead for Brighton and Hove Albion

Third division football club, Brighton and Hove Albion is hoping for an upsurge in supporters following the announcement of a partnership with Brighton-based record label Skint Records. Skint, which is home to acts like Fatboy Slim and Lo-Fidelity Allstars, will be jazzing up the team's strips by splashing its logo across the shirts. There are plans to launch a Skint/ Brighton and Hove Albion credit card and for the record company to organise club nights around the country to coincide with away games. Skint boss David Harris says the partnership will turn the usual sponsorship deal on its head.

Leisure Marketing
22 June 1999

Godmanchester's pioneering pool

A community school swimming pool which has been built with log instead of the more traditional brick has opened at Godmanchester Primary School. The new £400,000 facility received national lottery funding and will be used by both the school and the local community.

Sports Management, July 1999

Build your learning

Summary points

- Although the leisure and tourism industries are considered separately in this textbook, there are many links between the two.

- Both industries are interrelated and are often dependent upon each other for customers.

- Public, private and voluntary sector leisure and tourism organisations sometimes work in partnership to provide facilities, products and services to customers. Examples of links include dual and joint provision of facilities, grants and sponsorship.

Key words and phrases

You should know the meaning of the words and phrases listed below as they relate to the links between leisure and tourism organisations. Go back through the last eight pages to refresh your understanding if necessary.

- **Dual use**
- **Joint provision**
- **Partnership**
- **Sponsorship**
- **Patronage**
- **Grants**
- **Planning gain**
- **Charitable status**

SUMMARY ACTIVITY

In a locality of your choice, find three examples of how leisure and tourism facilities or organisations work together to improve the products and services they provide for local residents and visitors. You should consider a range of initiatives such as:

- dual/joint provision schemes

- sponsorship/patronage

- grants and planning gain.

Explain, using examples, how at least three components of the leisure and tourism industries from your area are linked.

PORTFOLIO ASSESSMENT

This unit is assessed through your portfolio work. The grade for this assessment will be your grade for this unit. These pages are designed to help you to review your work and to check whether you have covered the required tasks to the right standard. The assessment tasks show what your portfolio needs to contain. Your teacher can give you further advice on what you need to do for each task.

If you have completed the summary activities throughout this unit, you will have already done a great deal of work for your portfolio. Sometimes you may need to reorganise or expand upon the work that you have done before it is ready to be submitted for your final assessment. The table below shows which activities from the unit can help you build your portfolio.

Assessment tasks	Activities
Task 1	Activities on pages 4, 7 and 15
Task 2 – leisure industry	Activities on pages 15, 22, 31, 33, 40 and 46
Task 2 – tourism industry	Activities on pages 15, 48, 53, 58, 60, 64 and 68
Task 3	Activities on pages 46, 68 and 76
Task 4	Activity on page 85
Task 5	Activities on pages 46, 60, 68 and 74
Task 6	Activities on pages 81 and 85
Task 7	Activity on page 46

Assessment tasks

You need to produce findings of an investigation into the leisure and tourism industries in a chosen area. You may find it helpful to base this investigation on your local area. Wherever you decide to investigate, it is important that you choose somewhere that includes most of the components of the leisure and tourism industries. Your findings can be presented in many different ways, such as in displays, reports, presentations or guidebooks.

1 **Define the terms leisure and tourism, giving the sources of your definitions.**

2 **Describe the leisure and tourism industries in your chosen area. You should provide examples of facilities in each component of the leisure and tourism industries (see Figure 1.2, page 10). Note that if your area doesn't contain one or two of these components, highlight this in your description and provide examples from elsewhere.**

3 Give information about at least two organisations for each key component described in task 2. You could produce a map that shows the location of each organisation and you may find it helpful to display this information in a table, using the headings: component, name of organisation, sector, facilities, main activities.

4 Explain, using examples, how at least three of the components of the leisure and tourism industries from your chosen area are linked.

5 Give a detailed description of the products and services that at least two of the major organisations in your chosen area offer to local people and visitors. For Merit level work you will also need to compare and contrast the differences between the products and services offered by the two organisations.

To achieve a Distinction, you also need to do tasks 6 and 7.

6 Explain in detail how leisure and tourism organisations in your chosen area could work together to improve the products and services they provide.

7 Identify any gaps in provision in your area and explain how these could be addressed.

Collecting the evidence

You may be able to complete some of the tasks using your current knowledge of the area, however you will also need to find more detailed information, and can use a wide number of sources to do so, including tourist boards and information centres, the internet, libraries, local and national newspapers and visits to local leisure and tourism facilities.

When requesting information directly from leisure and tourism organisations within your chosen area, it is important to discuss your plans with your teacher before you start. You should plan how you are going to communicate with the organisation, identify exactly what you want to know about it, and decide how you are going to ask for the information.

Key skills

It may be possible to claim these key skills for this work, depending on how you have completed the tasks and presented your work.

Communication (2.2, 2.3)

Problem solving (level 2)

Improving own learning and performance (level 2)

Working with others (level 2)

Your teacher will need to check your evidence against the key skills specification.

Marketing in leisure and tourism 2

The leisure and tourism industries are becoming more and more competitive as the number of organisations offering products and services increases. This in turn means that customers are becoming more demanding, simply because they have a much wider choice of what they can do in their leisure time.

Marketing is therefore a key activity of all leisure organisations as it enables them to attract new customers and keep existing ones by developing products and services that will meet their customers' needs.

In this unit we look at some of the marketing tools that leisure and tourism organisations use such as:

- marketing research
- target marketing
- the marketing mix.

By the end of the unit, you should be able to identify how different leisure and tourism organisations use marketing to ensure that they are successful.

Introduction to marketing

The methods that organisations use to market their products and services are one of the most important factors in their future success. Large leisure and tourism organisations such as British Airways, Alton Towers and Thomsons Holidays spend millions of pounds each year on marketing activities. However, even the more modest providers cannot afford to ignore the importance of marketing and carry out activities on a smaller scale. Look at the two advertisements on this page. Lunn Poly, a large tour operator, has placed its advertisement in a national newspaper, while the other was placed in a local paper by East Coast Travel a small, independent travel agent. Both are effective in their own way and meet the needs of the respective organisations.

An understanding of the basic principles and practices of marketing is a necessity for anyone hoping to work in the leisure and tourism industries.

▶ All leisure and tourism service providers must pay careful attention to marketing

What is marketing?

Effective **marketing** involves getting the right product to the right people at the right price in the right place and at the right time. What does this mean in practice? The 'right' product (whether goods or services) is one people want to buy, that specifically meets their needs. Companies are continually developing new products and updating existing ones to meet the needs of customers. The 'right' price is one that people are prepared to pay, but it is also one that allows the company or organisation to achieve its income and profit targets. The 'right' place and time means that the product has to be accessible to customers so that they can actually buy it.

Marketing, therefore, involves the whole organisation. Larger organisations often have a specialist marketing department, whose main aim is to ensure that the organisation is effective in meeting customer needs. Marketing is a complex process and those who work in marketing usually specialise in a particular area, such as public relations, advertising or sales.

Marketing involves many functions, all of which combine to enable organisations to be effective. For example, a holiday brochure is the result of several activities, all of which are part of marketing. They include:

- the development and testing of new products
- responding to trends, new technology and opportunities
- understanding the market, including what competitors are doing
- analysing the needs of existing and new customers
- introducing promotional activities and sales campaigns
- evaluating marketing activities to see if they are successful.

Here are some quotes from people working in the industry that show the importance of marketing.

'We didn't bother with any market research because it takes too long and costs a lot. We were disappointed when no one seemed interested in our new under-16 soccer school and we had to stop offering it.'
Manager of a local authority leisure centre

'When we actually looked at the prices we were charging we realised that the competitors were charging a lot more and still getting as many customers. Now we've increased the entrance charge and the extra revenue means that we can afford to improve the catering facilities.'
Manager of an industrial museum

'We cannot afford expensive advertising but sending out mailshots to past customers was cheap, easy and very effective. Our bookings for next year have already increased by 25 per cent.'
Manager of a privately owned hotel

'Just looking through the local newspaper and seeing what other leisure and tourism providers were offering gave us lots of ideas about how we could develop and improve the services that we offer our customers.'
Local tour operator

ACTIVITY

Marketing responsibilities

Make a list of the types of things a marketing manager of a lesiure and tourism facility might do. To help get you started, look at the tasks below.

- Carry out marketing research

- Train staff in customer service skills

- Decide on prices for products and services

- Deal with customer payments

- Identify customers' needs and develop suitable products and services

- Design and use promotional materials

- Answer letters of complaint from customers

- Evaluate the effectiveness of marketing activities

- Contact and deal with the press

- Interview and select staff

- Look at what competitors are offering their customers

Marketing research

It is important to understand that before an organisation begins to think about the products and services that it is going to develop and promote, it needs to have a very clear idea about who its customers are and what they want. For example, it might seem a great idea when someone says 'this town needs a multi-screen cinema, the nearest one is 40 miles away – the locals would love it.' However, how do they know that enough people in the town agree with them? Why is there no multi-screen cinema in the town? Could it be because the cinema organisations do not think the local population would go often enough to make it profitable? To answer these questions, the person with the great idea needs to do some **marketing research**.

Marketing research is the tool that organisations use to find out what their customers really want. If it is done correctly it mcans that an organisation can develop and offer products and services that it knows will meet customers' needs. Marketing research can be carried out in many ways. Four of the main methods are:

- postal surveys
- telephone surveys
- personal surveys
- observation (including focus groups).

All of these methods may be useful in particular circumstances, so let's look at what each one entails.

◄ A market researcher conducting an interview in the street

Postal surveys

Postal surveys involve mailing a questionnaire to a number of selected people. Many leisure and tourism organisations use this type of marketing research. Organisations such as Thomas Cook send out questionnaires to customers who have booked holidays to see whether they are happy with the service that they have received (see Figure 2.1). The information collected from the questionnaires is then used to help improve the service offered to customers.

Figure 2.1: Thomas Cook postal questionnaire

One of the advantages of postal surveys is that people are able to fill in the questionnaire on their own and may therefore take more time over it. Many organisations encourage people to reply by enclosing a return stamped addressed envelope – and some even offer incentives such as prize draws for those who respond.

Postal questionnaires are relatively cheap to implement in comparison to other methods of marketing research. However, one of the big drawbacks of this method is that very few people actually return postal questionnaires. Some return rates are as low as 3 per cent, which means that if 1,000 questionnaires are sent out, as few as 30 may be returned. One of the questions that an organisation always needs to ask is 'are the opinions expressed by the people returning questionnaires representative of the opinions of all of our customers.'

> What do you think are the main advantages and disadvantages of postal questionnaires?

ACTIVITY

Testing demand for a multi-screen cinema

The person with the bright idea about the multi-screen cinema (see page 92) has sent out 5,000 questionnaires to the people in the town. (The town has a total population of 43,000.) The questionnaire asks if people would use a multi-screen facility if it were available in the town. Only 100 questionnaires are sent back; but 98 per cent of people replying to the questionnaire say that they would use the facility 'frequently'. Mr 'Bright Idea' says that this proves that a multi-screen cinema is needed in the town.

1 Can we assume from the research that 98 per cent of the local population will use the multi-screen cinema? If not, why not?

2 Why do you think 4,900 people did not return the questionnaire? Are they likely to be people who will use the facility?

3 What do you think people mean by 'frequently', and is this important?

4 Draw up a checklist setting out the factors that might make postal questionnaires unreliable.

Telephone questionnaires

Many leisure and tourism organisations use **telephone questionnaires** because they are quick to conduct and provide instant information. Although this method of marketing research is generally more expensive than postal surveys, it is cheaper than some other methods. A telephone questionnaire, unlike a postal survey, also has the advantage of allowing the market researcher to ask for further explanation when needed. For example, if a person says that he or she does not like a particular product or service, the researcher can ask how it could be improved.

However, there are disadvantages to telephone questionnaires – not least is the fact that many people contacted by the researcher will simply say 'sorry, I can't talk now; it's not convenient'. Even when people do agree to answer questions, few are willing to stay on the telephone for a long time. This means that questions need to be short and to the point. It is also much more difficult to follow a long and

◄ What do you think are the main advantages and disadvantages of telephone questionnaires?

detailed question when someone is reading it to you than when you are able to read it for yourself. A further disadvantage is that the interviewer and respondent obviously cannot see each other. Apart from the fact that body language cannot be used to help communication, it also means that the researcher cannot use visual information such as pictures.

Personal surveys

Personal surveys involve the use of questionnaires in face-to-face situations. Generally, people are more willing to respond to interviews that are conducted in person – it is easier to say no on the phone or to simply ignore a postal survey. However, a disadvantage of face-to-face interviews is that answers can be rushed. This is particularly important in a leisure and tourism context. If you are spending a day at a theme park, do you really want to spend 15 minutes answering questions when you could be on the new ride? A further drawback of this method is that it is very personal – the customer is talking face to face with a researcher (who may be a member of staff of the organisation) and, therefore, he or she may not want to appear to be too critical.

> ► What are the main advantages and disadvantages of personal surveys and observations?

Observation

In **observation**, trained market researchers watch how customers use and react to an organisation's products and services. This can be particularly useful in giving an organisation a better understanding of how its customers behave and what their needs are. Observation methods also include the use of **focus groups**, where a group of customers meet to discuss products or services.

When Madame Tussaud's was originally created, the wax figures were roped off and customers were not allowed to use cameras. However, through observation it was realised that what customers really wanted was to be a part of the experience rather than just to look at the figures. Today, the figures are accessible and visitors are encouraged to take photographs of themselves with the famous, life-like wax pop stars, actors and politicians.

Observation methods have the advantage that they often provide in-depth information about customers' needs and expectations. However, they can be very expensive because it requires a substantial amount of staff time to actually carry out the research.

▼ Madame Tussaud's

Marketing research on the internet

Many organisations are now using the internet to find out the opinions of customers. If you have access to the internet, look at the questionnaire placed on the net by Alton Towers (**www.alton-towers.co.uk**) to find out what customers think about the theme park's website.

See if you can find examples of marketing research by leisure and tourism organisations. You might start by visiting some of the website addresses given in the internet directory.

CASE STUDY

Marketing research at the Sea Life Centres

The Sea Life Centres are part of the Merlin Entertainments Group. The company has attractions in six countries and welcomes over five million visitors a year.

Merlin was formed following a successful management buyout of the former Vardon Attractions from London-based Vardon plc in January 1999.

Now based in Poole, Dorset, Merlin is Europe's leading multi-site visitor attraction operator. It also owns and operates the National Seal Sanctuary in Cornwall, and the London and York Dungeons. The dungeons are famous attractions covering everything from Jack the Ripper to the legend of Dick Turpin and they offer the chance to experience the ultimate trip as you are sentenced to death in the Judgement Day ride.

The first Sea Life Centre opened its doors on the banks of the picturesque Loch Creran, near Oban, in 1979. Since then, another 22 Sea Life Centres have been opened; there are

16 in the UK, with others in Germany, Ireland, Belgium, Holland and Spain.

Sea Life Centres are famous for producing marine life displays of diverse shapes and sizes, each cleverly themed to mimic the natural habitat of its resident sea creatures as closely as possible. They focus primarily on the environment and species specific to their nearest coastlines but also feature special exhibitions highlighting a range of more exotic tropical marine life. Several centres, along with the National Seal Sanctuary, are actively involved in rescue and rehabilitation work with both grey and common seals. They are also pioneers in the field of captive breeding, particularly with threatened species such as seahorses.

Sea Life carries out marketing research on a regular basis. The selection of methods is largely dependent on which are the most cost-effective. The company buys information from market research organisations about customer perceptions of visitor attractions. At Sea Life, information is stored on computerised customer databases and regularly analysed. These databases provide a range of information from customer profiles (who they are, where they have come from, who they came with) to frequency of visits. Valuable data is also collated from the customer details given on completed sales promotions, such as discount vouchers.

Each attraction conducts a regular visitor survey using a simple self-completion, multi-choice, 'tick box' format (see Figure 2.2). The questions in the Sea Life visitor's questionnaire are designed to evaluate visitors' perceptions of the attraction and its facilities. They explore how visitors heard about the attraction and their main reasons for visiting. The questionnaire also gathers demographic details such as the age of members of each group, area of origin, the type of accommodation that they are staying in within the area and the duration of their stay. Some attractions, including the new Seal Hospital in Scarborough, have introduced observational research methods by watching and recording the reactions and behaviour of visitors.

How do you think the Sea Life Centre might use the information that it gets from its visitor's questionnaires?

Figure 2.2: Sea Life Centre visitor's questionnaire

Build your learning

Summary points

- Marketing includes getting the right product to the right people at the right price in the right place at the right time.

- Marketing involves the whole organisation and everyone in it.

- Marketing research is the method that organisations use to find out what their customers want.

- Leisure and tourism organisations should always carry out marketing research before developing new products to make sure that there is a market for them.

- There are many different ways of carrying out marketing research.

- The most suitable type of marketing research to use in a given situation depends on the type of information being sought.

- In postal surveys, questionnaires are mailed to people.

- In telephone questionnaires, marketing research is carried out over the telephone.

- In personal surveys, people are asked questions in a face-to-face situation.

- In observation, trained market researchers watch how customers use and react to an organisation's products.

Key words and phrases

You should know the meaning of the words and phrases listed below as they relate to the marketing research. Go back through the last seven pages to refresh your understanding if necessary.

- **Postal surveys**
- **Observation**
- **Marketing research**
- **Marketing**
- **Telephone questionnaires**
- **Personal surveys**

SUMMARY ACTIVITY

As a group, select five local leisure or tourism organisations and either write a letter or visit in person to find out about the market research methods they use. Try to get copies of questionnaires that the organisations use. Ask each organisation for specific information about each of the four marketing research methods that we have discussed in this section. For each method, ask:

- do they use the method
- if so, what is it used for, what information is being sought
- how effective is the method?

Collate the information you obtain in a table.

Organisation	Postal survey	Telephone questionnaire	Personal survey	Observation

When you have collected all of the information, discuss as a group the various ways in which the leisure and tourism organisations use marketing research methods to identify their target markets.

Target marketing

When we talk about **target markets** we mean the group of customer who buy particular products and services. For most organisations the market is made up of different types of customer who have a range of needs and expectations. The different types are known as **market segments** and an organisation tailors its products to meet the needs of these different segments. For example, a tour operator's general product may be package holidays but it may offer different types of holidays for, say, families, young adults or retired people. Each different type of holiday has a separate image designed to appeal to a particular market segment.

Target marketing means developing and promoting products that appeal to a specific market segment. There are a number of ways that the market can be split into segments. Five of the most common ways of segmenting a market are by:

- age
- gender
- social group
- lifestyle
- ethnicity.

Let's look at target marketing in more detail and see the ways in which leisure and tourism organisations may target particular segments.

Age

Many products are aimed at people of a particular **age**. SAGA Holidays, for example, caters specifically for people over 50, while Club 18–30, as its name suggests, targets young adults.

ACTIVITY

Lesiure activities for all?

Many leisure activities appeal more to certain age groups than others. Decide which are the main age groups each of these activities targets.

- tenpin bowling
- golf
- visting a museum
- ice skating
- crown green bowling
- going to a gig
- roller blading
- snooker
- skiing

Gender

Some leisure activities and products, such as rugby or flower arranging classes, are aimed mainly at male or female participants. However, traditional **gender** distinctions are now becoming blurred. For example, many pubs and bars used to refuse to serve women in the saloon bar and were very male-oriented. Now, they often encourage women and families by providing a wider range of products and facilities.

ACTIVITY

Gender games

Working as a group, write a list of all of the leisure activities you like to take part in – you should include sports, visits to tourist attractions, socialising activities and home entertainment.

Separate the list into three columns, depending on whether the activities are done mainly by females, males or both. Some examples have been given in the table to get you started.

Activities mainly for females	Activities mainly for males	Activities for both sexes
Aerobics	Video games	Cinema

This activity gives you a general idea about how some leisure activities may be targeted at specific genders. However, it is important to understand that you should not make assumptions about gender. Many women play football, just as many men enjoy cookery courses.

Social group

Most people place themselves and others in a **social group** or class according to their job. For example, a waitress would be regarded as working class and a travel agent as middle class. One of the most widely used social class classifications in marketing was developed by the Institute of Practitioners in Advertising (see Figure 2.3).

Figure 2.3: Social class

Social class	Category	Examples
A	Senior manager and professionals	Doctors, lawyers
B	Middle-level managers and professionals	Teachers, leisure centre managers
C1	Supervisory and junior management	Computer operators, fitness instructors
C2	Skilled manual workers	Electricians, hairdressers
D	Semi-skilled and unskilled manual workers	Cleaners, kitchen porters, ride attendants
E	Others on low incomes	Casual workers, people on state benefits

Many leisure and tourism products are seen to be attractive to a particular class. For example, bingo is seen to appeal mainly to people in class C2, D and E, while opera is perceived to be more appealing to class A and B. However, in recent years, many traditional preferences have become blurred due to changes in the amount that people earn. Some manual workers have high incomes and can afford luxury holidays; public sector staff such as teachers and nurses have suffered pay restraint which may restrict the amount they can afford to spend on holidays.

Lifestyle

Lifestyle is a combination of work patterns, income, marital status, family commitments and leisure and social habits – in other words, lifestyle describes the way in which we live our lives. Many people would argue that lifestyle is one of the biggest influences on the type of leisure and tourism products that we buy. For example, a couple with young children are likely to have very different leisure needs to those of a retired couple or a single, young adult.

Ethnicity

Different **ethnic groups** may have specific leisure and tourism needs. For example, there is a growing network of cinemas specialising in showing Asian, particularly Indian, films. Religious beliefs can also impact on customer needs, creating separate market segments. For example, kosher or halal food menus are offered by some airlines to meet the dietary requirements of different religious groups.

Build your learning

Summary points

- An organisation's market is usually made up of several different groups of customers known as market segments.

- Different market segments have different needs that are met by different products.

- Target marketing means developing products that meet the needs of a particular market segment.

- Many organisations offer a range of different products and services targeted at different market segments.

- Products can be targeted at different market segments on the basis of age, gender, social group, lifestyle and ethnicity.

Key words and phrases

You should know the meaning of the words and phrases listed below as they relate to the target marketing. Go back through the last five pages to refresh your understanding if necessary.

- **Target markets**
- **Market segment**
- **Age**
- **Gender**
- **Social group**
- **Lifestyle**
- **Ethnicity**

SUMMARY ACTIVITY

Organisations spend a great deal of time and money identifying their different market segments and developing products to meet their needs.

To enable customers to select the holiday centre that will best suit their needs, Center Parcs has an interactive page on its website (**www.centerparcs.com**) called Design your Break. This asks customers to select the holiday features that are most important to them, and then suggests which Center Parcs villages would be most suitable.

If you have access to the internet, visit the Center Parcs site on 'www.centerparcs.com' and see how the system works. Identify the different facilities and services offered to different market segments.

If you do not have access to the internet, you may be able to complete the activity by using a Center Parcs' brochure. Alternatively, select a facility in your locality and identify the products and services that it provides for its different market segments.

The marketing mix

We have introduced some of the activities involved in marketing and considered why they are important. These activities work together in what is known as the marketing mix. This is one of the most widely used ideas in marketing and is a useful way of seeing how organisations go about their marketing activities. The **marketing mix** looks at the four main factors that need to be considered to make marketing successful. These factors, often called the four Ps, are:

> **P**roduct
> **P**lace
> **P**rice
> **P**romotion

Although each factor is important individually, it is the way that they are combined, or 'mixed', which is crucial. For example, an organisation may have an excellent product, but if customers cannot get to it or cannot afford it or have not heard about it then it will not sell. So, a good marketing mix means that an organisation:

- provides a product that customers want
- makes sure that the customer can buy the product
- charges a price that the customer is willing to pay
- promotes it effectively so that the customer knows about it.

In other words, an organisation aims to get the right product to the right people at the right price in the right place and at the right time.

Let's look at these four Ps individually and see some of the factors that an organisation needs to think about when planning its marketing mix.

Product

In marketing, the term **product** covers both goods and services. Goods are physical objects, such as food and drink, exercise equipment and sportswear. Services involve the combination of skills, information or entertainment, often associated with the use of facilities or equipment; examples include sports coaching, hotel accommodation, guiding services at a stately home, and a concert or theatre production. Essentially, goods are things that can be taken away, whereas services are things that are experienced at the time.

Some organisations offer both goods and services; for example, Macdonald's sells goods in the form of food and drinks and provides services such as a place to eat and children's entertainment.

ACTIVITY

Many leisure and tourism products are a combination of both products and services. Here are some of the things that you may expect to be provided at a pop concert:

- exciting atmosphere
- programmes
- listening/watching the concert
- first aid assistance
- merchandising (T-shirts, posters)
- comfortable seating
- heating and lighting
- refreshments
- clear signposts
- parking
- tickets
- advice from staff

Draw a table with two columns: head one 'products' and the other 'services'. Put each of the items listed above into the appropriate column. Can you think of anything else that could be added to either column?

Product and service features

When we talk about a **product's features** we mean the characteristics that the customer recognises as part of the overall product. For example, the product features of a theme park might include exciting rides, children's attractions, picnic areas, catering facilities, live entertainment and a well-laid out park. Organisations spend a lot of time ensuring that the products that they offer have specific features that will appeal to their target markets. These features are highlighted in promotional materials to persuade customers that the product will meet their needs.

◀ Britannia's advert lists the music club's ten distinct product features

10 great reasons to join Britannia

1. **5 CDs for £13.99 or 5 Cassettes for £9.99** (plus p&p)
2. **Save up to £80** now with this introductory offer
3. **No obligation** 10 day home trial
4. **Free Storage Unit** when you join
5. **Free magazines** with 1000s more titles to choose from
6. **CDs from £5.99** when you take advantage of Britannia's bonus prices
7. **Free albums** and special offers as a member
8. **24 hour customer service line**
9. **Fast delivery** in just 7 days
10. **There's no catch!** Simply choose six regular priced albums from the 1000s available within two years of joining, at least 3 in your first year. That's all. **You do not have to buy from every magazine.**

With over 2 million members we're Europe's biggest music club!

Registered Office:
60-70 Roden Street, Ilford, Essex IG1 2XX.
Registered Number: 1206311

Denotes double album, counts as one selection.

ACTIVITY

National Centre for Popular Music

The National Centre for Popular Music opened in Sheffield in 1998. Look at this extract from its leaflet and identify some of the product features that it offers.

The brand name

The **brand name** is the name given to a particular product or service to distinguish it from similar products. For example, sportswear products have brand names like adidas, Puma, Kappa and Nike.

It is important that a brand name suits the product and sums up the product features. Organisations invest a lot of money in promoting particular brands, in the hope that customers will automatically think of their product rather than that of a competitor. For example, which brand do you immediately think of when buying jeans?

Many organisations combine their brand name with a **logo** to make it instantly recognisable. A logo is a symbol that helps

> What brand name do you think of first when buying a package holiday? Why did you think of this brand?

identify an organisation. Look at the logo for Planet Hollywood below. The name has a young and trendy appeal, mixing space travel with the glamorous American film industry. The way that the name is written reinforces this image with the use of bold primary colours and informal letters that grab attention. Clearly the name and logo are designed to appeal to youth markets.

▼ Logos of some well-known leisure and tourism brands

ACTIVITY

Brand names

Get a copy of a national newspaper and find some well-known brand names of leisure and tourism products and services. To what extent does the brand name sum up the product's features? Do you think the brand name is designed to appeal to specific market segments? If so what type of customer does it particularly appeal to and why?

After-sales service

It is important to understand that when a customer buys a leisure and tourism product the buying experience does not always end when the customer leaves. Many customers require additional **after-sales service**. Organisations recognise that after-sales service is an important part of the overall product. For example, you (or your family) may have bought some home entertainment equipment such as a computer, television, video recorder or CD player. Organisations which sell these products understand that many customers may have problems or questions about the product once they get them home. Therefore, they may provide a telephone helpline, as after-sales service, to enable customers to get the most out of their new purchase. Another example of a product with after-sales service is travel insurance. Many insurers offer customers a 24-hour emergency assistance service (see Figure 2.4).

◄ Why do you think that it is important for an organisation to provide its customers with good after-sales service?

> **Figure 2.4: Lunn Poly's emergency service for customers who take out travel insurance**
>
> ## Contract of travel insurance
>
> **Assistance International - 24 hour Worldwide emergency service**
> If you need medical help in an emergency (see section 2), please call:
>
> ### Southampton
> ### (1703 from abroad) 644633.
>
> From 22 April 2000 the 'phone number will change to 23 80 644633
>
> The number from the countries most often visited is:
>
> USA and Canada   01 144   1703 644633
> Spain   07   44   1703 644633
> France, Greece, Portugal and Italy 00   44   1703 644633
>
> The telex number is U.K. 477429 - Answerback - G
>
> The fax number is (1703 from abroad) 644616
>
> From 22 April 2000 the fax number will change to (international dialling code) 23 80 644616.
>
> **This service is only for real medical emergencies.**

The product mix

Many leisure and tourism organisations offer several products so that they can satisfy the needs of different types of customers. This is known as the **product mix**.

A tour operator, for example, may offer coach and air tours, full service (holidays with board and lodging) and self-catering holidays. Other organisations might take the same basic product but describe it in different ways so that a wider range of customers are encouraged to buy it.

For example, the British Tourist Authority is constantly looking at new ways to market the country to different groups of customers to improve the product mix. The rock and pop map (Figure 2.5), sponsored by Rock Circus, is a guide to Britain showing where famous rock musicians have lived or performed and locations of specific musical interest. The campaign uses the world-renowned British pop music scene to attract visitors from the 18–25 youth market.

On a smaller scale, local authority tourism departments have promoted visits around unique local events and features. For example, Bradford has developed special 'curry weekends' to encourage more visitors, exploiting the fact that the city boasts some of the best Indian food in the country. The curry weekends add to Bradford's existing product mix, which includes business and conference facilities.

Figure 2.5: Rock and pop map

The product mix

Large tour operators often have quite complicated product mixes with a range of products being sold through different holiday brochures. Select one well-known tour operator such as Thomson or Airtours. Collect a range of the company's different brochures. As a group, discuss which particular group of customers each brochure targets. Can you identify any target markets that the tour operator does not cater for?

Price

The second 'P' in the marketing mix is **price**. It is important that organisations get the price right – if it is too high customers may not be able to afford it, but if it is too low the organisation may not make a profit.

The actual selling price

The **actual selling price** of a product refers to how much the customer is charged. In deciding the selling price, an organisation has four main considerations:

- how much it costs to provide the product
- what customers will pay
- what competitors are charging
- the required profit margin (if any).

Prices in leisure and tourism often vary depending on the time of year or day that the product is offered or the type of customer that is being targeted. Actual selling prices are affected by a number of factors. We examine these next.

Peak and off-peak pricing

Prices may be set higher during peak times when demand is highest and lower during off-peak times when demand is lower. This encourage customers to use facilities at quiet times. For example, many theatres offer lower prices during weekdays than at weekends, railway companies charge higher fares to travellers departing before 9.30 a.m. than they do to those travelling later in the day and many pubs have 'happy hours' when drinks are cheaper. Many popular package holidays to Europe are most expensive during the school holidays (known as the high season) because this is when most families want to take their holidays. Lower prices during winter are intended to encourage people to take holidays at a time when demand is low (referred to as the low season).

Group and special discounts

Many leisure and tourism facilities offer discounts to some customers such as organised groups, school parties, children, pensioners, the unemployed and students. The intention is to attract customers who might not otherwise buy the product, or to fill places through bulk (or group) sales, thereby reducing the cost of administration per customer. For example, the Jorvik Viking Centre in York offers a wide range of different admission charges (see Figure 2.6).

Figure 2.6: Admission prices for Jorvik Viking Centre (to 31 March 2000)

Admission charges		
	Jorvik only	Joint ticket (see note 1)
Adult	£5.35	£7.35
Child	£3.99	£5.99
Family (2 adults, 2 children)	£17.00	£23.00
Senior citizens	£4.60	£6.60
Students	£4.60	£6.60

Premium charges (see note 2)		
	Jorvik only	Joint ticket
Adult	£6.35	£8.35
Child	£4.60	£6.60
Family (2 adults, 2 children)	£20.50	£26.50
Senior citizens	£5.10	£7.10
Students	£5.10	£7.10

Note 1: During the school holidays, customers can save money by puchasing a **joint ticket** for the Jorvik Viking Centre and the Archaeological Resource Centre.

Note 2: **Premium prices** apply for pre-booked time slots between 10.00 and 16.00 and to all pre-booked time slots during the Jorvik Viking Festivals.

ACTIVITY

Seasonal pricing

Look through a range of holiday brochures and identify when prices are at their highest and lowest.

Discuss the reasons for any sudden and short-term rise in prices, (for example, prices often rise dramatically at school half-term breaks).

Try to compare different types of holiday, such as European winter sports breaks, European summer sun holidays and long-haul holidays (to Asia and Africa, for example).

You will find that the peak and off-peak times are not necessarily at the same time of the year. (For example, holidays in Mexico are often cheaper in the summer months; this is because it is the rainy season!)

Special offers

A facility may offer reduced prices to all its customers for a limited period. For example, theme parks sometimes offer reduced prices to customers who produce vouchers or discount coupons that have been issued in sales promotions. Travel agents usually advertise special offers and late availability holidays to increase sales. Pricing amongst airline companies is particularly competitive and newspapers are full of advertisements offering reduced fares.

▶ British Midland advertising its sale prices

Credit terms

Many leisure and tourism organisations offer **credit terms** that allow customers to pay for products over a period of time. This is particularly useful for the more expensive products that a customer may not be able to afford all at once, such as a time-share apartment or home entertainment equipment.

When setting their prices, providers of leisure and tourism attractions are often keen to be seen to be providing good value for money to their customers. One way of doing this is by looking at what is known as **dwell-time**. This concerns the amount charged in relation to the length of time that a customer spends at the attraction. For example, if a museum charges £4.50 per visitor and each visitor stays for approximately three hours, the dwell-time cost is £1.50 per hour.

ACTIVITY

Dwell-time at TechoBlast

TechoBlast is a new interactive sci-fi museum aimed mainly at the family and young adult markets. Activities make use of the latest computerised systems including virtual reality and the internet. Customers travel through a series of experiences based on well-known scenes from sci-fi television programmes and films.

The owners of TechnoBlast are keen to promote the attraction as good value for money as well as an exciting and unique experience. They have estimated that the approximate 'dwell-time' will be six hours and have looked at other family attractions in the area to compare their admission charges and expected dwell-time.

Attraction	Admission price	Dwell-time	Dwell-time cost per hour
Theme park		8 hours	
adult	£14.50		
child	£12.00		
Stately home with zoo		5 hours	
adult	£9.99		
child	£6.50		
Industrial museum		4.5 hours	
adult	£8.50		
child	£5.99		
Swimming pool		1.5 hours	
adult	£4.50		
child	£2.50		
Working farm		1.5 hours	
adult	£3.00		
child	£2.50		
Premiership football		2.5 hours	
adult	£25.00		
child	£15.00		

Work out the dwell-time cost per hour for each of the attractions in the table. How much do you think TechnoBlast should charge for adult and child admission if it wants to offer good value for money?

Place

The third 'P' of the marketing mix, **place**, is concerned with how goods and services are distributed to the customer. In other words, how the customer goes about actually buying them. One of the big differences between goods and services is that a customer usually has to travel to the provider to experience a service. For example, if you wanted to swim in a local pool, see a cinema film or eat a restaurant meal you have to go to the actual facilities – they cannot be brought to you.

Types of outlet

The **location** of a leisure and tourism facility often influences the type of outlet used. For example, a sports retailer would have a very different type of outlet in an out-of-town shopping mall than in the high street of an historic town such as Chester or Bath. Choosing the right type of outlet and location depends on the type of product offered and the target markets. One of the main considerations is whether the type of outlet fits in with the general image of the organisation and its customers.

Location of outlets and facilities

The physical location of the product is often very important. Many people have suggested that the initial lack of popularity of the Disney development outside Paris was due to its situation in a relatively cool and expensive part of the world, certainly it is in a cooler part of the world than the Disney facilities in Florida and California.

Several factors need to be considered when deciding on a suitable location.

- Is there sufficient public transport in the area?
- How much car parking space is there and what does it cost?
- Are there other facilities nearby that will attract people?
- Are there already similar facilities and, if so, will there be enough customers to go round?
- What is the climate like?
- Will the organisation be able to find staff and suppliers in the area?

Location does not just mean where a leisure or tourism facility is but also the ways in which a customer can buy it – this is known as distribution. For example, if you are going on holiday to Benidorm the location of the product would be Spain. However, you would probably buy the holiday in a travel agency – so this is how the tour operator distributes the product. Alternatively, you might buy the holiday directly from the tour operator or via the internet.

ACTIVITY

Janice Brownlow's pizza and burger bar

Look at the map of Nuttingford town centre. Janice Brownlow has just opened a takeaway pizza and burger bar in the town (shown by the arrow). It will be open seven days a week from 10 a.m. to midnight. What do you think are the advantages and disadvantages of the location she has chosen? Pay particular attention to other businesses nearby.

Janice's Burger Bar

Beach

Key

1 Railway station
2 Italian restaurant
3 Large housing estate
4 Industrial estate
5 Cinema
6 Local college
7 Night club
8 Yacht club
9 Park and gardens
10 Indoor shopping mall
11 Ice skating rink
12 Bus station

Scale (miles)
0   1   2

117

▼ Instructions on how to get to the Yorkshire Museum

Many organisations include details about their location in promotional materials. For example, Yorkshire museum's leaflet provides a detailed map and instructions on how to get to the museum by road, rail and bus.

OPENING TIMES
Open daily 10.00am - 5.00pm.

ADMISSION
Joint ticket - Myths & Monsters and Tracking Dinosaurs
Adult - £4.25   Child - £2.70

Myths & Monsters only
Adult - £3.75   Child - £2.40

Group bookings and school parties welcome. Group rates available.

York residents are entitled to free entry to the Yorkshire Museum collections and reduced entry to Myths & Monsters and Tracking Dinosaurs (on presentation of yorkcard). For further details, telephone 01904 629745.

VISITOR FACILITIES
All principal galleries accessible to wheelchairs. Toilet facilities are available for all users.

MUSEUM GIFT SHOP
A superb range of gifts are available to remind you of your visit.

HOW TO FIND THE YORKSHIRE MUSEUM

The Yorkshire Museum is situated in the Museum Gardens in the centre of York.

By Road: A regular Park and Ride service operates from three sites near the A64, A19, A1079 and A166 roads into York. There are also three car parks within a short walk of the Yorkshire Museum.

By Rail: The Yorkshire Museum is just a short walk from York Station. Follow the signs to city centre. For rail travel information telephone 0345 484950.

By Bus: Buses to York city centre run regularly from surrounding areas. For longer distance travel details telephone 0990 808080.

For further information, contact:
Yorkshire Museum, Museum Gardens, York YO1 7FR

E-mail
yorkshire.museum@york.gov.uk

Telephone 01904 629745

Fax 01904 651221

York Internet site
http://www.york.gov.uk

YORK
kokoro

© City of York Council 1999. Published by the Marketing and Communications Group for Leisure Services. Printed on environmentally friendly papers. The cost of producing this leaflet is 4.2p per York resident.

ACTIVITY

Evaluating location

Evaluate the location of some leisure and tourism facilities near to you. Select five leisure and tourism facilities – try to make sure that they are spread well apart. Visit each facility and evaluate how accessible the location is. You should think about:

- the types of outlets and facilities in the area

- public transport to the facility (including the types available and the times that they run)

- roads for car users (for example, are the approach roads very busy or is there a complicated one-way system)

- parking (cost and number of parking spaces)

- signs to the facility (would it be easy to find if you were visiting it for the first time)

- is it accessible to the people who use the facility?

Promotion

The fourth 'P' of the marketing mix is **promotion**. This involves telling customers about products and persuading them to buy them. It covers a wide range of activities, which are likely to be used in combination as part of a promotional campaign. In the next section of this unit we look at some of the most commonly used promotional techniques and materials and discuss how they can be used effectively in promotional campaigns.

Build your learning

Summary points

- The marketing mix is made up of the four Ps – product, price, place and promotion

- The marketing mix ensures that the organisation gets the right product to the right person at the right price in the right place at the right time.

- A product can be goods (physical objects) or services (skills, information or entertainment).

- Product or service features are the characteristics that the customer recognises as part of the overall product.

- The brand name is the name that an organisation gives to its particular product or service.

- After-sales service is an additional service provided by an organisation after a customer has purchased a product or service.

- The product mix is the range of products offered by an organisation.

- There are a number of different pricing strategies such as peak/off-peak, group and special discounts.

- Many organisations offer credit terms to encourage customers to buy a product by spreading the cost over time.

- The type of outlet is affected by its location.

- The location of outlets and facilities can have an effect on the types of customer who use it.

- Organisations consider a number of factors when choosing the location of outlets or facilities.

- Location also refers to channels of distribution or how the product is brought to the market.

- Promotion involves telling people about an organisation's products and persuading them to buy them.

Key words and phrases

You should know the meaning of the words and phrases listed below as they relate to the marketing mix. Go back through the last 15 pages to refresh your understanding if necessary.

- Product feature
- Brand name
- Marketing mix
- Product mix
- After-sales service
- Actual selling price
- Credit terms
- Price
- Location
- Promotion
- Product
- Place

SUMMARY ACTIVITY

In pairs, visit a local leisure and tourism facility or attraction and identify the four Ps of its marketing mix.

- Describe the products and services that it offers.
- Describe how its products and/or services are made available.
- Explain how the products and/or services are priced.
- Describe the promotional techniques and materials the organisation uses.

Promotional techniques

Promotional techniques are the ways that an organisation promotes its products. All successful leisure and tourism organisations, whether they are multinational companies or small local providers, use a range of promotional techniques. Some of the most commonly used are:

- advertising
- direct marketing
- public relations
- personal selling
- displays
- sponsorship
- demonstrations
- sales promotions.

In this section we examine each of these techniques in turn and see how they are used by leisure and tourism organisations.

Advertising

Advertising is the paid-for publication, display or broadcast of information that describes a product or service in a favourable way. It can be carried out in a number of ways. For example, an advertisement can be national and, therefore, seen across the whole country. Alternatively, it may be regional and shown, for example, just in the London area, in the south of the country or in Yorkshire. It may just be restricted to a local audience, say within a particular town or city.

There are also choices about which medium to use for advertising. The **medium** is the way in which the advertising information is given to the customer. The options include:

- radio
- television (both terrestrial and satellite)
- cinema
- Teletext (the information service on commercial television)
- newspapers
- magazines
- billboards
- the internet.

All of these media may be national, regional or local. However, you need to remember that television and radio advertising can only be run on commercial channels. Public service broadcasters like the BBC do not carry commercial advertising.

Advertising can be found in many forms. In addition to the media listed above, there are, for example, advertisements on buses, trains and other forms of transport. At sports grounds there are advertisements on hoardings, electrical signs, loudspeaker announcements, inside programmes and brochures and on tickets.

◀ Poster site at a sports stadium

ACTIVITY

Advertising media

Copy and fill in the following table giving examples of national, regional and local advertising media in a locality of your choice. Some national examples have been given to get you started, but also include ideas of your own in this section.

Advertising medium	National	Regional	Local
Radio	Atlantic 252		
Television	Granada		
Cinema	Warners		
Teletext	Skytext		n/a
Newspapers	Daily Mail		
Magazines	Cosmopolitan		

With such a wide range of advertising media, the main problem for marketing staff is to identify which one is likely to be the most effective. The answer is usually to decide which customers the advertisement is aimed at and then to identify the medium or media these target customers are most likely to read, watch, hear or look at. For example, if an advertiser wants to promote its product to you, which magazines and newspapers should it use? Would it be successful if it tried to attract you through radio advertising? If it used television advertising, it would need to consider which programmes are you most likely to be watching.

41 are pencilled in for lunch

At one time, a sandwich board man was the closest you got to a living advertisement. But now a San Francisco restaurant has gone one better – by offering free lunches for life to customers who agree to be tattooed with its logo. So far, 41 people have braved the needle so they can tuck in for nothing at the Casa Sanchez. Its 45-year-old owner, Marty Sanchez, said: 'The old saying is wrong – there really is such a thing as a free lunch.

'But most of those who've had the tattoo get embarrassed about not paying and leave large tips anyway.'

◄ Do you think this restaurant seriously sees tattoos as an advertising method or has it simply done this as a gimmick to get some press coverage?

ACTIVITY

Choosing advertising media

Discuss which media you think would be most effective in each case for advertising these products:

- national coach holidays offered to senior citizens

- a local sports centre

- luxury wedding package holidays to destinations such as Barbados and the Seychelles

- a pop concert at a major outdoor arena

- forthcoming films at a local cinema

- a national chain of three and four-star hotels.

Specify whether you think the advertising needs to be national, regional or local, or would a combination be more appropriate?

Direct marketing

Direct marketing is one of the fastest growing areas of promotion. It involves sending or giving promotional material directly to individual customers. This can be done in a number of ways such as by post, over the telephone or door to door. One of the great advantages of direct marketing is that organisations can target those customers that they think will be particularly interested in the products on offer. For example, a theatre might send out a direct mail letter about a forthcoming production to customers who have seen similar productions in the past. The increasing use of computers has greatly helped direct marketing because companies can store huge lists of names, addresses and customer details – known as **customer databases**. Details of any particular type of customer can be quickly found at the touch of a few keys. These can be used to provide a mailing list for direct marketing.

▼ A direct mail leaflet

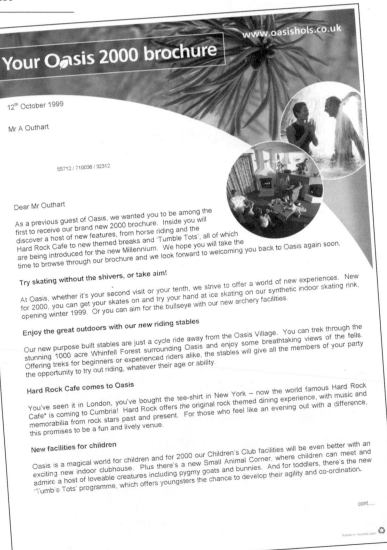

www.oasishols.co.uk

Your Oasis 2000 brochure

12th October 1999

Mr A Outhart

55712 / 710036 / 32312

Dear Mr Outhart

As a previous guest of Oasis, we wanted you to be among the first to receive our brand new 2000 brochure. Inside you will discover a host of new features, from horse riding and the Hard Rock Cafe to new themed breaks and 'Tumble Tots', all of which are being introduced for the new Millennium. We hope you will take the time to browse through our brochure and we look forward to welcoming you back to Oasis again soon.

Try skating without the shivers, or take aim!

At Oasis, whether it's your second visit or your tenth, we strive to offer a world of new experiences. New for 2000, you can get your skates on and try your hand at ice skating on our synthetic indoor skating rink, opening winter 1999. Or you can aim for the bullseye with our new archery facilities.

Enjoy the great outdoors with our *new* riding stables

Our new purpose built stables are just a cycle ride away from the Oasis Village. You can trek through the stunning 1000 acre Whinfell Forest surrounding Oasis and enjoy some breathtaking views of the fells. Offering treks for beginners or experienced riders alike, the stables will give all the members of your party the opportunity to try out riding, whatever their age or ability.

Hard Rock Cafe comes to Oasis

You've seen it in London, you've bought the tee-shirt in New York – now the world famous Hard Rock Cafe* is coming to Cumbria! Hard Rock offers *the* original rock themed dining experience, with music and memorabilia from rock stars past and present. For those who feel like an evening out with a difference, this promises to be a fun and lively venue.

New facilities for children

Oasis is a magical world for children and for 2000 our Children's Club facilities will be even better with an exciting new indoor clubhouse. Plus there's a new Small Animal Corner, where children can meet and admire a host of loveable creatures including pygmy goats and bunnies. And for toddlers, there's the new 'Tumble Tots' programme, which offers youngsters the chance to develop their agility and co-ordination.

cont....

Printed on recycled paper

ACTIVITY

I'm talking to you!

One of the problems with direct mail promotions is that customers can realise that the same letter has probably been sent to hundreds of other people, so they simply throw it in the bin without reading it. One way of overcoming this is to try and personalise the letter by using the words 'you' and 'yours' as often as possible so that customers feels as if they are being written to personally. Using the customer's name rather than just 'Dear Sir or Madam' is also effective.

Look at the letter shown here – it's fairly impersonal, isn't it? Can you rewrite it, using the words 'you' and 'yours', to make it sound more personal?

> **The Occupier**
> **Calendar Cottage**
> **Merrydown**
> **Hants**
>
> Dear customer
>
> Many of our customers use us year after year because they know that we can offer a personal service at competitive prices. Every year we receive dozens of letters from customers telling us how much they have enjoyed the holidays we have arranged for them.
>
> This year we are able to offer a special introductory offer to new customers – anyone booking a summer package holiday with us receives a guaranteed discount of 20 per cent on the total package holiday price. In addition, we are able to provide holiday insurance and currency exchange at very reasonable charges.
>
> Anyone wishing to take advantage of this amazing offer should call in to our branch in town and produce this letter. Our friendly staff will be pleased to serve you.
>
> Yours sincerely
>
> Manager

Public relations

Public relations (or PR as it is often referred to) is the planned attempt to create a favourable image of an organisation. One of the main advantages of PR is that it is free! It often involves liaising with the media (newspapers, radio, television) and persuading them to publicise information about an organisation and its products. This may be achieved by issuing press releases, where 'story' ideas are given to journalists to provide them with ready-written articles or feature material. The general aim is to create a good public image of the organisation and get the name of the organisation better known. Some press releases are good PR for a number of organisations or individuals who may be working together on a particular project or event.

> ▼ How many organisations and individuals might benefit from the story described in the article below in terms of public relations?

Cameras roll as pub turns into a recording studio for the day

Paul Ingle's manager Frank Maloney will become a television chat show host for a series of programmes being filmed in Scarborough on Sunday.

Frank on Sport will be recorded at the New George Hotel in Eastborough and one of the show's guests will be Paul Ingle himself.

The chat shows will be recorded by the Sheffield-based production company MWTV, who are aiming the half-hour videos towards the tourist market.

The videos have so far been sold to two airports so they can be shown to waiting passengers in departure lounges and there are hopes that they will be sold to a television channel.

Chris Edwards, assistant producer of the chat show, said it was Mr Maloney who chose Scarborough.

Mr Edwards said: 'Frank is good friends with Rocky Rowe who runs the New George Hotel and he has developed strong ties with the town. He feels very comfortable in Scarborough.'

The first programme will feature Britain's only professional female boxer Jane Couch.

The second will include interviews with Paul Ingle and jockey Keiron Fallon, who used to be based at Malton.

The third features bodybuilding and the last an interview with Sheffield Strikers, a team in the fledgling World Indoor Soccer League with players like Chris Waddle and Peter Beardsley.

Scarborough Evening News
23 April 1999

The effects of good public relations can be beneficial for sales. For example, if a television holiday programme includes an enthusiastic report about a travel destination, this may be followed by an increase in customer enquiries. Many resorts and holiday companies give journalists 'free' holidays in the hope of a complimentary 'write-up'.

ACTIVITY

Positive public relations

This article is a good example of how a leisure and tourism provider uses positive public relations.

1 What general image of the hotel will newspaper readers get from the article?

2 What impression do you get of Bill Soames and of his relationship with his staff?

3 How does the use of quotes from Sue Kirk and Bill Soames create a positive image?

4 What effect do you think the article might have on:

- existing customers

- locals who have not used the hotel before

- existing staff

- local people looking for employment.

Jupiter Hotel is a real star!

The three-star Jupiter Hotel proved this week that it has a heart of gold. Hearing about the cancellation of the Care Bears Playgroup's Christmas party, reported in last week's Gazette, the Jupiter decided to play Santa Claus.

Jupiter's general manager Bill Soames offered the playgroup a free room at the hotel for the party and provided food and drink for the children. He even dressed up as Santa Claus and distributed presents from the hotel to all of the guests.

Playgroup leader Sue Kirk said: 'We cannot thank Bill Soames and his staff enough. It is the hotel's busiest time of the year but they still managed to fit us in and gave the chil-

dren a party that they will be talking about for months.'

The Care Bears Christmas surprise had to be called off when the church hall was discovered under three feet of water. The culprit was a burst water pipe, flooding the venue where the party was going to be held.

Bill Soames was modest about his role. 'Chambermaid Anne Tomlinson should take the credit. She read the report in the Gazette and persuaded me that we should do something.'

'I must admit that putting on a Santa Claus outfit and seeing the look on the children's faces as I handed out the presents was one of the highlights of the year for me,' he said.

Now get hold of a copy of a local newspaper. How many examples of good public relations can you find?

Personal selling

Personal selling involves direct sales contact between an organisation and its customers. It may be carried out face to face or over the telephone.

▶ Good telephone skills are an asset in the leisure and tourism industries

Most employees in the leisure and tourism industries are frequently involved in selling situations. It is important to understand that personal selling does not mean persuading customers to buy something that they do not want, simply to achieve a sale. For example, the travel clerk in a travel agency is constantly using personal selling skills when booking holidays for customers. However, it is not in the clerk's interest to recommend a holiday that will not meet the customer's needs and expectations. At the very least it is likely that the customer will be disappointed, but also highly likely that he or she will complain and choose not to use the travel agency in future when booking holidays. In addition, the customer will probably tell friends about the poor advice that was offered.

There are several stages to successful personal selling.

- Identifying customers' needs and expectations. This means asking the right questions and listening carefully to what customers have to say.
- Providing customers with honest and accurate information so that they can decide which product suits their needs.
- Explaining all of the alternatives to customers so that they can make an informed decision.
- Not pressurising customers into buying something they are unsure about.
- Describing the products and services in an enthusiastic and positive way. If you cannot sound enthusiastic you cannot expect the customers to be!
- Explaining to customers how they go about buying the product that they have chosen.
- Following up the sale, wherever possible, to check that customers are satisfied with what they have bought.

Practising selling skills

For this role-play activity, you need to have enough leaflets or brochures from local leisure and tourism attractions so that everyone in the group has a different one. Before you carry out the role plays, spend some time reading the information on your attraction carefully so that you can answer all questions.

In pairs, take the roles of a member of staff at the attraction and a potential customer who is interested in visiting the attraction. Role play the situation. The member of staff should use good personal selling skills to explain how the attraction can satisfy the needs of the customer. The potential customer should ask at least five questions. Here are some sample questions.

- What is there for children to enjoy?

- Is it good value for money?

- I don't have a car, how will I get there?

- What type of refreshments are available?

- Do you have facilities for disabled visitors?

The customer should also think of some specific questions that someone would ask about the particular attraction.

After the role play, discuss as a group how the member of staff used personal selling skills and what he or she could have done to improve the performance.

Displays

Many leisure and tourism organisations use **displays** to promote specific products and services. One of the most common types of display is to put posters in windows and on doors. For example, a pub might display posters showing the nightly entertainment on offer such as karaoke, quiz nights and singers; travel agencies use poster displays in their windows to let customers know about special deals and products.

The items used in a display are not limited to posters, and some organisations are becoming very imaginative at making displays effective. For example, many organisations have printed materials as well as sample products in a display to tempt customers to buy. Many swimming pools use a display board to tell customers about different swimming lessons and forthcoming special events. This type of display is known as a **point-of-sales display**. In other words, customers can actually buy the product being promoted. Point-of-sales displays are particularly effective because the customer can buy the product immediately instead of going away and possibly forgetting about it.

Travel agents are one of the main types of provider to use point-of-sales displays. The shop window displays are seen as very important for attracting customers into the agency to find out more about holidays, travel and other services offered. Some agencies focus on special cheap deals, whereas others prefer to show the wide range of services offered.

▶ Posters in the window of a travel agent

ACTIVITY

Travel agents' point-of-sale displays

Visit two different travel agencies in your area and compare their shop window displays.

1 What products and services are displayed in each?

2 What type of products and services seem to be most important (what, for example, are the first products you see)?

3 How effective is the point-of-sales display?

4 Can you suggest any ways in which the display could be improved?

Sponsorship

Sponsorship involves one organisation giving financial or other support in exchange for the association of its name with the product or event. For example, every team in the Carling Premier and Nationwide football leagues displays the name of its sponsor on the players' strip, and the Football League Cup has been sponsored by several companies in recent years, most recently by Worthington. Many arts and entertainment events are also sponsored.

◀ Football clubs have sponsors' logos on their shirts

Organisations have to choose carefully which event or product they might sponsor. They look for an opportunity to enhance the organisation's corporate image and to strengthen awareness among target audiences. For their part, event organisers have to think carefully about the public perception of any association with the sponsoring company. Some sponsors, such as tobacco companies, are potentially controversial.

Although large leisure and tourism organisations often pay millions of pounds in sponsorship, it can be just as effective on a smaller scale. Many privately owned organisations sponsor local causes or contribute a more modest amount to national causes.

ACTIVITY

Arranging sponsorship for Hotfoot's

Hotfoot's is a privately owned children's adventure park in South Wales. The manager feels that sponsorship could help to raise the profile of the park and show a caring side to the company. She has £500 in her promotional budget.

Over the last few months several organisations and individuals have asked the company to sponsor them.

- The local Vipers under-15 football team would like sponsorship to enable it to buy a new football strip for all players. The team will have Hotfoot's name printed on the front of the football shirts.

- The local non-profit-making theatre would like a donation of £250 towards its fund to provide programmes printed in Braille for the visually impaired. Three other organisations have already donated money and all sponsors will be listed in the programme.

- A local group is trying to raise £5,000 to send a five-year-old child to the USA for specialist treatment for a rare genetic disorder. The campaign has already had coverage in the local newspaper and it only needs a further £250 to reach its target.

- A part-time catering assistant at Hotfoot's is about to finish her Advanced GNVQ in Leisure and Tourism and plans to work as a volunteer teacher in Sri Lanka for a year before going to university. She needs to raise £2,000 in sponsorship.

- The hospice would like to hold a charity fashion show at Hotfoot's to raise funds. It has asked to use Hotfoot's restaurant on a Saturday afternoon in July and would like the company to provide free refreshments. The event will be heavily publicised in the local press and attended by several hundred local residents.

Each of these requests is for £250 sponsorship. The manager has to decide how to best spend the £500 budget.

As a group, discuss which two organisations or individuals you think Hotfoot's should sponsor, giving reasons for your choice. When making your decision remember the manager's sponsorship objectives.

Demonstrations and visits

One of the problems with many promotional techniques is that customers cannot really see or experience the product or service. For example, you can see photographs of a holiday destination in a tour operator's glossy brochure, but what is the resort really like? You may be thinking of buying a piece of exercise equipment, but can you actually tell how easy it would be to use by looking at the newspaper advertisement? For this reason, many leisure and tourism organisations arrange **demonstrations and visits** to enable customers to see and experience products and services.

- A leisure centre may invite new customers to try out the facilities before they actually join as members.
- Time-share apartment companies often take prospective customers on a visit to the time-share complex to allow them to experience the product first hand.
- Tour operators frequently provide travel agency staff with familiarisation visits to holiday destinations so that they will be able to describe the product more effectively to customers.
- A hotel might invite local business people to lunch so that they can look around the conference facilities.

◀ Open days give potential customers an opportunity to try the facilities

CYBERNET

Have you been to the new internet café in town?

CYBERNET

24 hour surfing on the net with free e-mail access.

Coffee bar and advice on hand.

Open day and free demonstrations on Saturday 15th July Ring (01654) 377254

or e-mail cybernet@hostmail.co.uk

ACTIVITY

Generating interest in the theatre

The John Arnold Theatre stages a wide range of productions, including traditional plays, new writers' work and musical events. The theatre also has a restaurant, coffee bar and souvenir shop.

Market research has shown that the average age of customers is gradually getting older – and 16–19 year olds rarely, if ever, visit the theatre. The theatre has therefore appointed an educational officer, Gianni Ponti, whose job is to encourage young people to go to the theatre more often.

Gianni has introduced a number of new ideas, such as Saturday morning theatre workshops, backstage tours and special discount rates for students and school groups. Despite this, the number of young customers has not increased very much.

You are at the John Arnold Theatre on work placement and Gianni has asked you to help him encourage young people to visit the theatre. He is particularly interested in GNVQ Leisure and Tourism students – there are 12 colleges which offer the qualification within an hour's drive of the theatre. As a test run he has invited a group of 15 Intermediate GNVQ Leisure and Tourism students to visit the theatre in two weeks time. The students will be at the theatre from 1 p.m. to 4 p.m.

Gianni would like you to suggest a programme for the three-hour visit. Can you think of activities that would appeal to this type of customer and which would encourage them to visit the theatre again? A small amount of money is available for refreshments – so specify when and how you would spend it.

Sales promotions

Sales promotions are short-term activities intended to encourage interest in a particular product. For example, travel agencies may offer discounts to customers booking a holiday well in advance. Other examples include:

- free gifts given with purchase
- money-off vouchers
- discounts
- price reductions
- free samples
- entry to competitions and prize draws on purchase
- incentives to buy in bulk (two free tickets when you make a block booking)
- loyalty schemes.

Sales promotions are often used with other promotional techniques. For example, an organisation may use a direct mail letter and include a money-off voucher, or place a newspaper advertisement that includes a competition.

▲ Money-off vouchers are just one example of a sales promotion

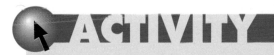

Surf Racers

Rachel Brown is about to open a jet skiing centre in Wales called Surf Racers. She has a very limited amount of money, so has decided to use the local press as her main source of promotion. She has already placed a number of advertisements in local papers and they have all also printed an article about the new centre based on an interview with her.

As the final (and hopefully best) piece of promotion before opening, Rachel plans to use a sales promotion. She has a budget of £500 for the sales promotion. Design a suitable sales promotion for Rachel and explain how it could be effectively advertised.

Build your learning

Summary points

- Promotional techniques are the ways in which organisations promote their products and persuade customers to buy them.

- Advertising is the publication, display or broadcast of information that describes a product in a favourable way.

- Direct marketing involves sending or giving promotional material directly to individual customers.

- Public relations is the planned attempt to create a favourable image of an organisation and its products.

- Personal selling involves direct sales contact between an organisation and its customers.

- Displays are a visual collection of promotional materials such as posters and leaflets.

- Sponsorship involves one organisation giving financial or other support in exchange for the association of its name with the product or event.

- Demonstrations allow the customer to see or experience what a product or service would be like if they bought it.

- Sales promotions are short-term activities intended to encourage interest in a particular product.

Key words and phrases

You should know the meaning of the words and phrases listed below as they relate to promotions. Go back through the last 16 pages to refresh your understanding if necessary.

- Advertising
- Direct marketing
- Public relations
- Point-of-sales display

- Personal selling
- Displays
- Sponsorship
- Customer database

- Demonstrations and visits
- Sales promotions
- Promotional techniques

SUMMARY ACTIVITY

You have completed a range of activities on how to use promotional activities and have probably realised that some of them are particularly suitable for specific types of organisations, products or customers. This activity asks you to suggest suitable promotional techniques for four different leisure and tourism events.

- A music festival featuring rock bands
- The opening of a new leisure centre
- A new year's eve dinner dance at a hotel
- A sponsored walk for Children In Need

In pairs, suggest how you could use the eight promotional techniques we have discussed in this section to promote each of the products. You do not have to use all eight techniques for each event.

Designing effective promotional materials

In the last section we looked at some of the techniques used in promotion. The effectiveness of these techniques depends largely on how well they are designed. In this section we are going to look at some of the factors that need to be considered when designing promotional materials.

One of the most common methods used to make sure that promotion is effective is an idea known as **AIDA**. This stands for:

Attention
Interest
Desire
Action

Let's look at these four stages in detail to see how they work in practice.

Attention

Attracting customers' **attention** is the first, and probably most important, part of AIDA, because if the promotion does not get their attention the whole promotion is wasted! This is often a lot harder than it seems. What do you usually do when the commercial break comes on during a television programme – make a cup of tea, zap onto other channels, have a chat? Unless a promotion can attract customers' attention and make them watch, read or listen then it will not be effective. Organisations use a lot of different methods to make their promotions eye-catching and to attract their customers' attention. We look at these next.

Colours

Colours give different impressions and organisations think carefully about which ones to use. For example, if you look at a summer holiday brochure or advertisement like the one for Guernsey you will see that bright blue and yellow are the dominant colours. This is because they are associated with sun, sea and sand.

Fonts and print style

The type of font used can create a strong image about the product. For example, a traditional font such as that used in this text is suitable for a book but may be a bit boring for a promotional title. Promoters will try to use a font that is in keeping with the image of their product. Some organisations use a combination of different fonts to create an unusual and effective impact

Bold titles and headlines

The use of an imaginative headline can often be very effective in attracting customer attention. Look at the P&O advertisement and see how a bold headline can attract attention.

Pictures and drawings

There is an old saying that a picture's worth a thousand words. Customers are often drawn more quickly to a well-chosen picture that sums up what a product is about rather than a detailed description. For example, look at the SkyDigital advertisement and see how it has effectively used a picture to get your attention.

Layout

Advertisers pay a lot of attention to the way that pictures and text are laid out. Slanted captions and pictures of varying size and angle all help to make promotional materials more eye-catching and attractive.

Celebrities

Many organisations use celebrities in their promotional materials to attract attention. The choice of celebrity will depend on the type of product and the target customers. For example, a boy band would be ineffective in attracting the attention of older customers.

▲ Advertisers use a range of devices to grab your attention

Humour

Humour is used widely in promotional materials – it helps attract attention and puts the customer in a good frame of mind. Many organisations use amusing pictures of young children or animals because they know that this generally raises a smile in the majority of the population!

ACTIVITY

Attracting customers' attention

Look at the leaflets shown here and opposite. Each is a good example of the methods leisure and tourism providers use to attract customer attention to their products. Remember there is no right way – different methods are effective with different products and different target audiences. Identify how the leaflets attract customer attention by use of:

- colour
- font
- bold headlines or titles
- layout
- pictures
- humour.

Can you spot any other attention-grabbing ideas in the leaflets?

As a further test of the attention factor, try this activity. Visit your local tourist information centre and find the leaflet rack. Quickly take the three leaflets that first attract your attention. What was it about these particular leaflets that made you pick them out?

Interest

It is clearly important to attract the attention of customers but if the content of the advertisement does not encourage them to carry on reading, listening or watching it is likely to be ineffective. Therefore, the next stage is to keep their **interest**. This is often achieved by slowly developing the features that originally attracted their attention, rather than bombarding them with lots of information.

Many advertisers use a humorous or fun element when designing the content to keep customers' interest and make sure that they keep reading to the end.

ACTIVITY

Maintaining interest

Look at the Virgin advertisement shown here. Attention has been gained by the use of bold colours, a question and an interesting, happy holiday picture. But when you start reading the smaller print you find that although some of the information is what you would expect from a standard holiday advertisement there is also a funny element to it – the chairman has a beard and flies balloons!

As a group, discuss why you think Virgin has introduced this humorous element to the advertisement. What does it say about its holidays and the sort of people who go on them?

Desire

The aim of the content of promotional material should not only be to create interest but also to make customers want to buy the product – this is the third stage of AIDA. Having attracted their attention and kept their interest, the promoter now needs to create a desire in the customer to actually buy the product. This is done by describing the product in a way that shows how it can meet customers' needs and expectations.

One of the ways in which a lot of leisure and tourism providers create **desire** in customers to visit their facilities (or buy their products) is to describe them in a way that makes customers feel as if they are already there. Using adjectives like exciting, thrilling and dangerous can do this. Similarly, the use of verbs, such as experience, hear, taste, join in, is very effective. Another way is to constantly personalise the information, making it sound as if the leaflet is talking to the customer directly by using words like you, your and our.

ACTIVITY

Creating desire

Look at this leaflet from the Thackray Medical Museum and identify what words are used to make the experience feel real to the reader and, hence, create a desire to visit.

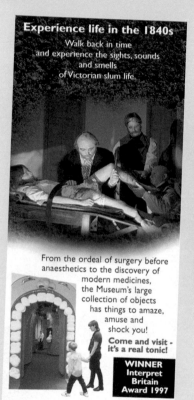

Action

The final stage of AIDA is to show customers how they can actually go about buying the product – in other words, **action.** Research has shown that the easier it is for customers to buy a product as soon as they have decided that they want it, the more likely they are to buy it. Alternatively, the longer the gap between deciding to buy something and actually buying it, the more likely they are to change their minds. Therefore, promotional materials need to make it as easy as possible to buy the product. When promotions are at the point of sale this is clearly easier. However, when they are not, organisations often give a phone number to ring or clear instructions on how to get to a facility.

To enable customers to take action, a promotion needs to include all of the information required for customers to actually buy the product. In effect it needs to anticipate any questions that customers might have before buying and give the answers. For example, will customers want to ask more questions about the product before buying and if so, how can they do this?

ACTIVITY

Taking action

Look at the booking information for Disney on Ice. How easy it would be for the following customers to take action and buy the product?

- Mr and Mrs Combes are senior citizens. They want rinkside seats for a Wednesday matinee. How much will it cost and when can they book in person?

- The Scarsfell Scout group (two adults and 15 children) want the cheapest seats available on a Saturday. How much will it cost and how do they book by post?

- Mrs Barker and two children (aged one and five years) want first level seats on a Sunday evening. How much will it cost and how can they book by credit card?

Disney ON ICE

PRODUCED BY FELD ENTERTAINMENT

Performances:
Tuesday November 16 at 7.30pm*
Wednesday November 17 at 2.00pm* & 7.30pm*
Thursday November 18 at 7.30pm*
Friday November 19 at 4.30pm* & 8.00pm
Saturday November 20 at 12 noon; 3.45pm & 7.30pm*
Sunday November 21 at 11.00am*; 2.45pm & 6.30pm*
*Group discount available at these performances

Ticket prices:

	Rinkside	1st Tier	2nd Tier
Tuesday - Friday perfs all tickets:	£21.50	£9.50	£7.50
Saturday & Sunday perfs all tickets:	£21.50	£12.50	£9.50

Booking Information:
All tickets will be subject to a 10% booking fee per ticket except to personal callers paying by cash or cheque at Sheffield Arena box-office.
By post - send remittance including booking fee to: The Box Office, Sheffield Arena, Broughton Lane, Sheffield S9 2DF
In person - at Sheffield Arena Box Office
(Mon - Sat 10.00am - 6.00pm)
By phone - call the Credit Card Hotline on: **0114 256 5656**
(Mon - Sat 9.00am - 9.00pm)
Coach Operators - please contact Alison on: **0114 256 0110** (Mon-Fri 9.00am - 5.00pm). Subject to 25p reservation fee per ticket.
Groups - groups of 15 or more save £2.00 on 1st & 2nd tier tickets at selected performances. Group bookings are subject to a 25p reservation fee per ticket unless payment is received with order. For further information, please contact Fiona Lakin or Cathy Kallis: Group Sales, Sheffield Arena, Broughton Lane, Sheffield S9 2DF; tel **0114 2560277/2560440.**

It is important to understand that AIDA applies to all types of promotional material, so let's go on to look at some of those used most frequently in the leisure and tourism industries.

Advertisements

As we have already seen, adverts can be used in a variety of media such as newspapers and magazines and on radio, television and billboards (poster sites). Advertisers need to remember that customers may not be willing to spend as long looking at advertisements as other forms of promotional materials such as leaflets and brochures. Therefore the information might need to be put across more simply and briefly. The important factor is to ensure that it follows the AIDA principles.

ACTIVITY

Effective advertising

Get a copy of a local or national newspaper and cut out all the advertisements from leisure and tourism providers. Identify how effective each advertisement is in telling you how you can buy the product that is being promoted.

- How many advertisements give an address and telephone number?

- Do they tell you how you can pay?

- Do they tell you the times when you can get information over the phone?

- Do they include a map or instructions on how to get to attractions?

- Are any further details included, such as the name of someone to talk to?

- Is an internet address given? If it is you might like to see whether the website gives you the information promised in the advertisement.

Brochures and leaflets

Brochures and leaflets are some of the most widely used promotional materials in the leisure and tourism industries.

Examples include:

- package holiday brochures
- hotel facilities
- sports centre programmes
- theatre productions
- transport timetables
- tourist attraction details
- holiday guides.

Unlike many advertisements, brochures and leaflets often contain a lot of information. This is because customers see them as a source of information rather than simply as promotional material.

ACTIVITY

Design a leaflet

Look at the leaflet for Courtney's. You will notice that its main focus is selling the product features and benefits to customers – in other words, what the customer will gain from joining Courtney's. Customers are being told that by using the clubs they will look and feel great, make new friends and enjoy the atmosphere and facilities.

Design a similar leaflet for a leisure or tourism facility in your area. You might like to choose a nightclub, cinema or sports centre that you use. Before designing the flyer think carefully about the product features. Why do customers use the facility and what do they gain from it?

Courtney's - the UK's leading chain of fitness centres is now open at Waterworld, York

Do you want to:

Look good and feel great?

Get fit in a relaxed and enjoyable atmosphere?

Achieve your own personal goals?

Meet new friends?

Experience the latest health and fitness products?

If you answered yes to any of the above then you need to join Courtney's

Benefits include:

No Joining Fee

Superb value for money

Free Fitness package to get you started worth £100.00

Free sunbeds

Direct debit easy payment scheme

Free parking

BEST OF ALL - THIS ONLY COSTS £31.00 PER MONTH THAT'S JUST £1.00 A DAY

adidas

Courtney's FITNESS PLUS

CALL 01904 642 162

Bugs and Beetles

Keep the kids amused at half term with our special creepy crawly exhibition. explore the insect world and discover the universe from a bug's eye view!

**Daily from
10.00 a.m. – 4.30 p.m.**

▲ A simple home-made poster

▶ Mobile posters

Posters and other point-of-sale items

Posters are probably one of the oldest forms of promotional material but still remain one of the most effective. They can be sited:

- on external buildings
- on transport (trains, buses, underground)
- at sporting stadiums
- on hoardings (special poster sites)
- at bus shelters
- at tourist information centres.

Many organisations will also agree to display posters; for example, hotels often display posters for local tourist attractions and facilities.

Posters can be very effective if they are sited in the right place: where potential customers are likely to see them and have the time to read them. One of the reasons that a lot of organisations pay for their posters to be displayed on bus shelters is that they realise that people waiting for buses get bored and are therefore likely to read the posters around them. However, to be effective, they would also need to make sure that the sort of customer they are trying to attract is the sort of person who uses public transport.

Many organisations use posters at the point of sale to tell existing customers about other products and services that they might be interested in. You need to understand that producing effective posters does not mean having to pay large amounts of money to an advertising agency. Many small organisations are able to produce very effective posters in-house – and, of course, it costs them nothing to display them at the point of sale!

ACTIVITY

Pronto Pizzas

Pronto Pizzas is a takeaway pizza and burger bar. Its main customers tend to be families and young adults. The owners are always looking for new and unusual ideas to keep their regular customers coming back. This year they have decided to offer a special Christmas pizza during December with slices of turkey, cranberry sauce and sage and onion seasoning. They have a very limited budget, so they plan to promote the pizza using posters in the shop at the point of sale.

Design a poster to promote the new pizza. You should think of a name for the pizza and include details of its ingredients and cost. Above all, remember AIDA!

Merchandising

Merchandising refers to materials that are sold or given away to customers that help to promote an organisation's main products. **Merchandising materials** usually feature the organisation's name. Examples of merchandising include:

- pens
- balloons
- bags
- T-shirts
- stickers
- posters
- drinks mats.

Merchandising materials were originally given away free to encourage customers to return and buy the product again. However, in the last few years, organisations have increasingly recognised that there are considerable profits to be made from selling merchandising associated with products like films and pop groups. One of the first organisations to realise the potential of selling merchandising was the Disney Corporation, which now sells a range of souvenirs at its theme parks, through retail outlets and through mail-order catalogues.

▼ Part of the Disney merchandising catalogue

ACTIVITY

Merchandising

Merchandising is used widely in the leisure and tourism industries. If you look around your home you will probably find that you have many examples of merchandised products bought as souvenirs of an event or visit. Count how many examples you can identify of merchandised products associated with each of the following:

- films

- television programmes

- pop groups or performers

- a tourist attraction.

Videos

As we have already discussed (see page 106), there is a difference between products that are goods and those that are services. Many leisure and tourism products are services that customers experience at the time rather than goods that they take away with them. For this reason many organisations feel that printed promotional materials are not enough when it comes to showing the customer what the experience is actually like. How much of an impression can you get of a foreign package holiday by looking at a few pictures and a written description in a brochure? Would you be able to appreciate how exciting an indoor skiing centre is by reading a leaflet? One of the ways that many organisations have overcome this difficulty is by producing **videos** showing customers actually using and experiencing the services and products. Some organisations are even putting videos on their internet sites.

Look at the pictures on the page opposite. They could be taken from any package holiday brochure. Now imagine that they are, in fact, shots from a video. If you could hear what the characters were saying and see what happened next, do you think that it would give you a better idea of what the holiday experience would be like?

▲ Photos from a holiday brochure

ACTIVITY

The video experience

For this activity you will need to get hold of a video from a holiday company. You may find that a travel agency has an out-of-date one that it will let you have, or it may be prepared to lend you one of its current videos. Some tour operators will send free videos on request; look for details in the holiday advertisement sections of national newspapers.

Watch the video and discuss the following questions as a group.

- What type of customer was the video aimed at?

- How successful do you think the video would be at persuading these customers to buy the holiday? Give reasons.

- Do you think the video would be more successful than another form of promotion such as a brochure or poster? Why?

- How was AIDA used to make the video successful?

- Can you suggest any ways in which the video could have been improved?

Look at the two examples ▶ of press releases on this page. Which do you think is the most effective and, more importantly, which is most likely to be printed by a local newspaper?

We are orginising a music festival in Greatholm Park in July. We hope that a lot of locle bands will vollunteer to play free of charge as the profits are going to a the childrens ward at the hospital. There will be refreshments and toilets provided. Please come and join us as it will be a grate day for all. If you are a locle band who would be interested in playing at the festival you can contact us on 367289.

June 15th 2000

Greatholm students aim for world e-mail record

A group of GNVQ Leisure and Tourism students at Greatholm College are hoping to enter the record books. As part of their course, they have to organise an event and they have come up with the novel idea of trying to enter the Guinness Book of Records for the longest sponsored e-mail session.

Students will work on separate computers, sending e-mail messages to each other. They have set themselves strict rules, having to reply to messages within 15 minutes, setting a minimum of 20 words for all messages and prohibiting sending the same message more than once to different people.

Student Mark Evans said, 'We spent ages thinking about what we could do that would be a challenge but also enjoyable and raise some money for local charities. The e-mail idea came about because we have all had to use computers a lot since starting this course and we wanted to use our new skills.'

The sponsored e-mail session is due to take place from 9 a.m. to 9 p.m. on Saturday July 26th at the college. Sponsors and spectators are welcome! For further details, course tutor Maria Combes can be contacted at the college on (01653) 623754.

Press releases

On page 126, we looked at how **press releases** can be used as part of a public relations campaign. One of the advantages of using a press release to get editorial coverage in a newspaper is that the customer is likely to spend longer reading it (because it is not seen as an advertisement), so it is therefore possible to include a lot more information. Another advantage, of course, is that it is free – so any organisation, no matter how small, can afford it!

Press releases also form part of organisations' promotional materials and the same rules of AIDA apply. When writing a press release you need to remember that it should read as if it is a proper newspaper article. Therefore, it has to be in the third person (for example, 'the Plaza cinema has recently invested in a brand new coffee shop') rather than the first person (for example, 'we are pleased to announce that...'). That is not to say that you cannot put in what you think, but it needs to be written as if a reporter were interviewing you and writing what you have said. Finally, the press release should include all of the relevant details, be titled and dated and not contain any spelling or grammatical errors!

ACTIVITY

Porchester Leisure Centre

Porchester Leisure Centre has recently introduced a customer care training programme to ensure that customers get the best possible service. The programme involves all the centre's staff. It includes an employee suggestion box for improvements to service as well as a monthly prize for the member of staff who has given exceptional service in some way.

All staff have attended the English Tourism Council's *Welcome Host* training day and received certificates to show that they have been trained in good customer service. The manager is very pleased with the results and would like to publicise the improvements that have been made in the form of a press release in the local newspaper.

Write a press release of about 200 words for the newspaper. You can make up any details, names and quotes that you need.

Computers and the internet

One of the greatest advances in producing effective promotional materials has been the widespread use of computers. You may already have used a computer to complete some of the activities in this unit. Even the smaller leisure and tourism organisations often have access to a computer that allows them to design their own promotional materials quickly and cheaply. However, there is another way in which computers have changed the nature of promotional materials. Many organisations now use channels such as the internet to send out promotional materials to customers.

Most local councils and many leisure and tourism providers in all areas of the United Kingdom have put some details about their area onto the internet. Some areas have a central website with lots of different sections allowing browsers to find specific types of information such as accommodation, attractions and transport. In other areas, browsers may find that different providers are all on separate websites.

Are you on the internet?

Use the internet to find out what information there is about your area, or a large town or city nearby. You might like to try to find out specific information such as:

- entertainment
- museums and art galleries
- hotels
- a map of the area
- restaurants.

Afterwards, discuss as a group how easy you think it would be for a visitor to find information in this way. To get you started try:

http://www.leisurehunt.com
http://www.whatson.com

Build your learning

Summary points

- Advertisements can be used in newspapers, magazines, radio, television and poster sites.

- Brochures and leaflets are widely used in the leisure and tourism industries and have the advantage that they can convey a lot of information.

- Posters can be very successful if sited in the right location.

- A point-of-sales display is a promotional display in the location where customers buy a product.

- Merchandising is sold or given away to customers to help promote an organisation's main products.

- Videos are useful as promotional materials in giving customers a better idea of the experience of using a leisure or tourism product such as a holiday.

- Press releases are newspaper articles written by an organisation about the company or its products. They have the advantage of being free and customers are likely to spend longer reading them than they would an advertisement.

Key words and phrases

You should know the meaning of the words and phrases listed below as they relate to promotional materials. Go back through the last 16 pages to refresh your understanding if necessary.

- **Advertisements**
- **Brochures and leaflets**
- **AIDA**
- **Posters**
- **Point-of-sales materials**
- **Merchandising materials**
- **Attention**
- **Videos**
- **Press releases**
- **Interest**
- **Desire**
- **Action**

SUMMARY ACTIVITY

For this activity each member of the group needs to arrange an interview with a member of staff at a local leisure or tourism organisation such as a travel agency, sports centre, theatre or tourist attraction. Try to select a wide range of different organisations. Ask the person you are interviewing to explain the various promotional materials that the organisation uses. Collect examples of:

- advertisements
- brochures/leaflets
- posters and other point-of-sale materials
- merchandising materials
- videos
- press releases.

When you have collected all of the information use it to create a display board showing the different promotional materials used in the leisure and tourism industries.

Describe how effective you think each promotional material is in terms of AIDA.

Planning promotional campaigns

We have looked at the promotional techniques and materials that are used by leisure and tourism organisations. You will have realised that organisations have a large number of different options to chose from when it comes to promoting their products and services. The techniques and materials that they decide to use will depend on a number of factors, such as how much money they have to spend, the type of customers that they are trying to attract and the type of product that they want to promote. In short, organisations aim to achieve the maximum effect by making the best use of their resources. To achieve this there are a number of factors that organisations need to consider when planning a **promotional campaign**:

- what the promotional campaign is trying to achieve
- who the target market is
- what promotional techniques to use
- what promotional materials to use
- how to monitor and evaluate the success of the campaign.

Let's look at these factors in more detail.

What does the campaign aim to achieve?

Before any promotional campaign can be designed and implemented, the first, very important step is to identify the **objectives** of the campaign – in other words what the campaign hopes to achieve. These objectives vary according to the type of product and organisation but might include:

- to make a financial gain such as an increase in sales or profits
- to achieve a social or community gain – some leisure and tourism organisations do not operate to make a profit but rather to provide a service for the community
- to raise awareness of the product or the organisation
- to improve, enhance or change the image of a product or the organisation
- to attract new customers
- to retain existing customers.

What are the target markets?

Having set the objectives for a promotional campaign, the next step is to identify the **target markets** that the organisation is trying to reach. This is obviously important because it will help the organisation decide which **promotional techniques** and **promotional materials** are most suitable. For example, if an organisation's objective is to attract new customers it would be ineffective to use point-of-sales promotions as potential new customers would not see them!

What promotional techniques should be used?

Having set the campaign's objectives and identified the target markets, the next step is to identify which promotional techniques and materials are going to be most effective. If the market research has been effective, the organisation will have identified its target market and the types of promotional materials that target customers are likely to see, hear or read. A variety of methods could be used, including:

- advertising
- sales promotion
- public relations
- sponsorship
- personal selling
- direct mail
- brochures and other promotional materials.

The type, or types, of promotional activities and materials selected for a campaign will depend on its nature and the target markets, as well as the resources available. The decision about which media are to be used should be made when target markets have been identified. For example, if a promotional campaign for a leisure centre aims to attract local customers, there would be little point in advertising in a national newspaper, or on television.

Monitoring the success of the campaign

Monitoring a promotional campaign means that those responsible for the campaign need to constantly check that the promotional activities are being carried out in the way that they had planned by asking appropriate questions.

- Has the newspaper printed the advertisement on the right night?
- Has the printer produced the information in the brochures as you requested?
- Is someone checking that the point-of-sales display is stocked with leaflets each day?
- Are the posters displayed still in good condition?

Obviously, the organisation needs to put right anything that is not going to plan.

Gemini Restaurant

Gemini Restaurant has paid for an advertisement in the local newspaper to promote its forthcoming Halloween masked ball. This is being held on Saturday 30 October. The event, which costs £19.50 per person, is due to run from 7.30 p.m. to 1 a.m. and includes a five-course meal with wine. Live music is being provided by The Ghouls and fancy dress is requested.

The manager monitors the promotional campaign and spots a mistake in the advertisement that the newspaper prints four weeks before the event. Look at the advertisement shown here and see if you can spot the mistake. What do you think the manager should do about it to ensure that the campaign is still successful?

GEMINI RESTAURANT
Halloween Masked Ball

Saturday October 30th

7.30 p.m. – 1.00 a.m.

Live dancing to the Ghouls

Five course dinner

Fancy Dress is required

£9.50 per person

Ring: 01532 545611 for further details and bookings

The final stage of a promotional campaign is **evaluating** how effective it has been – in other words, the organisation needs to ask if it has achieved the objectives set at the beginning. If those responsible for the promotional campaign have set specific and measurable objectives, this task should be easy.

One factor that needs to be remembered when evaluating success is that most promotional campaigns are a combination of several different techniques and materials. For example, an organisation may use press advertisements, direct mail and point-of-sale displays to promote one product – so how does it know whether all or some of them have been successful? One way is to ask customers how they heard about the product or what encouraged them to buy it – usually by using a questionnaire. This is useful up to a point, but it takes time and customers may not always be willing to answer questions.

A far more effective way is to use a promotional technique that lets the promoter know whether the customer has seen an advertisement or not. For example, if a tour operator advertises on television and gives out a free phone number that customers can ring for further details, it could count the number of enquiries that are received on that telephone line and therefore evaluate how effective the particular advertisement has been. If the advertisement is being screened over a number of nights, it could use a different telephone number each time to evaluate which particular nights are more effective.

ACTIVITY

Evaluating advertising campaigns

Look at the advertisements here. How easy do you think it would be for the organisation to identify whether or not customers had been encouraged to buy the product because they had seen the advertisement? Specify how they would be able to evaluate this in each case.

APOLLO CINEMA

Competition

The Apollo cinema is celebrating its first birthday by offering customers the chance to win free cinema tickets for a year. Simply answer the question below and return the coupon – you may be our lucky winner!

Question: Who was the first actor to play the role of James Bond?

....

Name..

Address..

Return to : Apollo Cinema, Esplanade, Heatherington

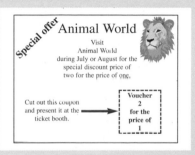

Special offer **Animal World**

Visit
Animal World
during July or August for the special discount price of two for the price of one.

Cut out this coupon and present it at the ticket booth. ⟶ Voucher 2 for the price of 1

Body Parts

Facial peel and scrub	Manicure/ pedicure
Indian head massage	Flotation therapy
Seaweed wrap	Colour analysis
Aromatherapy relaxation	Herbal reflexology

Castle Road, Tarcaster
Tel: (09775) 122342

THE NATIONAL TRUST

A marketing case study: the National Trust

The National Trust is a charity which was established more than 100 years ago with the aim of acquiring and maintaining places of historic interest and natural beauty. It protects over 575 miles of coastline, 271,000 hectares of countryside, as well as properties and gardens (see Figure 2.7). This case study has drawn extensively on material provided on the National Trust's website (**www.nationaltrust.org.uk**).

Mission statement
The National Trust's mission statement is:

> to promote the National Trust so far as to encourage visits to its properties which are both enjoyable and fulfilling for the visitor and profitable and sustainable for the Trust.

Marketing objectives
The National Trust identifies six main marketing objectives:

- to encourage visits to paying properties to a level of 12 million per year by the year 2000
- to encourage, in particular, visits to properties which need and can accommodate them
- to ensure that properties are as far as possible open at times when visitors wish to visit, subject to the necessary constraints which long-term preservation imposes
- to meet or exceed expectations on the part of our visitors
- to ensure a consistently high standard of visitor welcome, visitor attractions and visitor experience at all properties
- to achieve annual income targets arising from visitor admissions.

The marketing mix of the National Trust

Products
The products and services offered by the National Trust include:

- its properties
- membership of the National Trust
- merchandise in the National Trust shops and catalogues, including gifts, clothing, books, stationery and foods
- food and drink in National Trust tea-rooms and restaurants
- holiday cottages on National Trust properties, ranging from lighthouse keeper's cottages to renovated farmhouses
- educational activities.

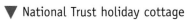
▼ National Trust holiday cottage

Figure 2.7: National Trust properties, 1998

Properties open to the public

Historic houses	164
Castles	19
Gardens	160
Mills, industrial archaelogy	47
Churches and chapels	49
Prehistoric and Roman sites	9
Landscape parks	73

Other assets

Land protected by the Trust	272, 659	hectares
Miles of coast protected by the Trust	565	miles
Listed buildings owned by the Trust	2,792	

▲ Cracking Haven, Cornwall

Place

The products offered by the National Trust are widely spread throughout England, Wales and Northern Ireland; the locations are obviously determined by where their properties and countryside areas are situated. The National Trust's website information pages separates the United Kingdom into nine areas, allowing customers to select an area that they are interested in and to find out about the properties in that particular area.

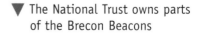
▼ The National Trust owns parts of the Brecon Beacons

Price

The National Trust decides property entrance fees based on five factors:

- inflation
- the entrance fees of other local attractions and competitors
- visitor figures over past years
- economic forecasts for the year ahead
- any resistance to existing prices.

Every year the National Trust reviews the charges, based on these five factors and may increase or, sometimes, decrease the entrance fee.

Promotion

The marketing section at the National Trust's head office in London has responsibility for the overall promotion of its products and services and uses a wide range of promotional techniques and materials. Regional National Trust offices are responsible for producing regional visitor guides and individual property leaflets.

Promotional techniques used by the National Trust

Advertising

Advertisements are largely local and are placed in regional newspapers and tourism brochures and newsletters. In some areas, such as Devon and Cornwall, this is aimed at visitors to the region, whereas other areas target local residents.

▶ National Trust press advertisement

Direct marketing

The National Trust has recently started to use direct marketing to attract new members. This includes inserts in selected magazines, mailings to lapsed members and direct promotions aimed at persuading existing members to encourage others to join the National Trust.

Public relations

The National Trust works hard to make sure that it has a positive public image by maintaining a good relationship with both local and national media. Each week it sends out press releases on a wide range of topics about its houses, gardens and countryside (see Figure 2.8).

Figure 2.8: National Trust press release

THE NATIONAL TRUST

McCartney family home in Liverpool: booking line opens for new season

The booking line for 20 Forthlin Road, Liverpool, the former home of the McCartney family where the Beatles met, rehearsed and wrote many of their earliest songs, is now open for the new season. Visitors can call the ticket line on 0151 486 4006.

Following a busy 1998, the booking line will open for business from Monday to Friday 9.30 a.m. – 4.30 p.m. until 26 March and Tuesday to Saturday 9.30 a.m. – 4.30 p.m. from 30 March. Visits to 20 Forthlin Road are by pre-booked ticket only and tours run from Speke Hall. The special Forthlin Road minibus, with its introductory video, will take people from Speke Hall to Forthlin Road, and back.

John Holliday, Custodian at 20 Forthlin Road, commented: 'I am looking forward to the new season. I enjoyed meeting the visitors to the house and showing them around last year. People have come from all over the world and I am so pleased to be able to share the history of the house with them.'

20 Forthlin Road is open from 31 March to 31 October on Wednesday, Thursday, Friday and Saturday; and from November to 11 December on Saturday only. Tickets cost £5 per adult and £3.50 per child (price includes admission to the garden and grounds of Speke Hall). National Trust members pay £2 to cover minibus and booking service costs.

Personal selling

Most members (90 per cent) join when they visit one of the Trust's properties. The main motivation for joining is the privilege, given only to members, of free admission to properties that the public has to pay to visit.

A specially trained sales force working face to face with visitors at the properties will aim to encourage paying visitors to convert into members. A conversion target of 8 per cent paying visitors to members is set nationally, although many individual properties exceed this.

Displays

Exhibitions are a key way of making contacts in the travel industry and the Trust exhibits at the British Travel Trade Fair and the World Travel Market. Both are well attended by group travel organisers as well as overseas travel trade. Exhibitions provide good opportunities for making new contacts and networking with existing ones as well as maintaining the profile of the National Trust in a very competitive industry.

Sales promotions and sponsorship

Sales promotions and sponsorships with leading companies can also help the Trust to promote property visits and membership of the Trust. For example, Barclays currently sponsors a whole range of countryside access projects with the National Trust under an imaginative programme called 'Barclays CountryFocus'. Under this, the National Trust receives:

▼ A National Trust guidebook sponsored by Barclays

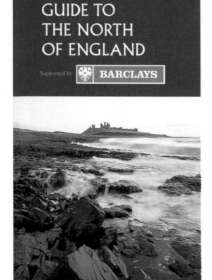

- much-needed money to fund new access routes (such as bridlepaths, cycle routes, footpaths both for able and less able visitors), to repair existing ones, and to provide information (free leaflets, interpretative panels) throughout England, Wales and Northern Ireland
- publicity for its extensive work in the countryside, through National Trust publications to its 2.5 million supporter base, publicity materials available to the general public and through press launches and photo calls.

As a major supporter of countryside conservation, Barclays benefits from media coverage and extensive exposure to National Trust members and visitors, and reaches local communities nationwide.

In addition, Barclays has run a savings promotion for two years. This has given the National Trust significant publicity on posters throughout all Barclays branches as well as promoting property visits and sales of National Trust memberships. It has also significantly increased the number of Barclays savings accounts opened during the promotion.

Each year the Trust also runs several 'on-pack' promotions which offer free admission to National Trust properties. The costs of the promotion are paid for by the company or publication running the promotion. This often provides national coverage on high profile goods, for example: Allinson Bread and Jordan's Cereals.

Marketing research

The Trust carries out market research on a regular basis. It is important that it knows:

- who its visitors are
- how they are getting their information
- whether they have enjoyed their visit
- how much they spend.

The results provide pointers for the marketing activities that the Trust undertakes. From research, it knows that word of mouth recommendation has proved to be one of the biggest influences in encouraging visitors to National Trust properties. This highlights the importance of excellent visitor care.

Figure 2.9: National Trust visitor questionnaire

National Trust Visitor Survey

Dear Visitor

Could you please help the National Trust by providing a few details of your visit today? We are constantly working to provide an enjoyable and informative experience at all of our properties. The information you provide will help us to do this well.

Our questionnaire is completely confidential and will only take a few minutes to complete. We are attaching a stamped, addressed envelope so that you can take it away and complete at your leisure.

Simply indicate your chosen answer by ticking the appropriate box or writing in the space provided.

We ask that one person fill in the questionnaire only.
Thank you for your help

Denise Melhuish

KILLERTON HOUSE

Q1 Please enter the date of your visit

Q2 Approximately what time did you arrive

Time

Q3 Please note the type of weather on the day of your visit

Q4 Are you a member of the National Trust?
Yes .... ☐
No .... ☐

Q5 Have you ever been a member of the National Trust?
Yes .... ☐
No .... ☐

Q6 If you are not a member of the National Trust how would you rate the admission charge in terms of value for money?

Value for money — Very Good ☐ Good ☐ Poor ☐ Very Poor ☐

Q7 Have you visited this property before
Yes .... ☐
No .... ☐

Q8 Approximately when did you last visit this property
This year .... ☐
1 year ago .... ☐
2 years ago .... ☐
3 years ago .... ☐
Don't know .... ☐
Other

Individual properties are encouraged to carry out ongoing market research to monitor satisfaction levels and to maintain accurate information on who their visitors are. National surveys are carried out on a regular basis in order to establish the national picture regarding visitors and Trust members. Occasionally research is carried out in the form of focus groups to test opinion on specific subjects. Recent research has been undertaken to assess members' reactions to the National Trust magazine and handbook, whilst a national visitor survey is currently being carried out to enable the National Trust to develop knowledge of its market segments. Accurate information on the Trust's main market segments allows limited resources to be targeted more effectively.

Target markets

The National Trust regularly analyses the types of customer who are members, to identify which segments are increasing or decreasing.

However, many of its customers are simply visitors rather than members of the Trust. To ensure that visitors go to a property or area that meets their needs and expectations, the Trust uses a system of symbols that shows the specific facilities and services offered at each location.

Figure 2.10: National Trust membership by category

Annual categories

	29 February 1988		28 February 1998	
	number	% total	number	% total
Individual	499,033	32.7%	673.570	27.1%
Additional	428,454	28.1%	652,828	26.2%
Pensioner	119,628	7.8%	261,727	10.5%
Family group	365,988	24.0%	724,029	29.1%
Child*	18,532	1.2%	2,686	0.1%
Young person*			31,271	1.3%
Totals	1,431,635		2,346,111	

* Prior to 1997 these categories formed the under 23 category.

The National Trust

Find out what National Trust properties there are within your area. If you have access to the internet you can do this by visiting the National Trust website (**www.nationaltrust.org.uk**). Alternatively, you could find out the information from your nearest tourist information centre or directly from the National Trust.

- Identify exactly what is offered at each local NT property.

- Compare the different entrance fees charged.

- Ask for copies of leaflets and brochures and discuss their effectiveness in terms of AIDA.

The case study about the National Trust gives you an insight into how a major leisure and tourism organisation uses marketing activities to promote itself.

Throughout this unit you will have realised that leisure and tourism organisations use marketing and promotions in different ways depending on the types of products that they offer and their target markets. You may already find that you look at marketing and promotions with a more critical eye and ask more informed questions.

- How have they used AIDA?
- Why have they used that colour and picture?
- Who do they hope to attract with that layout and font?
- What type of customer is this aimed at?
- Could any of these ideas be used in another type of advertisement?
- Have they given all of the information needed?

And, hopefully, on occasions you will have looked at a promotion and thought: 'They've not got that quite right – but I think I know what they should have done!'

Build your learning

Summary points

- Organisations have a large number of options when it comes to promoting their products.

- The promotional techniques that they choose will depend on cost, type of product and the type of customer that they are trying to attract.

- The first stage of any promotional campaign is to identify the objectives.

- It is important to identify which market segments are being targeted by a promotional campaign so that suitable techniques and materials can be used.

- The promotional techniques and materials used in a campaign depend on the objectives and the target markets.

- It is important that promotional campaigns are monitored to make sure that all is going as planned.

- It is important to evaluate the success of a promotional campaign to see whether the objectives have been met.

Key words and phrases

You should know the meaning of the words and phrases listed below as they relate to planning promotional campaigns. Go back through the last 12 pages to refresh your understanding if necessary.

- **Promotional campaign**
- **Promotional techniques**
- **Promotional materials**
- **Objectives**
- **Target market**
- **Monitoring**
- **Evaluating**

SUMMARY ACTIVITY

For this activity you need to set a time limit for gathering external sources of information. It is suggested that this should be two to four weeks. Split into small groups, with each group assigned to one of the following:

- effective use of AIDA

- use of colour and font

- use of layout – including graphics and symbols

- use of text – particularly looking at how passages of text help create interest and desire in AIDA

- use of pictures – including cartoons and celebrities

- use of unusual techniques – including humour and teaser campaigns.

During the period of research each group should collect as many good examples as they can find for their chosen area within the leisure and tourism industries. They should be from as many types of promotional techniques and materials as they can find. Each group might consider gathering examples by:

- collecting local leaflets and brochures

- evaluating local point-of-sales and poster displays

- keeping press advertisements and cuttings

- videoing television advertisements

- keeping examples of direct mail letters.

Once each group has collected enough examples it should present them to the whole group and discuss why it thinks each one is effective. In doing this, it should explain what it thinks the objectives of each piece of promotional material are and who the target markets are.

Assessment guidance

This unit is assessed through an external assessment that will ask you to show your understanding of the marketing activities of a leisure and tourism organisation. The grade for the external assessment will be the grade for the unit. The awarding body responsible for your school or college's GNVQs will set the style of the external assessment.

There is much that you can do to prepare for the external assessment. This book has been designed to help you learn new skills and knowledge. The table shows the unit's features that will be of most help in preparing for your assessment.

Feature	Learning
Build your learning	Summarises key concepts
Key words	Defines and lists marketing language
Activities	Practises marketing skills

Assessment tasks

The external assessment may be based on a case study. The table opposite sets out the tasks you are likely to be asked to do and shows which activities in this unit may give you opportunities to apply your marketing skills and knowledge, and help you to complete the external activities.

Other preparation

Everyday you encounter a great deal of promotional material, from posters on buses to the small advertisments in your local paper, from flyers through your letter box to sponsorship of major sports events. You can develop your understanding of the purpose and effectiveness of these types of promotion through collecting examples of leisure and tourism marketing and publicity material. You may find it helpful to:

- compare and contrast material that promotes similar products and services from different organisations
- follow particular campaigns from beginning to end
- visit leisure and tourism industry events, such as the World Travel Fair
- read discussions of leisure and tourism promotional campaigns in the national papers and in specialist magazines, such as *Leisure Manager* and *Marketing Week*
- interview people who promote products and services in the leisure and tourism industries.

Assessment tasks	Activities
Describe the products and/or services offered by an organisation	Activities on page 105, 111 and 120
Explain how the products and/or services are priced	Activities on page 113 and 120
Describe how the products and/or services are made available	Activities on pages 118 and 120
Describe the promotional techniques and materials an organisation uses, including the research methods it uses to identify target markets	Activities on pages 100, 120, 137, 154 and 167
Evaluate the success of an organisation's promotional techniques and materials	Activities on pages 140, 144, 149 and 167
Identify an organisation's target markets	Activities on pages 105, 109, 111, 159 and 167
Produce an item of promotional material	Activities on pages 145 and 147

Customer service in leisure and tourism 3

The main focus of all leisure and tourism organisations is to ensure that customers want and buy the organisation's products. One of the main ways in which organisations attract customers is by offering excellent customer service so that they will come back again and again. This unit looks at how this is done. It looks at the skills and knowledge needed to achieve this aim and enables you to assess and develop your own personal and communication skills in dealing with customers. You will learn about:

- the different needs of customers and how they are met
- the importance of personal presentation when dealing with customers
- handling dissatisfied customers
- the importance of keeping records.

By the end of this unit, you should be able to identify the important role you have to play in providing good customer service.

What is customer service?

So why do you want to work in the leisure and tourism industries? One of the answers that people in interviews most frequently give to this question is 'because I like meeting people'. Some of the better candidates may go on to say that they want to meet lots of different types of customers and that they hope this will be in a wide range of interesting and exciting situations.

Certainly you will meet lots of different people if you work in the leisure and tourism industries and you will definitely experience some unusual situations! However, some of the people you meet and the situations you find yourself in may not be quite as glamorous and exciting as you first imagined. Have you thought about the customers that you would probably rather not meet – the angry customer who blames you because his squash court has been double-booked; the young adult on a package holiday who has drunk too much and is feeling unwell; the visitor who asks you for the third time for directions to the local cinema; or the young children who want you to show them how the computer works when you just want to get on with booking their parents' holiday? These may be your customers and it is your job, and that of your organisation, to satisfy their needs.

So, what exactly do we mean by **customer service?** Customer service includes all contact with the customer, as well as the products or services that the organisation offers. In simple terms, it means putting the needs of customers first. In organisations that stress good customer service this should be the main aim of all staff.

Customer service may involve direct contact, such as when dealing with a customer face to face, or indirect contact, for example, in dealing with complaint letters. Good customer service requires you, as a member of staff, to put yourself in the position of your customers. You should be aware of how you would like to be treated if you were a customer and deal with your customers accordingly. You can learn a great deal from your own experience as a customer. What makes you feel you are being cared for well, and what annoys you and makes you decide not to use a service or buy a product again?

ACTIVITY

A word for service

If you tried to think of all the words to describe good and bad customer service it would be a never-ending activity. We have listed below just a few of the words that could be used. Put them into two columns – those that suggest good service and those that suggest bad service. Use a dictionary if you are unsure of the exact meaning of any of the words.

- accurate
- aloof
- apathetic
- attention
- churlish
- composed
- concerned
- confident
- controlled
- discreet
- hesitant
- hostile
- indifferent
- ineffective
- interested
- prejudiced
- responsible
- supportive
- tactless
- thoughtful
- vigilant

ACTIVITY

Experiences of customer service

Think of some leisure and tourism attractions or facilities that you have recently visited such as restaurants, shops, nightclubs or leisure centres. What sort of service did you receive?

Divide what was good and what was bad about the service into two columns headed 'good' and 'bad'. For example, you might have been made to feel welcome ('good'), you might have been kept waiting a long time ('bad').

When you have finished, compare your list with those of other members of the group. Are there similar points in your lists?

Discuss how many of the points that you have all listed were within the control of the member of staff serving you. You will probably find that most of them are!

Types of customer

The leisure and tourism industries offer a very wide range of products and services. Many appeal to a lot of different types of customer, others may be aimed at specific customers. Whichever sector you decide to work in, you will probably find yourself dealing with a wide range of customers with different backgrounds, ages, nationalities, interests and specific needs such as families with young children or disabled visitors. You need to learn that different customers have different needs. Therefore to provide excellent customer service, you have to be able to identify what customer needs are and then decide how you can meet them.

We now consider some of the main types of customer that you may have to deal with.

Individuals

You will often deal with **individual customers** on a one-to-one basis. For example, someone working in the ticket office of a stately home or at the reception desk in a sports centre deals mainly with individuals.

▶ Receptionist dealing with a customer

In some ways, this can be one of the easiest types of customer to deal with because you can give the person your full attention. On the other hand, it can be difficult if the customer is awkward or if you find it hard to understand the person's needs. You may feel somewhat exposed and isolated in dealing with the situation. It is important to understand that individual customers often have very different needs even if they are buying the same product or visiting the same attraction.

Any tourist resort or destination caters for two distinct groups of customers. In the first group are the visitors who come from outside the area for a holiday, on business, or to visit friends and relatives. The second group is made up of those people who already live in the area and who use the local leisure and tourism attractions and facilities. Both groups are equally important. The visitors may spend more money in a shorter period of time, but the residents' spending is usually spread out over the year and helps support the area's tourism industry during off-season months.

Visitor or resident?

In a recent market research exercise, people were asked for their views on town centres. They were asked for their opinions on the most important factors for town centre users. There were differences between the opinions of local residents and visitors to a town. The ten most important factors for visitors (in order of importance) were:

1 Variety of goods

2 Amount of car parking

3 Restaurants

4 Cleanliness

5 Location of car parking

6 Leisure facilities

7 Quality of tourist attractions

8 Cost of car parking

9 Visitor information

10 Historic architecture

As a group discuss what you think the top ten most important factors were for residents. Six of the factors are the same but they are not necessarily placed in the same order. (Answer on page 262.)

Groups

Staff in many leisure and tourism facilities have to communicate with **groups** of customers. For example, guides showing tourists around an art gallery or a heritage site deal with groups of people. This can save time, because it is possible to deal with several customers at once, but it requires special skills to take into account the needs of individual customers while dealing with the group as a whole. For example, an art gallery guide will need good communication skills to deal effectively with a group of visitors that includes young children, foreigners and art experts.

▶ A registered tourist guide with a group of tourists

In some situations, staff members find themselves talking first to a group, as they explain and demonstrate the basic techniques, then to individuals as they each try to apply skills. For example, an instructor at an outdoor pursuits centre may deal with a group first before undertaking individual instruction. Anyone who has tried this, especially with children, knows that you need 'eyes in the back of the head' to keep in touch with all that is going on.

People of different ages

When working in the leisure and tourism industries, you will almost certainly meet people from a wide range of **age groups**: they have different needs. Customers can be broken down into the following age groups:

- children – babies, toddlers, older children and teenagers
- adults – young adults, middle-aged adults, senior citizens.

However, you need to remember that you will often be dealing with groups of mixed ages, such as an adult with young children or senior citizens with grandchildren. This means that you will need to identify and satisfy the specific needs of each age group.

Children make up a large percentage of all leisure and tourism customers. They may visit some attractions and facilities on their own, but more often than not they will be accompanied by a parent or other adult. This presents a particular challenge for leisure and tourism providers. Obviously the children expect to enjoy themselves, but the adult wants an enjoyable time too. In addition, there will often be adults with no children who expect to have a good time without being bothered by other people's children. Providers are constantly looking for new ways to provide services that ensure that all customers are satisfied (see article below).

A class of their own

A nightmare or a brilliant new service? Kids Class is being introduced on some charter flights.

The plan is to segregate five- to 12-year-olds from other passengers by giving them their own block of seats at the back of the plane where a crew member will have the responsibility for entertaining and feeding them. The idea comes from the charter airline Airworld, which is part of Sunworld's operations.

A crew member hands out toys and comics, organises games, and, if needs be, helps the children with their menu of potato letters and chicken nuggets. All of which has worked pretty well so far, according to Airworld's marketing executives, who say that once-a-week trials on flights to Greece have been so successful that the company hopes to sell Kids Class to many other operators by next summer. Sunworld says it will also be expanding the service to other flights next summer.

The airline assures us that passengers who want to be seated well away from the children's area can request this, but in any case parents are seated near to their offspring, creating a buffer zone between Kids Class and the rest of the plane.

Holiday Which?
April 1999

Accommodating different age groups

Read the article on page 177, 'A class of their own'. This describes one of the ways that a tour operator has tried to ensure that children, accompanying adults and adults with no children can all enjoy a charter flight taking them to their holiday destination.

- How effective do you think this approach would be?

- Can you think of any problems that might arise?

- Can you think of any other leisure and tourism services or facilities where customers are separated to ensure that each enjoys the experience?

People from different cultures

Our cultural background influences our traditions, tastes, opinions and behaviour. In the course of your work in the leisure and tourism industries you may often find it important to recognise that people from different cultural backgrounds have different needs and behaviour. We often take our own cultural background for granted (simply because we have grown up with it) and assume that everyone else does the same as us. They don't! For example, did you know that:

- in South Africa a café is a grocery shop and won't sell you a cup of coffee
- in Japan you should change into a special pair of toilet slippers before using the bathroom
- if you take the lift to the first floor in the USA you will arrive at the ground floor
- in China it is considered very unlucky to leave your chopsticks in your bowl
- in India it is very insulting to show someone the sole of your shoe
- if you enter a Tunisian mosque you must remove your shoes, cover your arms and legs and avoid walking in front of someone who is praying
- in Turkey blowing your nose in public is very rude.

When dealing with people from **different cultures** it is important to respect and understand their beliefs but equally important not to make any assumptions based on culture.

Non-English speakers

You will often find yourself in situations in which you have to deal with customers who are **non-English speakers**. Obviously you cannot be expected to be able to speak all foreign languages, but even if you know just a little of the customer's language it shows excellent customer service to have a go. Simply knowing how to say hello, goodbye and thank you in key languages such as French, Spanish and German is a real help. Even when you and the customer have no language in common it is still possible to communicate and provide good service.

Many languages share similar words, so it is possible to work out what a customer is asking for if you both speak and listen carefully. For example, you might guess at what the following mean in French:

- *dîner* (dinner)
- *musée* (museum)
- *carte postale* (postcard)
- *autobus* (bus).

Gestures and facial expressions also help to convey many messages, as do the use of pictures, maps and diagrams. So, for example, if you were asked *'ou est le musée?'*, you could work out what was meant, draw the customer a simple map and of course give him or her a friendly smile!

▼ Using symbols rather than words helps overcome language barriers

ACTIVITY

Designing a sign

Many organisations use pictures and symbols on signs so that they can be easily understood by anyone, regardless of language. Can you design a sign for use in a leisure centre? The sign should only use pictures and symbols and should show the direction to the:

- swimming pool
- exercise studio
- squash courts
- cafeteria
- changing rooms
- male and female toilets.

LAKESIDE *Shopmobility*

FREE

Wheelchair Loan Service

▲ Lakeside's shopmobility scheme gives everyone access to shops on all levels of the centre

People with specific needs

Some customers have **specific needs** that might require special customer service. A specific need is anything that may require a bit of extra thought and assistance from staff. People in wheelchairs, those with visual or hearing impairments or people with young children have specific needs.

There is often a lot of misunderstanding about people with specific needs – they may need a bit of extra care but they do not want to be made to feel as if they are different or a nuisance. Dealing with these customers means understanding their particular needs and acting quickly to ensure that they are able to enjoy the product you are offering. For example, a young mother with a baby buggy or a customer in a wheelchair struggling to get through a swing door should not have to ask for assistance – any member of staff seeing the situation should react quickly and offer help.

ACTIVITY

Specific needs

Visit a leisure centre or swimming pool and collect promotional leaflets and any information available on the price list, opening hours, sessions available, etc. Using the information that you have gathered, identify all of the different types of customer who use the facility. List the types in one column and then fill in what you think their specific needs might be in a second column. An example based on a swimming pool has been given to start you off.

Type of customer	Specific needs
Children's beginners lessons	Supportive teachers High level of supervision

Businessmen and businesswomen

When we talk about leisure and tourism customers we usually think of tourists, holidaymakers or day visitors. However, people visiting an area on business are also leisure and tourism customers since they use many of the leisure and tourism facilities and services. For example, they may use public transport, stay in hotels, eat in restaurants and spend their spare time at tourist facilities such as cinemas, pubs, theatres, nightclubs and casinos. Many leisure and tourism organisations tailor the services they offer to meet the needs of **businessmen** and **businesswomen**. For example, some hotel chains have special executive bedrooms with desks and writing materials. They may also offer secretarial services and photocopying, fax, e-mail and internet facilities.

London

The Plaza on Hyde Park Hotel

The Conference and Business Centre is conveniently located on the ground floor. Providing secretarial and office support, this self-contained centre comprises two meeting rooms with natural daylight. Ideal for training sessions, presentations, breakfast meetings or formal board meetings. Whatever the occasion, the Business and Conference Centre will take care of your needs.

▲ Hotels compete strongly for business custom

Build your learning

Summary points

- Customer service is vital to all leisure and tourism organisations because it ensures that existing customers are kept and that new customers are attracted.

- Customer service is everyone's job and means putting the needs of the customer first.

- Customer service includes direct contact and indirect contact.

- There is a range of different types of customer and each has different needs which need to be met.

- It is your job to identify and satisfy the needs of different types of customer.

Key words and phrases

You should know the meaning of the words and phrases listed below as they relate to the different types of customers dealt with by the leisure and tourism industries. Go back through the last 10 pages to refresh your understanding if necessary.

- **Individual customers**
- **Groups**
- **Age groups**
- **Different cultures**
- **Non-English speakers**
- **Specific needs**
- **Businessmen**
- **Businesswomen**
- **Customer service**

SUMMARY ACTIVITY

Many leisure and tourism organisations offer different levels of customer service depending on the type of customer. Look at the extracts from the leaflets for Eurostar and British Midland. Both give details of special services offered to customers who pay more than standard fare customers.

As a group, discuss the similarities and differences between the service offered by the two transport providers.

- What does it tell you about the needs and expectations of their customers?

- What particular types of customers might be attracted to each service?

- Does one of the providers offer something that you think the other could include in its service?

Heathrow Manchester

A choice of service

For the first time ever, you now have a choice of service when flying between London Heathrow and Manchester.

British Midland is the only airline to offer you a business class service both on the ground and in-flight, with our prestigious Diamond EuroClass product.

On the ground

- Diamond EuroClass lounges for all business passengers at London Heathrow and Manchester, with complimentary drinks, snacks and modern business facilities

- Priority ticket sales and check-in

- Advanced seat assignment

- Chauffeured Parking Service available at London Heathrow and Manchester

In the air

- Separate Diamond EuroClass business cabin on every flight

- New wider seats

- Award winning in-flight cuisine, including hot breakfast

- Complimentary bar service, hot towels and newspapers

There's simply never been a better choice for the UK business traveller.

Our Premium First service to Paris

PREMIUM f I R S t

To travel Premium First is to experience the ultimate in quality and comfort. Features include:

- A dedicated Premium First ticket desk and check in up to 10 minutes prior to departure.

- Free parking at Ashford International.

- Before boarding, unwind in the peaceful atmosphere of our executive lounges.

- Take advantage of our porter service – Premium First passengers have priority.

- Relax in our extra-wide, reclining seats, with additional leg-room.

- Enjoy spacious work and meeting areas.

- A complimentary gourmet four-course meal, with a choice of fine wines and champagne. Hot and cold drinks are available throughout your journey.

- Choose from a selection of complimentary newspapers.

- Unlike a flight, you can use mobile phones and laptop computers during your journey.

- On-board telephones can be used with any major credit card.

Complimentary executive car service for Premium First passengers

You can book your complimentary executive car whenever it suits you: either at your departure station, in the Clubhouse lounge at London Waterloo International, the ticket desk at Ashford International or Salon Eurostar at Paris Gare du Nord.

When you arrive at Paris Gare du Nord we provide a complimentary executive car. Your driver will be waiting to take you to any central Paris arrondisement.

And when you return to London Waterloo International another car will be waiting to take you to any central London or Docklands address. A member of staff will give you payment vouchers to hand to your drivers.

The London postal areas that qualify for this offer can be obtained from Eurostar executive lounges on request.

The benefits of excellent customer service

A large part of the day-to-day operation of any leisure and tourism organisation involves dealing with customers and satisfying their needs. Therefore, it makes sense that providing a high level of customer service is a top priority. However, you need to be aware that when we talk about customers we do not just refer to the person who actually buys or uses the product. There is a difference between what are known as external customers and those known as internal customers.

External customers are what we have traditionally meant by customer: they are individuals, groups and businesses who use the facility in which you work and to whom your organisation sells goods and services. **Internal customers** are other people and departments who work in the same organisation as you do and who may need to draw on your services. Internal customers also include other organisations which help to supply your products and services.

ACTIVITY

External or internal?

Imagine that you work as a waitress or waiter in a hotel. Which of the following people are external customers and which are internal customers?

- The hotel receptionist

- The manager

- A person attending a conference

- A member of staff from the local tourist information centre who supplies the hotel with leaflets on local attractions

- A member of the public who comes in asking for directions

- The delivery man who supplies bread to the hotel

- A member of staff drinking in the hotel bar

It is important to understand that good customer service needs to be provided to both internal and external customers if an organisation wants to be successful and effective.

Figure 3.1: Effective customer service is essential for leisure and tourism organisations

Enhanced reputation	Customer satisfaction	Customer loyalty (repeat business, recommendations)
Safe environment for customers and staff	**Effective customer service promotes...**	Increased sales (new and existing customers)
Secure environment for customers and staff	Job satisfaction of staff	Increased profitability

▲ Draw a diagram like Figure 3.1, but this time make the box in the middle read 'poor customer service promotes...' and change the other boxes accordingly.

The benefits of providing excellent service for external customers

External customers are undoubtedly the most important part of any leisure and tourism organisation because without them there would be no organisation! Let's look at some of the specific benefits to the organisation of providing excellent customer service for external customers.

Increased sales

All leisure and tourism organisations aim to maximise the number of customers who buy their products. **Increasing sales** (or usage) means that an organisation is more likely to achieve its business targets. One of the benefits of excellent customer service is that it helps to increase sales and therefore profits. You have probably already realised one of the ways in which this happens:

Excellent service
▼
customer loyalty/repeat business
▼
recommendations/new business
▼
more customers

However, it is also necessary to think about the costs involved when customer service is not excellent – because this comes out of profits. Not only will fewer customers visit the organisation but it may find that it needs to spend a lot of money dealing with dissatisfied customers. This is why many leisure and tourism organisations monitor and evaluate the effectiveness of their customer service.

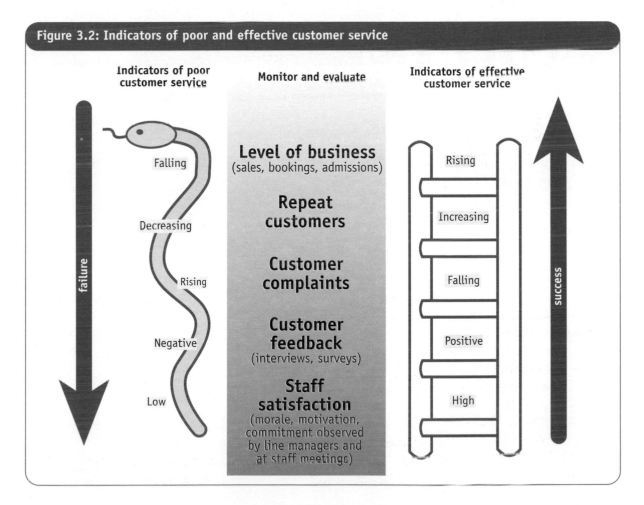

Figure 3.2: Indicators of poor and effective customer service

Satisfied customers

What do we mean by **customer satisfaction**? A dictionary might say that satisfaction is to adequately meet needs and expectations, but this is not enough, as the word adequate suggests that only the minimum has been done! Excellent customer service should aim to exceed customers' expectations so that they cannot think of anything more that could have been done to make them more satisfied.

Repeat business and recommendations

In essence your aim is to provide excellent service so that your customers will have such a good time that they will stay loyal to your organisation and want to come back again and again. This is known as **customer loyalty** and **repeat business**. In many situations, this also means that customers will tell lots of other people about your product and service and recommend that they visit. Of course, the opposite is also true. If customers receive poor service they probably won't come back. They may well tell other people about the bad service that they received, which will put others off visiting the organisation in the future.

ACTIVITY

Read the following conversation between two friends.

Joan: Hello Sarah. You're looking well, have you lost weight?

Sarah: Only a few pounds, but actually I'm feeling great since I started going to the Trendsetters health club twice a week.

Joan: I've seen their advertisement in the local paper and walked past a few times but it looks a bit fancy to me – all those skin-tight leotards in the window and a receptionist who looks as if she's just walked out of Gladiators. I'm sure that they'd take one look at my cellulite and send me packing!

Sarah: I know what you mean, I felt a bit like that to start. But once you get there they couldn't be nicer. They're so friendly and helpful. James and Irene who run the club are always around to talk to everyone and advise them on what exercise programme would be best. And the instructors have us all laughing so that you don't feel that it's too serious – in fact they often come with us for a drink after classes. I started going there to get fit but now it's because I just enjoy it so much.

Discuss how excellent customer service in this case may encourage repeat business and a recommendation.

A better public image

Leisure and tourism organisations that always provide excellent customer service will find that in time they gain a good reputation. This means that their **public image** will be improved. Existing customers will be proud to use these organisations and new customers will be encouraged to try their products and services. Of course the opposite is also true – poor levels of customer service mean that customers will not want to use the organisations and new customers will be put off trying them for the first time.

If you have not already done so, watch one of the consumer programmes on television. These often deal with complaints from customers about package holidays and charter flights, which greatly damage the reputation of the organisations concerned. See what specific aspects of the service customers most frequently complain about.

▲ Richard Branson's activities ensure a high profile for Virgin

ACTIVITY

Rating customer service

Select five leisure and tourism facilities in your area that everyone in your group has either visited at least once or heard about from someone else.

Each group member should rate the customer service at each of the facilities based on what he or she knows or has heard. Use a scale of one to five, with one being poor and five being excellent.

Add up the total scores for each facility and present them in a list, going from the highest score to the lowest. (For example, the group might score a local swimming pool: 2, 3, 2, 2, 3 making a total of 12. The group might score a cinema: 3, 4, 4, 4, 4 making a total of 19.)

When you have finished you should have a clear idea which organisations in your survey have the better public image for customer service with your group.

An edge over the competition

We have already seen that customer service is one of the main concerns of leisure and tourism organisations simply because customers are the business. Many of the products offered in leisure and tourism are very similar. For example, think about nightclubs or fast food takeaways in your area – is there really any big difference in the products that they all offer? What often distinguishes one from another is the level of customer service offered. In many situations customers choose one organisation rather than another simply because it provides better service. If you and your organisation are able to provide better service than your competitors you will have gained a **competitive edge**.

ACTIVITY

Which travel agency has the best service?

In this activity you are going to have a go at identifying which of your local travel agencies has the competitive edge.

Identify three local travel agencies. Split into three groups and each visit one of the agencies. When you visit suppose that you are on a limited budget but would like to go on a young adults holiday next summer. Typically, you are looking for something offered by tour operators such as Club 18–30, Escapades or Twenties.

Before you go, decide on five factors that each group will rate their travel agency on. For example, these might be:

- the attractiveness and layout of the travel agency

- how long you had to wait before being served

- the attitude of the staff

- the display of relevant brochures

- the ability of staff to answer your questions.

You can think of other factors if you prefer, but make sure that they are based on excellent customer service.

A good way of comparing the travel agencies would be for the group to use a common rating scale of 1–5; with 1 being very poor, 2 poor, 3 satisfactory, 4 good and 5 excellent.

As a group, discuss your experiences of the customer service at the three travel agencies and decide which you think has the competitive edge.

A safe and secure environment

Public swimming pools have lifeguards to ensure that customers don't get into difficulties

In any leisure and tourism situation, health, safety and security have to be the main concern of customer service. If the health, safety or security of customers is ignored or put at risk in some way, then no amount of good customer service skills is going to put it right. A good customer service policy identifies any possible risks, ensures that there are recognised procedures for dealing with them and, above all, ensures that staff are fully trained to avoid risks or deal with emergencies when necessary. The clear benefits to the organisation are that customers can be confident that they can use the facilities and services without any personal risk.

Pool drama – eight year old saved!

Darren Purvis had a lucky escape when he went for a swim at Gedsborough swimming pool on Tuesday night. Darren, who is asthmatic, got into difficulties in the deep end of the pool and was pulled to safety by two of the pool's lifeguards.

Darren had visited the centre as an eighth birthday treat with six friends. They had planned to enjoy themselves in the pool with the inflatables that are provided as part of the pool's Splashnight and follow it with a meal at a pizza restaurant. Darren's mother Christine said, 'Due to the quick action of the lifeguards, Darren was absolutely fine and after a short rest was able to enjoy his pizza.'

The pool's manager, Stephanie Cook, said, 'We were very sorry to hear that Darren's birthday treat was interrupted by an asthmatic attack but are glad that our safety procedures proved so effective. All of our lifeguards are fully trained and constantly vigilant to ensure that all swimmers are perfectly safe in the pool.'

Darren and his friends have been invited back for a free Splashnight session.

Do you think the Gedsborough pool's attitude towards providing a safe and secure environment would encourage you to use the facility?

ACTIVITY

TROLLEYS

- THAT FREE BAGGAGE TROLLEYS WILL ALWAYS BE AVAILABLE IN THE SHORT STAY AND MULTI-STOREY CAR PARKS AND AT ALL ENTRY POINTS TO OUR TERMINAL BUILDINGS INCLUDING THE BAGGAGE RECLAIM HALLS.

CLEANLINESS

- THAT THE HIGHEST STANDARDS OF CLEANLINESS ARE MAINTAINED EVERYWHERE ON THE AIRPORT AT ALL TIMES.

COMMUNICATIONS

- THAT OUR INFORMATION SERVICES INCLUDING ALL SIGNAGE ARE CLEAR, ACCURATE AND HELPFUL.
- THAT FLIGHT INFORMATION PROVIDED BY THE AIRPORT AND THE AIRLINE HANDLING AGENTS IS ALWAYS UP TO DATE AND ACCURATE.
- THAT AN INFORMATION DESK AND A DUTY MANAGER ARE BOTH AVAILABLE 24 HOURS A DAY TO PROVIDE ASSISTANCE TO PASSENGERS AND TO DEAL WITH ANY PROBLEMS.
- THAT OUR INFORAMTION DESK STAFF ARE TRAINED TO DEAL WITH CUSTOMER ENQUIRIES IN A COURTEOUS AND FRIENDLY MANNER AND THAT THE MAJORITY SPEAK AT LEAST ONE FOREIGN LANGUAGE.
- THAT THERE IS A PLENTIFUL SUPPLY OF PAYPHONES AND CARDPHONES WHEREVER NEEDED.

CHECK IN

- THAT PASSENGERS ARRIVING AT CHECK-IN WILL QUEUE FOR AS LITTLE TIME AS POSSIBLE WITH A TARGET OF NO MORE THAN 12 MINUTES.

FACILITIES FOR ALL CATEGORIES OF CUSTOMER

- THAT ALL OF OUR CUSTOMERS INCLUDING CHILDREN OF ALL AGES, THE ELDERLY AND THOSE WITH HEARING, VISION OR MOBILITY DIFFICULTIES CAN USE ALL OF OUR FACILITIES WITH EASE AND THAT ANY NECESSARY ASSISTANCE WILL BE PROVIDED.
- THAT IN ALL AREAS OF OUR PUBLIC BUILDINGS NON-SMOKERS ARE ABLE TO AVOID TOBACCO SMOKE AND SMOKERS WILL HAVE A REASONABLE OPPORTUNITY TO SMOKE.
- THAT BABYCARE FACILITIES ARE AVAILABLE IN BOTH TERMINALS, BOTH LANDSIDE AND AIRSIDE.

A promise to customers

Like many leisure and tourism providers, Birmingham Airport sets out its standards for external customer service in a leaflet called a customer promise. Read the leaflet extract and identify the type of standards set.

The final page of the airport's leaflet has the following headings:

- catering and shopping
- security
- baggage delivery and transfer
- first aid facilities
- comments (customer complaints).

As a group, discuss what sort of standards Birmingham Airport might have set for each of these areas.

The benefits of providing excellent service for internal customers

Very few leisure and tourism organisations employ only one member of staff. The vast majority have a number of employees who need to work as a team, both to support each other and to provide excellent external customer service.

As we have already seen, internal customer service looks at the way in which the staff in an organisation work together to provide service both to each other and to their external customers. Internal customers are colleagues or anyone that you work with and rely on to help you provide excellent customer service.

If you have already had a job which involved working with others to provide customer service, you may have a few nightmare stories to tell about some of your colleagues! You may have already met some of the following types of employees who manage to get jobs in the industry (but don't keep them for long).

Figure 3.3: Unhelpful colleagues

Johnny Jobsworth – He always answers every customer's enquiry with 'sorry, I'd like to help but it's more than my job's worth'; so you end up dealing with it instead.

Tessa Teabreak – She always manages to be just going off-duty when something really difficult needs doing.

Sandra Short-Term Memory Disorder – She can remember the year that man first landed on the moon but forgot to tell you that an urgent message came through ten minutes ago that the wedding party had been held up in traffic and would be an hour late.

Malcolm Management Material – He may only be a trainee but plans to be the manager (in about the year 2056) and therefore uses every situation to show how great he is and how useless the rest of you are.

Ivor Reason For Not Doing This – No matter what the job is and however you ask, he can think of a reason why he cannot do it.

Disorderly Deirdre – You all know she is not really up to the job but everyone feels sorry for her, so they cover up for her mistakes so she doesn't lose her job.

Mandy Mayhem Management – She knows it all but passes on very little to the staff and then asks why they are not doing their job properly.

If you have come across any staff like these you will know that they make your job much harder, often causing others to make mistakes and waste time as well as badly affecting the level of customer service that you are able to provide. Fortunately such staff are rare. The majority of people who work in leisure and tourism are employed because they are skilled at working with others and understand the benefits of good teamwork and effective communication.

One of the obvious benefits of excellent internal customer service is that staff who work well together are much more likely to provide excellent customer service to their external customers. But let's look at some of the benefits to the staff themselves of providing good service to each other.

A more pleasant place to work

Simply being friendly, helpful and supportive to colleagues creates a far more pleasant working atmosphere. It is also very noticeable to external customers, who can usually tell whether staff are enjoying their work and get on with each other.

Helpful colleagues?

If you have had a part-time job or work placement, think about how staff did (or did not) help to make your working environment more pleasant. Can you identify any Johnny Jobsworths, Disorderly Deirdres or other staff that you and your colleagues recognised for particular faults?

Discuss your ideas with the rest of the group and suggest what you could have done to persuade or help the weaker staff to provide better internal customer service.

A happy and efficient workforce

Working well together means that staff are happy to carry out their duties. A further, very important, benefit is that a more **efficient workforce** is able to provide excellent customer service to external customers.

Job satisfaction

Good internal customer service usually means that staff get more **job satisfaction**. Job satisfaction simply means enjoying your work and the duties that you are expected to carry out. Most people are much better at doing things that they enjoy, so if you get job satisfaction from your work you are more likely to give better customer service.

Promotion

The better you are at doing your job the more likely you are to do well in your career. Staff in more senior positions in organisations always need to be able to prove that they can provide good internal customer service. They are responsible not only for providing good service themselves, but also for motivating the staff who work for them. Therefore, if you are able to give good service to internal customers you are far more likely to be promoted to a position with more responsibility.

ACTIVITY

Good internal customer service

Read these comments from staff who work in the leisure and tourism industries.

> The entertainments manager is really good at letting us know what's going on. We have a daily briefing meeting each morning and if anything changes during the day she tells us straight away.
> **Jason, holiday camp host**

> When I first started working here I used to really panic when it got busy – especially on Saturdays. But now I know that there is always someone around to give a hand if I need it. We all look out for each other and step in if someone needs help.
> **Stacey, sports equipment shop assistant**

> A few months ago I had lots of problems at home and had to take time off at short notice. The other staff were great, covering for me when I couldn't get in and always asking how things were at home.
> **Raschid, waiter**

> Like anyone, I sometimes make mistakes in my work but the manager is always very understanding, so I'm never afraid to own up when I've done something wrong. He will always help me sort out the problem and then spend time showing me how to do it properly next time.
> **Caron, advance reservations computer operator**

Each of the staff mentions something that has increased their happiness or efficiency in their job because of the good internal customer service of the people that they work with. After reading the comments, draw up a list of some of the things that colleagues can do to provide good internal customer service.

Josie's aerobics classes

Josie Frames is an aerobics instructor at a council-run leisure centre. She is employed on a part-time basis and runs five aerobics classes a week – two for beginners and three advanced sessions.

Bookings for the sessions are taken by the duty receptionists, who have been trained to advise customers on the sessions which would be most appropriate for their needs. If any customers have any medical conditions that they think may prevent them from doing aerobics, they are advised to speak to Josie personally for advice. There is a limit of 30 customers per session.

The aerobics classes are held in the main gym, which is also used by a number of other instructors throughout the day for sessions such as badminton, volleyball, line dancing and trampolining. The centre's duty manager is responsible for checking the gym after it has been used to ensure that it is ready for the next session. An outside cleaning company cleans the gym twice daily.

Josie's classes require mats to be laid out and a music system to be set up. This is done by the caretaker. There is a changing room for customers to get dressed and shower. At the end of the sessions Josie usually joins her customers in the centre's coffee bar for a drink and a chat.

Because Josie works part time at the centre and works for other organisations, she often arrives only 15 minutes before each session. This gives her just enough time to get changed and into the gym before the customers.

1 Identify all of Josie's internal customers.

2 In what ways does she rely on each of them to help her provide the standard of service that her customers would expect?

3 Can you give some examples of how customer service might deteriorate if the other staff do not support Josie?

A safe and secure environment

We have already discussed the importance of ensuring the health, safety and security of external customers but of course it is equally important to do the same for your colleagues. All leisure and tourism organisations should have a staff health and safety policy and ensure that all staff receive training.

Build your learning

Summary points

- External customers are those who buy or use an organisation's products, services or facilities.

- Internal customers are the people that you work with and who may need services from you.

- It is just as important to give good internal customer service as it is to give good external customer service.

- Good external customer service helps to increase sales, create customer satisfaction, encourage more customers, create a better public image, create an edge over the competition and ensure a safe and secure environment.

- Good internal customer service creates a more pleasant place to work, a happier workforce, improved job satisfaction, improved chances of promotion and a safe and secure environment for staff.

Key words and phrases

You should know the meaning of the words and phrases listed below as they relate to the benefits of providing excellent customer service. Go back through the last 12 pages to refresh your understanding if necessary.

- **External customers**
- **Internal customers**
- **Increasing sales**
- **Customer loyalty**
- **Customer satisfaction**
- **Repeat business**
- **Recommendations**
- **Public image**
- **Competitive edge**
- **Efficient workforce**
- **Job satisfaction**

SUMMARY ACTIVITY

If you have a part-time job or do a work placement you can carry out these summary activities based on your experience. If you do not, you will need to visit a leisure or tourism organisation and arrange to speak to the manager or a key member of staff.

1 Identify all the external customers that the organisation provides for and decide how the customer service provided helps to:

   • increase sales

   • satisfy customer needs and expectations

   • attract more customers through repeat business and recommendations

   • create a better public image

   • gain an edge over the competition.

2 Identify the ways in which the organisation provides good internal customer service and how it ensures:

   • a more pleasant place to work

   • a happier and more efficient workforce

   • improved job satisfaction

   • improved chances of promotion within the organisation.

3 Can you make any suggestions as to how the organisation could improve the service it provides to both external and internal customers?

4 Describe ways in which the organisation meets the needs of its customers.

5 Describe how the organisation deals with complaints.

6 Provide examples of the types of customer records used by the organisation.

7 Give a basic evaluation of the customer service provided by the organisation. You may find it useful to rate the organisation using the same scale as in the activity on page 188.

Personal presentation

Because such a large part of any job in the leisure and tourism industries involves dealing with people, the way in which you present yourself is very important. Your personal presentation says a lot about the sort of person you are and how you feel about your job and it has a big effect on whether your customers are likely to be satisfied with the service or product provided.

There are four key features to good personal presentation:

- dress
- personal hygiene and appearance
- personality
- attitude and behaviour.

Let's look at each in turn.

Dress

▼ It is important to be appropriately dressed in the leisure and tourism industries

Appropriate **dress** depends on what the job actually is. Whether you wear a uniform will vary from job to job; some jobs call for a more casual clothing style than others, but you should always take care with your appearance. How would you feel if the pilot flying your plane wore dirty jeans and a T-shirt and smoked a cigarette? You would certainly think that he or she was not very professional and you might also worry that he or she could not do the job properly. You would also probably think that it reflects badly on the airline and the rest of the staff that it employs.

Appearance tells customers how members of staff feel about their job, the organisation that they work for, themselves and the customer. A neat and tidy appearance is likely to reassure customers that staff are professional in their attitude and can do their job well. Equally, it helps them to take a pride in their job and the organisation that they work for.

ACTIVITY

Appropriate dress?

Look at the pictures shown here. For each picture, try to suggest three jobs in the leisure and tourism industries where the person would be suitably dressed.

Personal hygiene and appearance

Appearance does not only concern a clean and tidy uniform. It also involves **personal hygiene**, and clean hair, hands, fingernails and shoes. Make up and jewellery may be important, and employers may have rules about what can be worn, as well as about the permissible length of hair and of beards and moustaches (see Figure 3.4).

Requirements regarding personal hygiene and appearance vary according to context. For example, people responsible for handling food have additional responsibilities that include keeping their hair covered, wearing protective uniform and washing their hands thoroughly between tasks.

Figure 3.4: Extract from staff handbook of personal appearance

Go-Europe Travel

All travel agency staff are provided with a company uniform which they are expected to keep clean, pressed and in good condition. In addition you are expected to maintain the following standards.

Male staff

Hair
Short, clean, no hair gel

Jewellery
Wedding ring only

Make-up
None

Hands
Clean, well-manicured nails

Shoes
Black, polished, no trainers, dark socks

Female staff

Hair
Clean, tied back if below shoulders

Jewellery
Wedding ring, small earrings

Make-up
Subtle

Hands
Clean, well-manicured nails

Shoes
Black, polished, no trainers, black or natural coloured tights or stockings

ACTIVITY

An appearance code for town guides

Sandcombe is a seaside resort in Norfolk. Some leisure and tourism providers are sponsoring town guides during the peak summer months. The idea is that between 10 a.m. and 7 p.m. guides should be available throughout the area to give advice and directions to tourists. The guides are students, recruited from the local college.

All guides will be given training in customer service skills. They will also be provided with a uniform of a yellow T-shirt, sweatshirt and baseball cap, so that they are easily recognised. They are responsible for keeping the uniform looking clean and tidy. They are expected to wear a pair of their own dark blue or black trousers and clean trainers.

Although the guides have been told what to wear, it has been decided that further information on general personal hygiene and appearance would be useful. Design a poster explaining the main points that the guides need to remember on personal appearance.

Personality

The word **personality** simply means having a distinctive character. However, we usually use it in a positive way as in 'he or she has lots of personality', meaning that the person is likeable, outgoing and good to be around. In giving excellent customer service it is very important that customers see you as someone with a pleasant and caring personality.

Of course, different jobs require different sorts of personalities, which is why interviewers usually try to have a clear idea of the type of person that they are seeking for a particular job. For example, a resort representative for young adults' holidays would need a very different type of personality than one working with elderly customers.

Attitude and behaviour

Your **attitude** and **behaviour** towards customers are a very important part of your overall personal presentation. Customers are very sensitive to the ways staff react and behave towards them. You have probably been in a situation where you have gone into a shop and felt that the sales assistant was not really interested in serving you. If you have, then you know that no matter how good the product was that you bought, you went away an unsatisfied customer.

There are lots of things that you can do to convince customers that your attitude and behaviour says 'I really want to serve you'. You can:

- attend to them straight away
- show that you are interested in what they have to say
- ask them questions to make sure that you know exactly what they want
- avoid being distracted by concentrating on the customers all the time that you are serving them
- be friendly and encouraging
- smile!

It is important to understand that all aspects of personal presentation – dress, hygiene and appearance, personality and attitude and behaviour – apply to any customer service situation, whether you are dealing with the customers face to face, over the telephone or in writing. Admittedly the customer on the other end of the phone or a letter cannot see whether you have ironed your shirt and washed your hands! But, of course, you should have done this because it is all part of being professional and always maintaining excellent personal presentation.

> ► What sort of personality do you think is required to be an overseas resort representative?

Build your learning

Summary points

- The way in which you present yourself is very important because you are constantly dealing with customers.

- Personal presentation has a big effect on customer satisfaction.

- Appropriate dress means clothes that are suitable for a particular job.

- Personal hygiene is an important aspect of personal presentation.

- Your attitude and behaviour towards customers will affect their level of satisfaction.

- Different types of personality are suited to different types of job, however all jobs in the leisure and tourism industries need people with a pleasant and caring personality.

- Personal presentation is important in all customer service situations, including both direct and indirect contact.

Key words and phrases

You should know the meaning of the words and phrases listed below as they relate to personal presentation. Go back through the last five pages to refresh your understanding if necessary.

- **Dress**
- **Personal hygiene**
- **Attitude**
- **Behaviour**
- **Personality**

SUMMARY ACTIVITY

1 Visit a local leisure and tourism organisation that you have not been to before. Rate the staff that you come into contact with on their:

- dress/uniform

- personal hygiene

- personality

- attitude

- behaviour.

You might like to design a form before you go so that you can record your impressions. You might rate each aspect of personal appearance on a five-point scale:

   1 very poor

   2 poor

   3 acceptable

   4 good

   5 excellent

2 Suggest ways in which the organisation could improve its image.

Dealing with customers

Whatever your job in the leisure and tourism industries, at some time you will be in contact with customers and you will need to know how to communicate with them effectively. Some situations will be expected and can be anticipated, such as when a receptionist or waitress deals with customers. At other times the contact may be unexpected, such as when a customer asks a cleaner or member of maintenance staff for advice or assistance. You need to develop good communication skills to deal with the customer effectively, whatever the situation. These skills include:

- language
- pitch and tone of voice
- pauses and silences
- body language.

Let's look at each of these skills and see how you can use them effectively when communicating with customers.

Language

Understanding the most appropriate **language** to use in customer service situations is very important. We all use different types of language and words depending on the person we are talking to. For example, think of the different language that you might use when talking to a friend, a tutor, your doctor or an elderly relative. Similarly, when dealing with a customer you may have to change the language that you would normally use to suit the type of customer and his or her specific needs. Some situations may require a more formal approach, such as when dealing with a complaint or talking to a businessman or businesswoman. In other instances it may be more appropriate to be less formal, such as when talking to children or young adults.

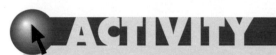

Appropriate language

Three of the most common communications that you will have with customers are:

- greeting them
- asking them what they want
- thanking them.

As a group, brainstorm all of the different words and phrases that could be used in these three situations. List all that you can think of, even if they are slang, such as 'hiya' and 'ta'. Then decide which are the most appropriate when providing excellent customer service.

Pitch and tone of voice

It is one thing to make sure that you use appropriate language but quite another to ensure that you say it in a way that sounds as if you mean it. Staff in leisure and tourism organisations sometimes say the right words but spoil the good impression by the **tone** and **pitch** of their voice. They may sound bored, disinterested or even aggressive.

Tone and pitch

In pairs, try repeating the following phrase to each other several times:

Good morning sir, how may I help you?

Each time, use a different tone and pitch to your voice so that you sound:

- bored

- angry

- nervous

- impatient

- happy to serve the customer.

See if you can make your partner guess which one it is.

Pauses and silences

When we talk about communication most people think of how they talk to others. However, it is just as important to understand how the other person can communicate back to you. The deliberate use of **pauses and silences** gives customers the chance to ask you questions and also allows you to show that you are listening to them. Perfecting good listening ability is a skill that takes practice. It means that you have to learn to recognise when customers might want to ask a question or make a comment. Sometimes you will need to encourage customers by saying 'does that answer your question?' or 'is there anything else I can tell you about?'.

Body language

Body language is the term used to describe how we communicate with others using posture, gestures and facial expressions. It is important to recognise that a great deal is communicated between people in this way. Body language can be put into two categories – open and closed. **Open body language** is when your expression, posture or gestures show that you are interested, relaxed, confident and friendly. It would include good eye contact, smiling, relaxed posture and confident gestures such as using your hands to emphasise a point. **Closed body language** says that you are unfriendly, ill at ease, hostile and disinterested. It might include avoiding eye contact, tightly crossed arms, hands in pockets, expressionless face and nervous fidgeting.

ACTIVITY

Body language

Have a look at the cartoons shown here. What can you tell about the person's attitude from his or her body language?

Discuss which of the following words might apply to each cartoon and explain how you can tell this from the body language:

- confident
- friendly
- hostile
- interested
- nervous
- disinterested
- bored
- unsure
- in control
- relaxed
- superior
- enthusiastic
- displeased
- professional
- happy

When communicating with customers you also need to be able to:

- work accurately
- listen to and respond to questions
- ask appropriate questions.

Working accurately

Working accurately means making sure that you get all of the details that you need, that you record them correctly and that you pass them on to the appropriate people. If you are in any doubt, it is important that you are able to clarify the details – even if it is just to ask the customer how to spell his or her name. Remember that incorrect details are usually worse than having no details at all. Imagine how Mr Tollet would feel if you sent him a letter addressed to Mr Toilet!

Listening and responding to customers' questions

You will often find that while you are dealing with customers they will ask questions about the product or service being offered. You need to be ready to answer these questions as they arise. Remember that no customer wants to feel as if they are being put through a process, so be ready to react to customers' questions.

Asking appropriate questions

Clearly, you need to ask enough questions to make sure that you have all of the details that you need to provide a customer with the best service. You also need to make sure that they are asked in an appropriate manner. This means ensuring that customers do not feel as if they are being put through a standard process and treated as though they are 'just another customer'. It is the difference between saying:

- *Can I take your name, sir?* rather than *What name?*
- *How would you like to pay for the tickets, Mrs Graves?* rather than *Method of payment?*
- *Do you have any medical condition that we should know about before you start aerobics classes?* rather than *Any medical conditions?*

In perfecting your own questioning technique you will find it useful to understand the difference between open and closed questions.

- An **open question** is one where the answer has to be an explanation, such as 'what sort of holiday are you looking for?' or 'which rides did your children enjoy?'.
- A **closed question** is one where the answer is just one or two words, such as 'do you like swimming?' or 'have you been here before?'.

It is important to realise that both types of question are useful in certain situations. Open questions are best when you want to strike up a conversation with a customer and encourage him or her to talk. These types of question are also useful when you want to find out how customers really feel about something, as they give them the chance to explain their thoughts fully. However, closed questions may be more appropriate when you want customers to give you a lot of routine information, as when completing a booking form. It would be fairly ineffective to say 'Tell me about yourself', when all you really want to know is the customer's name, address and telephone number!

Build your learning

Summary points

- Language, pitch and tone of voice, pauses and silences and body language can all help to communicate effectively with customers.

- Different types of language may be appropriate in different customer service situations.

- Pitch and tone of voice can help you to sound as if you really mean what you are saying.

- Pauses and silences allow customers to talk to you and ask questions, but you need to look interested and caring.

- Body language involves communicating with gestures, facial expressions and posture.

- It is important to work accurately to ensure that you get all the necessary details correct.

- Listening and responding to customers' questions helps to identify and satisfy the customers' needs.

- You need to ask the right sort of questions to identify customers' needs.

Key words and phrases

You should know the meaning of the words and phrases listed below as they relate to dealing with customers. Go back through the last six pages to refresh your understanding if necessary.

- **Language**
- **Pitch**
- **Open body language**

- **Tone**
- **Pauses and silences**
- **Closed body language**

- **Body language**
- **Open question**
- **Closed question**

SUMMARY ACTIVITY

This summary activity is a role play designed to help you to practice and evaluate your verbal communication skills. It might help your evaluation to record your role plays either with a video camera or a tape recorder. Most of us are surprised to find out how we sound and look to others!

Imagine that you are working in a tourist information office in your area and have just been asked by a visitor, who is new to the area, to describe some of the attractions and facilities that he or she could go to. In pairs, role play the visitor and information clerk. Make sure you both have a go at playing each role.

Try the role play first in a face-to-face situation and then sitting back to back as if you were on the telephone.

After the role plays, evaluate each person's communication skills in terms of:

- language used
- pitch and tone of voice
- pauses and silences (listening effectively)
- body language.

You might like to evaluate each other using a scale of 1–5, with 1 being very poor, 2 poor, 3 satisfactory, 4 good and 5 excellent.

Customer service skills

Customer service skills are used in a wide range of situations including:

- providing accurate information
- giving advice
- receiving and passing on messages
- providing assistance
- keeping records
- dealing with problems
- dealing with dissatisfied customers
- offering extra services.

We now look at each of these in turn and see how you can use good customer service skills to deal with customers.

Providing information

One situation that you will face time and time again in the leisure and tourism industries is **providing information** to customers. For example:

- visitors to a tourist information centre expect the staff to be knowledgeable about local facilities and services
- guides at a heritage site should know and be able to answer questions about the history of the site
- a travel agency clerk should be able to answer customers' queries about things like health and visa requirements for visiting other countries.

Anyone working in the leisure and tourism industries needs to be aware of the sort of questions that customers ask and how they can find out the information.

Computers are becoming more and more important as a way of providing information. Some people argue that this form of communication lacks the personal touch and reduces the level of customer service. Nevertheless, in many situations, it is a quick and efficient way of meeting customer needs when they want information about opening times, train times or prices of admission.

Most travel agents provide information on holiday availability and prices by means of computer systems linked to those of tour operators, and many tourist information centres now provide a computerised information system that visitors can use for themselves to find out details of local facilities and services. All airlines, most tour operators and many hotel groups use computers for making reservations. Only by using

▼ Many staff need access to computers to gain information

information technology can they manage and control the sales of airline seats, holidays and hotel beds on a national or worldwide basis and provide customers with the most up-to-date information.

Finding out information

The tourist information centre in your area takes a lot of GNVQ Leisure and Tourism students on work placement. Many of the situations that the students deal with in the centre involve answering customers' questions and providing information. There is usually a full-time member of staff available to help students who do not know the answers to customers' questions, but sometimes they have to deal with the situation on their own for a short while.

The manager has decided to write a customer service staff book specifically for students on work placement. One of the pages will deal with how they can find out information for a customer.

Can you design the 'sources of information' page? The most frequent questions that guests ask are about:

- hotel facilities and services

- local attractions and facilities

- transport

- doctors, dentists and other medical services

- directions in the area.

The centre has a good supply of local timetables and maps, the local evening newspaper, phone books, Yellow Pages and a what's on guide, as well as a leaflet rack containing details of local facilities and attractions.

Design the sources of information page for work experience students telling them how they can answer customers' questions. The page should start:

If you do not know the answer to a customer's question ask your supervisor for help. If he or she is not available you can often find information yourself from the following sources:

Giving advice

In many situations customers want more than simple information – they expect you to be able to advise them on the suitability of products or services. For example:

- a customer at a sports centre might want to know which sessions are best for people with mobility impairments
- a customer in a restaurant might want advice on which dishes are suitable for vegetarians
- a visitor to a cinema may ask whether a film is suitable for young children
- a customer in a travel agency may want to know where to go in December that is sunny but not too expensive.

◀ Waiters can advise on the restaurant's specialities

Giving advice to customers is a big responsibility; they are relying on you to give them accurate and honest advice. Therefore, if you are unsure it is always better to ask for help from a colleague or supervisor, rather than give the wrong advice.

The sort of advice that customers require from staff varies greatly depending on the type of customer as well as the type of attraction or service being offered. Customers on foreign package holidays frequently ask the tour representative for advice on health and safety issues, for example. This may be because a particular problem has happened or simply because they are in an unfamiliar country and are unsure of how things work. Many tour operators produce safety leaflets for customers but representatives still find that guests ask them for advice.

ACTIVITY

Alcohol

Some of us like to indulge, especially during our holidays, but there are times when alcohol is best avoided. Do not drink alcohol before swimming in the pool and try to avoid it when sun bathing as it will dehydrate you. Never drink if hiring a car as drink-driving laws exist in most countries.

Sea/Beaches

Playing and swimming in the sea can be great fun. At times, however, especially during rough conditions, dangerous currents may be present. We therefore recommend that you follow the flag warning signals available on most beaches and swim in the designated areas. Should these not be in place, please consult your Representative who will be able to provide full details. Be especially careful if you have small children.

Here are a few tips:

- Familiarise yourself with the local flag warning system.
- Seek local advice on which beaches are the safest.
- Check to see if the beach has lifeguards in attendance.
- Swim parallel to the shore, within your depth.
- Beware of local conditions (e.g. tides, winds and currents).
- Supervise children at all times.
- Swim before eating and drinking, not immediately after.
- Do not swim at night.
- Find out what the appropriate emergency procedure is.
- Beware of any "zones" for power boats, jet skis etc.
- Remember to always use adequate protection against the sun's rays.

Safety first

Thomson Holidays provides guests with a safety leaflet. Some extracts from the leaflet are shown here. Read these carefully before starting this role play activity.

In pairs, take turns at playing a resort representative and a package holiday customer. For each of the following situations the resort rep should give the appropriate advice to the customer. You can refer to the leaflet if you want.

1 I'm worried that we have a third floor room with a balcony. Our two children are two and five. Is it safe?

2 I'm not a very strong swimmer but I would love to go in the sea as it looks so inviting. Can I swim safely here?

3 I've seen programmes about how dangerous foreign swimming pools are. Is the one at the hotel safe?

4 Our hotel lift does not have internal doors, which seems very dangerous. Should I stop my children using it?

For a Safe and Healthy Holiday

Part of the enjoyment of travelling abroad is experiencing a different way of life. Please remember though, that it may also mean experiencing different safety and hygiene standards from those you are used to at home. Our standards are among the highest in the world, but many developing countries and resorts still have a long way to go to bring their transport, accommodation and services up to the level you normally take for granted. This applies to many European resorts, as well as more exotic destinations. We are working to raise safety standards overseas and will of course do our best to ensure that your holiday is safe and trouble-free, but we do ask that you take extra care while you are away. Therefore, please read this leaflet carefully.

Balconies

If you are travelling with young children, make sure they are not left unsupervised on balconies. Keep balcony furniture away from the railings so that they are not encouraged to climb up.

Glass Panels

Few hotels and apartments are legally obliged to install "toughened" or safety glass in their windows, doors and glass cabinets etc. Please take particular care when walking through patio doors; in bright sunlight it can be difficult to spot if they are closed. Identifying stickers should be in place on balconies, and other large glass doors. If they are missing, please bring this to the attention of your Representative.

Fire Safety

Different countries have different fire safety regulations and procedures. Please read carefully all fire safety information available in your hotel room or apartment and in the Holiday Information Guide. When you first arrive, please make sure you familiarise yourself with the location of the fire exit nearest to your room or apartment.

Bathrooms

Few hotels and apartments provide non-slip mats in their baths and showers. Bathroom floors are often tiled so you will be using a bath or shower tray which is unfamiliar to you, please take extra care to ensure you do not slip.

Lifts

Some hotel and apartment lifts do not have internal doors. This means that the inside of the lift is exposed to the lift shaft. As the lift travels up and down, a "moving wall" effect is created. If your hotel or apartment has this type of lift, make sure that you stand clear of the "moving wall" and never allow children to travel inside any lift without an adult.

Swimming Pools

You will find that most hotels and apartments do not employ a lifeguard. You will need to adopt a sensible attitude around the pool and make sure that children and non-swimmers are supervised at all times. Before diving, please check that the water is deep enough. Take care when walking around the pool, as pool surrounds are often slippery when wet. You should not enter the pool after drinking alcohol.

Here are some tips to ensure safety at all times when using the swimming pool:

- Always check the pool design and layout before getting in.
- Check your height in relation to the pool depth.
- Find out where the deep and shallow areas are, plus any slopes.
- Check for any "hidden" obstacles in the water such as rocks or ledges.
- Never dive from the pool side into less than 1.5m of water, and never dive from bridges, rocks or other decorative features.
- Check to see if the pool has a lifeguard and when they are in attendance.
- Do not use the pool if you cannot see the bottom.
- Swim before eating and drinking, not immediately after.
- Check what you should do in an emergency. If it is not stated, ask.
- Always supervise children.
- Do not swim at night (or when the pool is closed).
- Remember to always use adequate protection against the sun's rays, even when swimming.

THOMSON

Safety First ✓

For a safe & healthy holiday.

Portland DIRECT

Skytours

Receiving and passing on messages

In many customer service situations you will be asked to take and pass on a message. This may be from one member of staff to another, from a member of staff to a customer, from a customer to a member of staff or from a customer to another customer. In all these situations it is important that full and accurate details of the message are recorded and passed on as soon as possible. Many organisations have a set procedure for **receiving and passing on messages**. They use a specially designed message pad and system for making sure that the message gets to the right person.

Designing a message form

Go back to the activity on page 194 about Josie's aerobics classes and refresh your memory about how her customers' classes are booked.

Josie has been unhappy about the amount of information that the centre's receptionists are passing on to her about new customers to her classes. She has found that:

- some messages do not include the customer's full name, address and telephone number

- there is no information about when the customer rang up or visited and booked into a class

- no information is given about whether the customer has attended one of Josie's classes before – she would like to know this so that she can welcome them back

- often there are no details about customers' medical conditions that Josie needs to know about

- it is unclear which receptionist took the message, so Josie does not know who to ask if she wants further information.

Josie has complained to the centre's manager that the receptionists are not taking the right information. He suggests that she design a message form for receptionists to use when dealing with an aerobics class booking.

Design a suitable message form that would prevent Josie needing to repeat her complaints above.

Providing assistance

In many leisure and tourism situations customers need special **assistance** from staff to meet their needs and allow them to enjoy the product being offered. Examples include:

- a customer in a wheelchair who is not able to use the lift and requires help to reach another floor of the building
- a visitor to the cinema who expects to receive assistance in finding a seat
- a businessperson at a conference who needs help in operating an overhead projector.

ACTIVITY

Special assistance

Read this extract from a GNER leaflet. Note what special assistance is offered to:

- people with special needs
- mothers with babies
- unaccompanied children.

At Great North Eastern Railway all our customers receive the best possible care and attention at all times. You can enjoy the advantages of dedicated customer care, designed to make your journey one to remember.

Dedicated **customer care**

Assistance *for customers with special needs*

If required, customers can book assistance in advance for help at stations and getting on and off trains.

Our **dedicated service** *offers:*

- Wheelchair space in First Class and Standard accommodation
- A toilet and washroom on all 225 trains for wheelchair users
- Disabled toilet facilities at many stations, please see table
- A dedicated booking line for train tickets, seat reservation and assistance booking. Please call 0345 225 444 between 0800 and 2200 hours daily.
- Deaf customers can call our Minicom (textphone) number on 0191 233 0173.

Discounts *for people with disabilities*

The Disabled Railcard costs only £14.00 a year and, dependent on the type of disability, entitles the holder and a companion to discounts of up to 50% on First Class and Standard rail fares.

More details about the benefits they offer can be obtained from principal rail stations, or by telephoning the enquiry number.

Railcard price and discounts subject to change. Correct at June 1998.

Mothers *with babies and children*

All trains have baby changing facilities, as do many of our stations. Please see the table of facilities available at each station on the back page.

To make your journey even more rewarding, children under 5 can travel for free.

Please note that for hygiene and safety reasons GNER on-train staff are not permitted to warm babies' bottles.

Kids *Go First*

We have developed an "unaccompanied minor" train travel service. This is available on direct journeys on GNER services to most stations on our route.

Customers should phone the dedicated booking line below. Your child must be aged 8 to 15 years and can travel on a service which departs between 1000 and 1500 hours, anyday. Your child will be escorted to and from the train by GNER staff and a regular check is made on the child during the journey. However this is not a baby-sitting service and therefore is not suitable for children who require close and constant supervision. The fare is the appropriate Standard Child fare plus an administration charge, for which your child is reserved in a dedicated seat in First Class and provided with a beverage. For more information and conditions, pick up a leaflet at GNER stations or call 0345 225 444 daily between the hours of 0800 - 2200.

GNER Special Needs enquiries **0345 225 444**

GNER Group Travel enquiries **01904 523615**

Can you identify the special assistance that these three types of customers might need when travelling by plane?

Remember that one of the big differences between rail and air travel is that at an airport only the traveller can go through passport control and into the departure lounge, unlike on a train where someone can accompany the traveller his or her seat.

Keeping records

Keeping records is a vital part of good customer service. A good record keeping system allows organisations to operate efficiently and meet the needs of their customers. This area of customer service needs to be explored in some detail, and we cover it in a separate section on page 227.

Dealing with problems

In an ideal world, all customers would buy the product or service that you are providing, everything would run smoothly and you would not have to deal with any problems. Unfortunately, in reality, **dealing with problems** will be a skill you must acquire.

Sometimes problems may be the fault or direct responsibility of the organisation, such as the fire alarms sounding, a passenger's cases going astray or a lift getting stuck between floors. At other times, problems may arise that are outside of the control of the organisation, for example guests may have locked themselves out of their bedroom or a customer may have lost his or her coat.

Whatever the situation, it is your responsibility to do everything you can to resolve the problem for the customer – even if this means putting yourself out and providing extra service. As you become more experienced, you will find it easier to deal with problems. Training can also help, and the role play activity on page 216 is designed to help you practice dealing with problems in a variety of situations.

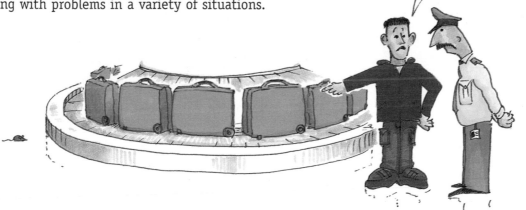

THE GREEN SUITCASE!

Dealing with dissatisfied customers

Sometimes problems arise, and customers will be dissatisfied with some aspect of the service and they will complain to you. The ability to **deal with dissatisfied customers** and to handle complaints is a very important part of providing excellent customer service. This topic is covered in a separate section and we consider it in some detail on page 221.

Dealing with problems

This activity is a role play that you should carry out in pairs. It would be useful to perform the role plays in front of the rest of the group so that they can comment on the way you dealt with each of the problems. Different pairs can perform the same role play to see the various ways of dealing with customer problems.

1 You are a waiter or waitress in a restaurant. A couple have just finished an expensive meal with champagne to celebrate their engagement. Having been presented with the bill the man says that he has accidentally left his wallet at home and has no money with him. Neither does his fiancée.

2 You are a clerk in an information centre. An elderly visitor to the area comes in, clearly in a state of distress. He has parked his car in one of the town's car parks but cannot remember which one it was. He has spent the last two hours walking around looking for his car.

3 You are a ride operator at a theme park. A six-year-old girl comes up to you in tears and says she has lost her parents.

4 You work in the ticket office of a theme park. It is a very busy day so there are long queues to get in. A customer from the back of the queue pushes to the front demanding to be served straight away.

5 You work at a swimming pool. A customer claims that his wallet has been stolen from his locker whilst he was swimming. When he returned the locker was open but he thinks he locked it properly.

6 You are an usher at the local cinema. A group of young boys have talked loudly and giggled throughout the film, despite being asked to be quiet. They have now started making more noise and other customers are becoming annoyed.

Offering extra services

Leisure and tourism customers usually want no more than any other customer and well-trained staff should find it straightforward to provide excellent service. However, situations sometimes arise in which customers need more than what is usually offered and it is the staff's responsibility to react effectively. **Extra services** may vary widely but might include:

- a nervous, new member of a beginners swimming class who needs extra reassurance and help
- a parent who needs baby food heating up
- a hotel guest asking for help in working his or her television
- a museum visitor wanting more information on a particular exhibit
- a theatregoer asking for a taxi to be booked.

In such situations it is up to the staff to do their best to meet the customer's needs – without making the customer feel that he or she is a nuisance! Of course, it may not always be possible to provide the extra service – in these cases, your refusal should always be polite and you should give a good reason, such as 'I am very sorry, but we do not have any cooking facilities here to heat baby food' rather than 'it's not company policy' or 'that's not part of our service'.

If it is not possible to provide the extra service requested, you might be able to suggest an alternative. So rather than say 'I can't book you a taxi because there isn't an outside phone line here', you could say 'I'm sorry, I would book you a taxi if I had an outside phone line, but there's a taxi rank just around the corner which will have plenty of taxis available after the show'.

Leisure and tourism organisations are always looking for ways to improve or add extra service. For example, until a few years ago the level of service on charter flights tended to be fairly standardised and did not vary a great deal between different airlines. However, research has shown that the charter flight has an important bearing on some package holiday customers' overall enjoyment of their holiday. As the following case study shows, tour operators and airlines have realised that offering extra services on flights can greatly improve customer satisfaction.

CASE STUDY

Britannia's 360 service

Britannia Airways has introduced a new type of in-flight service called 360. Here's how the airline introduces the service in its in-flight magazine.

We've had a great response to our new in-flight service. It's called 360, and it's designed to make sure your holiday starts here. So why not relax and get in the mood.

The thinking behind 360

360 is the name of our new in-flight service which we launched last summer. It's the result of months of research to discover what you, our passengers, hope to find during your flight. The package we've come up with builds on Britannia's reputation for professionalism and reliability but makes everything brighter, modern and more fun. We hope you find your onboard environment relaxing, comfortable and entertaining. Have fun on your flight, and remember that your holiday starts as soon as you board the plane!

New treats

Along with a traditional range of wines, spirits and soft drinks, our new 360 drinks service offers holiday cocktails, a selection of snacks and even a chance to win our Holiday Hunt scratch cards.

The kids are alright

We've captured children's imagination by listening to what they want, and not what we think they want. OBK is their own club, with fun-packed features and activities, meals and drinks, OBK radio and television programmes, and two great OBK magazines with transfers or crayons. If the kids are happy, their parents are too!

The shop in the sky

Skystore offers simply the best in-flight shopping opportunity, with a wide range of duty-free spirits, fragrances and tobaccos as well as jewellery and gifts with a holiday feel, all at bargain prices.

Real people

Our confident, friendly cabin crew blend approachability with professionalism. The new uniforms they are wearing were created by top fashion designer Elizabeth Emmanuel, who has come up with a look she calls 'classic but funky'.

Plenty to entertain

We've won awards for our approach to in-flight entertainment. We have eight hours of your favourite television programmes and 10 radio channels offering a range of musical styles – and it's all free. On many flights there is even ice-cream for sale and a free national newspaper – all designed to help make your journey a real pleasure.

Thought for food

Having listened to your needs, we've thought up menus to match the time of day, length of flight and destination. There are tasty, traditional breakfasts, Sunday roasts, three- or four-course hot lunches and dinners, cream teas with sandwiches, scones and clotted cream, satisfying suppers and, on longer flights, our snack attack service where you can help yourself to a buffet. And it's all attractively and imaginatively presented.

ACTIVITY

Britannia's 360 service

Read carefully the case study about Britannia Airways' new 360 in-flight service. List all of the extra services that 360 provides. As a group, discuss which aspects of the service would appeal to you if you were travelling as a passenger with Britannia.

Build your learning

Summary points

- It is important to understand the sort of information that customers may require and to know how you can find it out.

- You should be accurate and honest when giving customers advice.

- It is important to pass on messages accurately and quickly to the right person.

- Keeping accurate records allows an organisation to operate efficiently and to satisfy customers' needs.

- Many customers need assistance when buying or using leisure and tourism products or facilities.

- Staff have to be ready to deal with and resolve customers' problems.

- Dealing effectively with dissatisfied customers is a very important part of customer service.

- Some customers require extra services and staff should ensure that this is provided wherever possible.

Key words and phrases

You should know the meaning of the words and phrases listed below as they relate to customer service skills. Go back through the last 11 pages to refresh your understanding if necessary.

- **Providing information**
- **Giving advice**
- **Keeping records**
- **Receiving and passing on messages**
- **Assistance**
- **Dealing with problems**
- **Dealing with dissatisfied customers**
- **Extra services**

Handling complaints

For most of the time you will find dealing with customers a pleasant and interesting experience – in fact it will probably be the aspect of your job that you enjoy most. However, regardless of how good you are at providing excellent customer service there will be times when you have to deal with a **customer complaint**. This may be over the phone, in a letter or (perhaps the most difficult of all) face to face with the customer. No one enjoys dealing with complaints, but knowing how to do it properly can make the experience a lot easier.

Figure 3.5: A complaints procedure

Go-Europe Travel

Complaints procedure

It is likely that all staff will have to deal with a customer's complaint at some time whilst working for the agency. Dealing with the complaint efficiently and effectively is an important part of the service we provide to our customers.

You should remember the following.

√ Listen carefully to what the customer is saying and write down the details.

√ Do not interrupt the customer, argue back or try to make excuses.

√ Be sympathetic, express concern that the customer has had to complain.

√ Try to sort out the problem straight away. If you cannot, tell the customer that you will investigate the complaint and contact them when you have solved the problem.

√ Always follow up a complaint with the appropriate action.

√ Make sure that you have a record of the customer's full name, address and telephone number.

√ Ensure that all details are filled in on the company complaint form and that copies are sent to the manager.

√ If you feel you cannot deal with the complaint contact a supervisor for assistance immediately.

Most organisations give their staff training in complaint handling and some have a set procedure for staff to follow (see Figure 3.5). This is because organisations realise the damage that can be done when customers' complaints are not resolved effectively. For a start, it is unlikely that the customers will return and they will probably also tell a number of other people about their bad experience, which will discourage new customers from visiting. However, if complaints are handled well customers will leave satisfied and impressed by the level of care and attention that they have received. They are therefore much more likely to return, and to tell others about the service in positive terms. In other words, when dealing with a complaint you should see it as an opportunity to show the customer just how good your service is.

The key to dealing with any customer complaint is to find a solution so that the customer leaves satisfied with the service that he or she has received. There are eight stages of successful complaint handling. These are listed opposite – each stage in the process begins with one of the letters of of the word solution.

It is important to understand that while the eight stages of the solution (see Figure 3.6) will help you deal with complaints, many organisations have additional procedures for staff to follow. You may well find when you first start working in the industry that you are not expected to solve customer complaints on your own. In fact, a lot of organisations train their staff to contact a supervisor if a customer complains. This is because supervisory and management staff are more experienced in dealing with complaints and usually have more authority to put things right.

Because organisations realise the importance of listening to and handling customers' complaints, most organisations ensure that there are channels to allow customers to complain. Many organisations provide comment cards for customers to list any aspects of the product or service that they are unhappy with so that they can be dealt with quickly.

Another option is to make use of modern information technology. Oxford City Council is one of a growing number of organisations that have put complaints forms on their websites. Oxford's website (see Figure 3.7) outlines the various ways that a customer can contact the council with a complaint and sets out the actions that customers can take if they fail to receive a satisfactory reply within a specified period.

Figure 3.6: Dealing with complaints – the solution

S
O
L
U
T
I
O
N

- Show that you are **listening carefully**. This means maintaining good eye contact, making sure that your body language is positive and above all not interrupting customers when they are talking. Listening carefully to the customer's complaint is vital because if you do not know and understand all of the details you cannot do anything about it.

- Offer your **apologies**. In other words, show that you are concerned that the customer is dissatisfied by saying something like 'I'm very sorry to hear that you are unhappy about... I'm sure that I can do something about it'.

- Let the customer know that the complaint will be fully **investigated** and, if possible, put right. Sometimes this can be done at the time, but often you may have to reassure the customer that you will contact him or her as soon as you have looked into the matter.

- Understand the situation from the **customer's point of view**. Put yourself in his or her position and ask yourself 'if I were complaining about this how would I feel and what would I want done about it?'.

- Take control of the situation by **staying calm**. The reason that the customer has complained to you is that he or she expects you to be able to do something about it. The worst thing you can do is to panic or to lose your temper and argue with the customer. This shows that you have lost control of the situation and is likely to make the customer even more dissatisfied.

- Identify a suitable solution if possible. This will depend on the customer and the nature of the complaint. Sometimes the customer may require nothing more than a sincere apology and a reassurance that the problem will not happen again in future. Other complaints may require further action, such as offering a refund to the customer or replacing a product.

- Offer to **solve the problem** if possible and make sure that the customer is satisfied with your solution. If it is within your power to solve the problem straight away then you should do it. It is always better to act quickly rather than let the customer leave without knowing what action is going to be taken.

- Note what needs to be done to ensure that the customer is fully satisfied and that the problem does not happen again. Most organisations keep a complaints book to **record customer complaints**. This ensures that management is fully aware of dissatisfied customers and can take action to improve the level of customer service.

Figure 3.7: Oxford City Council's complaints procedure

I Want To Make A Complaint....

How to complain about Council services

Oxford City Council aim to give you quality services. If you are not happy with a service you have received, let us know. We have a Complaints Unit which is there to help put things right and to give you a chance to have your say.

You may want to complain because:

- you are unhappy with the service you have received;
- you disagree with a Council policy;
- you have been kept waiting.

What to do

If possible, you should complain to the person who provided the service. But, if you don't know who that is, you don't want to speak to them, or you are not happy with their response, you should get in touch with the Complaints Unit.

You can:

- fill in and return an Oxford City Council complaints form (available from any Council reception area);
- detail your complaint in a letter;
- phone us to tell us your complaint or to ask for advice;
- call in to see us to tell us your complaint;
- e-mail your complaint to us from this Web page.

You should keep a note of everyone you speak to and when, and keep copies of all letters or e-mails you send.

If you want to discuss your complaint with a Councillor who represents your area, or with your local MP, we can tell you how to get in touch.

What happens next?

Within 3 working days of receiving your complaint we will write to let you know how it is being dealt with.

Within 10 working days of us acknowledging your complaint the Head of Service will send you a written reply or, if a full response is not possible within this time, we will let you know what is being done about your complaint and when you can expect a full reply.

What to do if you are still not happy

If you are unhappy with the reply from the Head of Service, get back in touch. We can arrange for the Council's Chief Executive to look at your complaint and investigate it further.

If you are still not happy, you can take your complaint to the Local Government Ombudsman. This person is not part of Oxford City Council and will have an independent view.

The service is confidential and free of charge. Ask the Complaints Unit for a copy of the leaflet *How to complain to the Local Government Ombudsman* or collect one from any Oxford City Council reception area.

Source: **www.oxford.gov.uk**

A complaint handling check list

The manager of Barkdale Leisure Centre Rick Stevenson has recently received this memo from his boss Sarah Harris, the director of leisure services.

Can you design the complaint handling check list for the staff induction booklet?

To: Rick Stevenson

From: Sarah Harris

Date: 10.10.1999

Subject: Complaint handling

During the last three months I have received a number of complaints about various aspects of the service at the Barkingdale Leisure Centre. In all instances the letters have been sent directly to me because the customers felt that your staff were unconcerned about their complaints and failed to take any action. This is a situation that cannot continue, as we are in danger of losing some valued customers as a result of your staff's inability to handle complaints correctly.

I would like you to hold a formal training session for all full and part-time members of staff to ensure that they know the procedure for dealing with complaints. I would also like you to write an additional page for the staff induction booklet to include a checklist of how staff should behave and act when faced with a customer complaint.

Will you please let me have a copy of the staff booklet page by this Friday.

Build your learning

Summary points

- All staff need to know how to deal effectively with customer complaints.

- If customer complaints are not dealt with well it can result in the loss of the customer and a bad reputation that will put off other customers.

- It is important to listen carefully to customers' complaints, so that you understand all of the details.

- You should always offer your apologies to a customer who is complaining.

- Customers should be told that their complaint will be fully investigated and put right.

- You need to put yourself in the customers' position and see the complaint from their point of view.

- Staying calm and not arguing back will help you keep control of the situation.

- Wherever possible you need to identify a solution and agree it with the customer.

- You should always make sure that you do what you have promised.

- You should always contact a supervisor for help if you feel unable to deal with a customer's complaint.

Key words and phrases

You should know the meaning of the words and phrases listed below as they relate to handling complaints. Go back through the last five pages to refresh your understanding if necessary.

- Listening carefully
- Apologising
- Investigating
- Customer complaint
- Customer's viewpoint
- Staying calm
- Recording complaints
- Solving the problem

SUMMARY ACTIVITY

This is a role play activity. Use the following opening sentences, each spoken by a customer to a member of staff, as the basis for a role play. In pairs, role play each situation, with the customer making up all further details about the complaint. Take time at the end of each complaint to discuss how well the complaint was handled and what, if anything, could have been improved.

1 'We've already been waiting three hours and now you're telling me that the flight is delayed by a further two hours at least. My young children are tired and I've run out of English currency to buy any food.'

2 'When I rang up yesterday I was told that this film was suitable for young children. My two sons were absolutely terrified – they've spent most of the film hiding behind the seat in front.'

3 'When I booked to go on the Greek night I was told that there was unlimited free wine. Well the stuff you've been serving tastes like paint stripper – I think it's a big con!'

4 'You advertised these aerobics lessons as a way to get fit and lose weight. I've been coming for six months now and I still weigh 12 stone.'

5 'The brochure said that the weather was hot and sunny at this time of the year. We've had 12 days of solid rain and spent all our holiday money on warm clothes.'

6 'I was just getting changed in my bedroom when the hotel maintenance engineer barged into my room. He said that he knocked but I certainly didn't hear him.'

7 'I made it quite clear when I booked the table that three of my party are vegetarians – what do you mean you can only do them a plain omelette?'

8 'I've been waiting to pay for these trainers for the last 15 minutes while you've been talking on the phone. Why didn't you tell the customer that you would ring them back and serve me first?'

Keeping customer records

Good customer service is not just about being able to talk to customers. A large part of the process involves writing information down so that it can be used by other staff to help them provide good service to customers. All leisure and tourism organisations keep records on their customers and knowing how to maintain and use these records is an essential part of excellent customer service.

Records may be kept for any number of situations. For example:

- a travel agency keeps files containing the customers' holiday reservation details
- a theatre keeps files on existing customers showing what performances they have attended
- a health club has details on customers, including any medical conditions
- a hotel has records of guests who have stayed before, with details of any special requirements
- an organisation may have records of past customer complaints and the action taken to satisfy the customer.

Creating customer records

When keeping customer records you need to know how to **create customer records**. Any organisation that uses customer records will have standard procedures, whether paper based or on computer. You need to know how to create and store records for new customers. If you are unsure, always ask another member of staff for help rather than guessing. Incorrect records can have disastrous results, as you can see!

Finding and changing existing records

Customer details are constantly changing, which means that you need to know how to **find and change records**. Records may be keep in a filing system in a filing cabinet, on a computer database, on record cards or in books and files. Organisations often keep different types of records in different places so it is important that you know where they are. For example, customer complaints may be in a book, reservations may go into a diary and customer details may be stored on a computer.

You also need to be careful when changing details and make sure you follow the correct procedures. One (not very funny) example of this going wrong was when an elderly gentleman contacted his travel agent to say that his wife had died, so could they take her name off all future letters they might send to him. The eager new receptionist found his file on the computer database and typed in 'died' after the wife's name. The computer automatically addressed all further letters to 'Mr and Mrs (died) Johnson'.

Accuracy and confidentiality

The details in customer records are only of any use if they are 100 per cent **accurate**. If they are 99 per cent accurate, then all of the information is useless because it is not possible to be sure which details are correct and which are not. It is therefore your responsibility to make sure that everything you enter in a customer record is correct and to double check before you enter it if you are unsure.

Customer records often contain personal information about customers which is given to the organisation in the belief that it will not be passed on to anyone else. It is your responsibility to make sure that you keep all such information **confidential** to save the customer any embarrassment or difficulty. Even a casual remark to a customer in front of others about something that you have read in his or her record could be seen as a breach of confidentiality and result in a very dissatisfied customer. For example, you shouldn't make these kind of casual remarks.

- 'I'd never have guessed you were 50.'
- 'Have you had any luck in finding a new job yet?'
- 'Our fitness programme must be working, I see you're down to 15 stone.'
- 'Have you fully recovered from that little accident you had in Tenerife?'

Build your learning

Summary points

- Keeping customer records helps organisations operate efficiently and provide good service to their customers.

- Records can be kept in a filing cabinet, on a computer database, on record cards or in books and files.

- Different types of records are suitable for different situations.

- When creating new records it is important to record information accurately and clearly.

- It is important to know how to find specific information in records.

- The correct procedures should be followed when changing information in records.

- Staff should always treat information in customers' records as confidential.

Key words and phrases

You should know the meaning of the words and phrases listed below as they relate to keeping customer records. Go back through the last three pages to refresh your understanding if necessary.

- **Create customer records**
- **Accurate records**
- **Find and change records**
- **Confidentiality**

SUMMARY ACTIVITY

1 By law, all leisure and tourism organisations must keep records of any accidents that happen to people on their premises. Many organisations keep an accident book in a central place, so that staff can fill in details immediately after an incident.

Using the accident book below, fill in the details of the following accidents. Make up details of address, telephone number, dates and times. If you think that any further action should have been taken, other than what is described in the scenarios, add it to the last column.

- Mrs Cooper slipped on some water spilt by a cleaner. Madge Brown, the cleaner, called the staff first aider, who decided that Mrs Cooper had twisted her ankle. He arranged for a taxi to take her to the local casualty department.

- Ben Thomas, canteen assistant, burnt his hand when he fell against a hot plate in the kitchen. The head chef cooled the burn with cold water and sent Ben home for the rest of the day.

- Two part-time staff, John Michaels and Rob Sartin, were fighting in the car park when Rob got pushed to the ground, badly cutting his head and temporarily losing consciousness. The staff first aider called an ambulance and Rob was kept in hospital overnight for observation. Following an interview with the manager, both staff were issued with a written warning about their conduct.

- Mr North fell down a small flight of stairs and broke his hip. The manager, who was present at the time, called an ambulance immediately. Mr North claimed that the reason for his fall was a piece of loose stair carpet. The manager contacted the maintenance engineer, who inspected the carpet but could not find anything wrong with it.

Accident book						
Date	Time	Name of Victim	Address/ Tel No.	Details of Accident	Witnesses	Action taken

2 Select a leisure and tourism organisation of your choice and provide examples of customer records, other than accident records, that the organisation uses.

PORTFOLIO ASSESSMENT

This unit is assessed through your portfolio work. The grade for this assessment will be your grade for this unit. These pages are designed to help you to review your work and to check whether you have covered the required tasks to the right standard. The assessment tasks show what your portfolio needs to contain. Your teacher can give you further advice on what you need to do for each task.

If you have completed the summary activities throughout this unit, you will have already done a great deal of work for your portfolio. Sometimes you may need to reorganise or expand upon the work that you have done before it is ready to be submitted for your final assessment. The table below shows which activities from the unit can help you build your portfolio.

Assessment tasks	Activities
Task 1	Activity on page 196
Task 2	Activities on pages 190 and 196
Task 3	Activity on page 196
Task 4	Activities on pages 196 and 231
Task 5	Activities on pages 187, 188, 196 and 202
Task 6	Activities on pages 208 and 216
Task 7	Activity on page 227
Task 8	Activity on page 196
Task 9	Question on page 184
Task 10	Activity on page 208

Assessment tasks

There are two parts to the assessment evidence for this unit. You need to produce a review of the customer service provided by a selected leisure or tourism organisation (tasks 1–5) *and* provide a record of your involvement in a variety of customer service situations (tasks 6–7). These can be real, such as from a work placement or your part-time job, or could be simulated through role plays. There is also a lot of evidence that you can collect from the viewpoint of the customer. The organisation you choose to investigate must be one that provides customer service in a variety of different ways, such as face to face, on the telephone and in writing. Your findings can be presented in a variety of different ways, for example reports, displays or oral presentations. Your record of your performance in customer service situations can be written, such as a witness statement, or recorded on video or audiotape.

1 Explain why customer service is important to an organisation and identify the benefits of delivering it effectively. For a Merit, you will also need to clearly explain the employee's responsibility to provide good customer service.

2 Describe, using relevant examples, ways in which an organisation meets the needs of internal and external customers. For a Merit, you will also need to compare and contrast the ways in which the organisation serves its internal and external customers.

3 Describe fully how an organisation deals with complaints.

4 Provide relevant examples of the type of customer records used by an organisation.

5 Evaluate the customer service provided by an organisation.

6 Provide detailed evidence of your dealings with customers that shows you can communicate clearly with them in a friendly and helpful manner.

7 Provide detailed evidence that shows how you dealt with a customer complaint. For a Merit, you will need to provide customers with valid information and handle their complaints appropriately.

To achieve a Distinction, you need to do three further tasks.

8 Produce a detailed description of the way in which an organisation provides for different customer needs.

9 Analyse the consequences to an organisation of poor customer service.

10 Evaluate your own performance in the customer service situations that you have undertaken. Consider:

- What types of customer were you dealing with?
- What was the customer service situation?
- What were the main customer needs?
- How did you satisfy customers' needs?
- What do you think that you did well?
- How could you have improved the way in which you dealt with customers?
- What did you learn from dealing with this customer service situation?

Key skills

It may be possible to claim these key skills for this work, depending on how you have completed the tasks and presented your work.

Communication (2.1a, 2.1b, 2.2, 2.3)

Problem solving (level 2)

Improving own learning and performance (level 2)

Working with others (level 2)

Your teacher will need to check your evidence against the key skills specification.

Jobs in leisure and tourism

Leisure and tourism, taken together, are Britain's biggest growth industries, directly employing over 1.7 million people. By 2000, it is forecast that leisure and tourism will be the largest employer worldwide. Few industries can match it for the range of employment opportunities offered people of all ages. Taking account of both direct and indirect employment, the list of jobs is vast.

   This section provides a general overview of job opportunities and then sets out how to apply for jobs in your chosen area of the industry. It suggests ways of presenting information about yourself to prospective employers and how to compile a curriculum vitae (CV).

Jobs in leisure and tourism

There are many jobs at a basic level or operative level and relatively few in management. If you are a school or college leaver starting out on your career your first job will probably be at the operative level. Figure A.1 shows some typical examples of jobs at this level.

Figure A.1: Entry level jobs in leisure and tourism

Leisure and recreation	Travel and tourism
Sports centre assistant	Hotel receptionist
Pool attendant or lifeguard	Waiter or waitress
Bar staff	Travel agency clerk
Sports leader or coach	Tourist information centre clerk
Parks or garden ground staff	Tourist guide
Playscheme assistant	Coach driver
Cinema box office cashier	Airline cabin crew

The leisure and tourism industries offer good promotion prospects and many people progress from basic jobs to supervisory and higher management positions. Some examples of career progression are shown in Figure A.2.

Figure A.2: Career progression in leisure and tourism

Operative	Supervisory	Management
Sports centre assistant	Sports centre duty manager	Sports centre manager
Waiter/waitress	Head waiter/waitress	Restaurant manager
Hotel receptionist	Front-of-house manager	Hotel manager
Lifeguard	Swimming pool duty manager	Swimming pool manager
Travel courier resort rep	Head courier resort rep	Resort manager

For some people, promotion from operative to supervisory and management levels can be relatively quick, although competition for jobs at all levels is often intense. For example, thousands of people apply to airline companies every year for cabin crew positions, but only a small proportion are accepted.

Another feature of work in the leisure and tourism industries is the potential for changing career paths. For example, if you work for an employer who owns a range of facilities, such as hotels, pubs, restaurants and leisure facilities, it may be possible to move from one to another. Even if this is not the case, there are numerous opportunities to diversify into different areas.

Identifying suitable jobs

Your starting point is to decide what your personal aims and interests are and then identify jobs and career paths which suit these aims and interests. This will involve doing some research to find out about jobs, qualifications, prospects and employers. When identifying suitable job roles you should consider a range of criteria.

Am I being realistic?

Most employers expect prospective employees to be ambitious but you must also be realistic about the level at which you will enter the industry. As we have seen, for most people this is initially at the operative level. It is best to discuss your plans with a careers adviser or your teacher.

What are my circumstances?

You must take your personal circumstances into account when you are considering jobs. How far are you prepared to travel to find employment? Is your age an important factor? Some employers specify that you must be willing to work anywhere in the country, and some jobs have minimum age requirements. For example, bar staff and lifeguards must be 18 or over and most airlines and tour operators require cabin crew or resort representatives to be at least 21, and often require staff to have a second language.

If you are a 16 or 17-year-old school leaver the range of full-time job opportunities in the industry is limited, unless you are taking a training scheme which is sponsored by an employer. One such scheme is the ABTA Travel Training Company training programme, which recruits over a thousand young people every year and trains them for work in various occupations in the travel industry. The case study overleaf gives details about the scheme.

CASE STUDY

The Travel Training Programme

Each year, the Travel Training Company arranges travel training courses throughout Britain at over 60 regional training centres. All of the courses provide the opportunity to achieve National Vocational Qualifications at levels 2 and 3.

The Travel Training Programme is regarded nationwide as a well-run, quality scheme and should not be confused with other non-ABTA training programmes. A large number of travel companies have decided that the only method of entry for young people into their organisation will be through the programme. It is an equal opportunity scheme which does not discriminate on the grounds of race, religion, sex or disability.

The Travel Training Company offers training in three different areas of the travel industry, each leading to a National Vocational Qualification or Scottish Vocational Qualification.

- **Business travel**
  This part of the industry looks after the businessperson, mainly working behind the scenes and using the telephone to arrange flights, car hire and hotel reservations.

- **Tour operations**
  Opportunities exist in the field of tour operations. However, there are far fewer tour operators than travel agents, and therefore the number of openings is correspondingly lower. At present the company runs courses in central London and Manchester.

- **Retail travel**
  This is by far the most popular programme, and this area has the most openings for young people. All trainees work towards qualifications in travel services at NVQ/SVQ levels 2 and 3. This includes air fares and ticketing, travel geography, package holidays and car ferry costings, and ongoing assessment of performance in the workplace.

Source: The Travel Training Company

What are my interests?

Consider your current interests when looking for suitable jobs. This may involve an evaluation of your leisure pastimes and activities. For example, if you are interested in sport you may consider working as a coach, instructor or sports centre assistant. Similarly, if you enjoy travel and meeting people you may decide to seek employment as a holiday resort representative or a sales consultant in a travel agency.

What qualifications, skills and experience are required?

It is important to obtain advice on the qualifications, skills and experience required for your chosen job. A useful starting point is to list the relevant qualifications, skills and experience you already have, identify what others you are in the process of obtaining and, finally, list any others you think you will need in the future. This may involve undertaking more training and work experience at school, college or another training provider before you are ready to seek employment. You must also consider the type of person required by prospective employers: ask yourself whether you have the personal qualities employers are looking for.

What opportunities are available?

You must also consider what opportunities are available for gaining employment. For example, if you live in a popular tourist area you may be readily able to identify a number of opportunities in the travel and tourism industry within your locality. Alternatively, you may need to look outside your locality for suitable employment opportunities. Make sure you keep up to date with current developments by looking in newspapers, magazines and journals, as they can be a useful source of information on employers and potential job opportunities.

Gaining skills and experience

Qualifications and training opportunities will help you gain employment in the leisure and tourism industries. In addition to taking qualifications at your local school, college or training provider, you may be able to acquire useful skills and experience from part-time or voluntary work or through work placements.

Due to the seasonal nature of the industry there are many opportunities for temporary and part-time employment, particularly in the travel and tourism industry. If there is no way of finding part-time or temporary paid work you may be able to find voluntary work in order to learn about the job and make useful contacts. Moreover, in undertaking voluntary work you will have gained experience and shown commitment to the industry.

If you already have a job in the leisure and tourism industries your employer may provide you with on-the-job training. For example, lifeguards often receive first aid training from their employers to meet health and safety legal requirements. Similarly, staff who have face-to-face contact with customers may receive some form of on-the-job training to

◀ What job in the leisure and tourism industries do you think would be suitable for you?

develop their skills in dealing with customers in a variety of situations. Some employers also encourage their employees to undertake qualifications and training programmes at local colleges and training providers through day or block release.

Whatever your chosen career path and personal circumstances, the acquisition of qualifications, skills and experience is of vital importance. Remember to seek advice before committing yourself to a particular training course or job; careful career planning at this stage could enable you to establish a successful career in your chosen field.

ACTIVITY

Knowledge and skills requirements

Study these comments from six people actually working in the leisure and tourism industries. Each person was asked to describe the most important personal qualities, skills and knowledge requirements for his or her job.

1 'I must understand how to motivate people and this means finding exactly the right approach for each individual. The most important skills are the ability to communicate, teach others and inspire confidence.'

2 'I need business acumen and flair to develop new ideas and increase use of facilities. It is important to be able to handle people, both employees and customers. Good communication skills are important. Numeracy and information technology skills are needed in order to cope with the financial and management information aspects of the job. Finally, there is a high level of responsibility as I am accountable for the day-to-day running of the facility and for the health and safety of visitors and staff.'

3 'I have to be confident and outgoing whilst at work. It is important to get on well with people and deal tactfully and diplomatically with dissatisfied customers. I am very much in the public eye, so smart appearance and good social skills are vital. Also important are organisational ability, business skills, competence in financial matters and knowledge of a range of related practical skills such as cookery, food and beverage service and housekeeping. At peak times the work is hectic and the ability to work under pressure is vital.'

4 'I need an eye for detail and must be neat and thorough in my work. I work as part of a team so it is important to get on with colleagues. A reasonable level of physical fitness is necessary due to the nature of the work.'

5 'Talent, creativity, adaptability, stamina, confidence and a lively outgoing personality are the most important requirements for my line of work. The ability to sing or dance can improve prospects. You must be prepared to go anywhere in the country to find work which can mean spending time away from the family.'

6 'Many people think the work is glamorous, but it is frequently very demanding with long hours. The main requirement is the ability to communicate well with all types of people, combined with common sense. It is important to have a confident, outgoing personality and to get on with customers. Languages are also useful.'

These comments are from people employed as a:

- hotel manager
- holiday resort representative
- sports centre manager
- sports coach
- hotel room attendant
- entertainer.

Match each description with the job role. Then, in small groups, discuss what knowledge and skill requirements are common to all of these jobs. Record the main requirements in a table like the one below. Discuss how your course covers these common skill requirements.

Description	Job role	Knowledge/skills required
1		
2		
3		
4		
5		
6		

Sources of careers information and guidance

Whether you are looking for your first job or contemplating a career change there are many sources of information to help you make the right decisions. Here are some of the main providers of careers guidance and information.

Careers services

Your school or college should have someone responsible for providing careers education and guidance who can help you. Alternatively, careers services have extensive libraries and computer databases which provide information on most types of jobs. Careers service offices also display vacancies for employers and, in some cases, will arrange interviews for you. Addresses of careers service offices are listed in the telephone directory.

Libraries

There are numerous books and publications on jobs and careers. Your library is likely to contain a selection dealing with the leisure and tourism industries, together with information on how to apply for jobs. One title to request is the *Handbook of Jobs in Leisure and Tourism*, published annually by Hobsons.

Jobcentres

Jobcentres display information on vacancies that have been notified to them by employers. Their staff can also advise you on job opportunities in your area and on education and training schemes. Jobcentres are listed in the telephone directory under Employment Services.

Employment agencies

Many employers choose to place vacancies with private employment agencies rather than to advertise in local newspapers or jobcentres. Some employment agencies specialise in particular areas of the leisure and tourism industries, such as catering and accommodation. Employment agencies in your locality will be listed in Yellow Pages.

Professional bodies

If you are a member of a professional body, such as the Institute of Leisure and Amenity Management (ILAM), you may be able to obtain specialist careers advice and guidance. ILAM has a student category of membership and distributes a weekly appointments bulletin to its members. It also produces careers information and guidelines on its website **www.ilam.co.uk**.

▼ Some on-line sources of careers information

Talking to people already doing the job

Talking to people already employed in your chosen area can be an effective way of finding out about jobs and career opportunities. Ask them how they got started and what skills and qualifications are required for a particular job. Many schools and colleges arrange visits to leisure and tourism facilities to find out how they operate and what sort of jobs are available.

Writing to employers

Many of the larger employers in the leisure and tourism industries provide information about job opportunities, the skills and qualifications required, and how to apply. Jarvis and First Choice are just two of the many employers who provide careers information.

Finding information on vacancies

Once you have sought careers advice and decided what type of job is of interest to you, the next stage is to find information on specific job vacancies. Careers services, jobcentres and employment agencies are useful sources of information on job vacancies as well as providing careers advice.

Many organisations also advertise vacancies in a variety of newspapers, magazines and trade journals. The type of advert, and where it is placed, depends on the nature of the job, its level and the type of employer. Places to look for details of job vacancies in the leisure and tourism industries include:

- local, regional and national newspaper advertisements in the situations vacant columns
- careers service noticeboards and databases
- jobcentre noticeboards
- local radio advertisements
- school and college careers noticeboards
- television job advertisements (on Teletext)
- the internet
- trade journals and magazines, such as *The Caterer and Hotelkeeper, Travel Trade Gazette, Leisure Opportunities*
- publications issued by the industry lead bodies, including the Association of British Travel Agents and the Institute of Leisure and Amenity Management

ACTIVITY

Looking for jobs

Study this list of jobs. Match each job with the most likely publication (in the second column) in which you would find details about vacancies.

Jobs	Publication
1 Hotel manager	A Museums bulletin
2 Travel agency clerk	B *Caterer and Hotelkeeper*
3 Part-time bar worker	C *Travel Trade Gazette*
4 Museum guide	D *Leisure Opportunities*
5 Sports centre manager	E Local newspaper

Applying for jobs

Competition for many jobs in the leisure and tourism industries is intense. Many people may apply for a particular job, but few will get interviewed and, usually, only one person actually gets the job. It is important, therefore, for you to understand how to present personal information to prospective employers in order to increase your chance of being considered. This section gives you some useful tips on applying for jobs and producing a curriculum vitae (CV).

When you hear of a job, or see one advertised in a newspaper, you usually have to write or telephone for further details. Remember, writing this letter or making the telephone call is the first chance you have of impressing the employer, so it is important to get it right. Always apply for a job as soon as you hear about it; it shows that you are genuinely interested and are actively looking for work.

When you have received more information, the next stage is to write a letter of application, complete the employer's printed application form, or send a copy of your curriculum vitae. It is important to do this well. The quality of your letter or form, both in terms of what it contains and how it is presented, often determines whether you get an interview. Always take steps to ensure that your application is with the employer before the closing date, as most will not consider late entries.

Writing letters of application

In writing letters of application, follow these guidelines.

- Make sure you set the letter out in the correct format (see Figure A.4, page 247), with your address, the date and the full address of the employer. Write to a named person if you have been given this information.
- Always write neatly and clearly, and make a practice copy first. Better still, type your letter.
- Use plain, unlined white or cream paper and blue or black ink. Envelopes should match the colour of the paper. If you find it difficult to write straight on unlined paper, use bold lines under the paper to guide you.
- Always use a first class stamp on the envelope.
- Check spelling, or get someone else to check it if you are not certain. When wordprocessing, use the spellcheck function.
- Letters addressed to 'Dear Sir' or 'Dear Madam' end 'Yours faithfully'; letters addressed to a named person ('Dear Mr Johnson') end 'Yours sincerely'.
- Make your signature clear and print your name underneath.
- Always say what job you are writing about, using a reference code if one is given in the job advert, and stating where you saw the advert. This is particularly important if a firm has several vacancies at the same time.
- Keep a copy of your letter, so that you can refer to it if you get an interview.
- If you include the names of people who will give you a reference, make sure you ask their permission first.

It is important to write the 'right' letter. If you are responding to a job advert, follow the instructions given. For example, do not include personal details if the advert requests you to write for further details or send for an application form. However, if you are asked to 'apply in writing' you should give details about yourself and state clearly why you are applying for the job. Look at Anytown District Council's advert (Figure A.3), which requests the applicant to apply in writing.

Even if no suitable job vacancy is being advertised, it is still worthwhile writing to a company to enquire if there will be any job opportunities in the near future. With this type of letter, too, you will need to include details about yourself (or provide a CV) and identify areas of work you are interested in.

Figure A.3: Some job advertisements ask you to apply in writing

Anytown District Council

Anytown Leisure Centre

We require three full-time trainee leisure assistants to work in our purpose-built leisure centre. Each post will focus on a particular area of the complex. The posts are:

leisure assistant: swimming pool **(Ref la1)**
leisure assistant: sports hall **(Ref la2)**
leisure assistant: health and fitness centre **(Ref la3)**

We are looking for energetic, enthusiastic young people with relevant academic or vocational qualifications who are eager to start a successful career in the sport and recreation industry.

Apply in writing to:
Mrs J Arkwright, Personnel Manager, Anytown District Council, 17 High Street, Anytown, AD1 3PQ.

Please quote job and reference number.

Closing date for application: 5 October 1999

Figure A.4: When replying to prospective employers, make sure that letters are properly laid out

29 Westfield Road
Anytown
AL6 7DD

24 September 1999

Mrs J Arkwright
Personnel Manager
Anytown District Council
Central Chambers
17 High Street
Anytown
AD1 3PQ

Dear Mrs Arkwright

Trainee leisure assistant (Ref la2)

I would like to apply for the post of trainee leisure assistant, sports hall, as advertised in the Anytown Evening News on 17 September 1999.

I am 17 and left Anytown College this June after completing a General National Vocational Qualification (GNVQ) in Leisure and Tourism at intermediate level, gaining an overall grade of Merit. During the one-year full-time course, I studied a range of leisure and tourism-related subjects, including customer service, marketing, organising events and tourist destinations, as well as developing skills in information technology, communication and numeracy.

I would really like to work at Anytown Leisure Centre because it is a well-established local facility. I am also keen to gain further vocational qualifications and would welcome the opportunity to work towards NVQs in Sports and Recreation during the training programme.

Since leaving college, I have worked at Shades Fitness Centre restaurant as a part-time instructor at weekends and in the evenings. During my GNVQ course, I completed a three-week work placement at Elstree Sports Centre in Bambry. I thoroughly enjoyed this experience and found it very useful to observe experienced sports coaches and to assist in the recreation programme.

I am a friendly, outgoing person who enjoys meeting people. My personal interests include hockey, football, eating out and keep-fit. I am a member of Emperors Health and Fitness Centre and regularly attend step classes. If you wish to obtain references, please contact:

Mr R Deacon	Mrs J Rose
GNVQ Co-ordinator	Manager
Anytown College	Shades Fitness Centre
Anytown	High Street
AD8 6DL	Anytown
	AL5 7PQ

I am available to come for interview at any time.

Yours sincerely,

Jane Cook

Key

1. Do not forget your address and the date.
2. Make sure you reply to the named person (if given) and correct address.
3. Say what job you are applying for.
4. Say where you saw the advert.
5. Give your age.
6. List your qualifications (you may also wish to include your GCSEs).
7. Say why you want the job.
8. Give details about any relevant skills and experience you have. Remember to include details of previous jobs or work placements.
9. Give brief details, including information about your main interests.
10. Give two references, remembering to ask their permission first.
11. Make sure you finish the letter in the correct manner ('yours sincerely' in this example), and print your name clearly below the signature.
12. The envelope should be the same colour as the paper (preferably white or cream) and a first class stamp should be affixed.

ACTIVITY

Responding to job advertisements

Study this job advert for a trainee travel consultant with Faraway Travel Agency which was placed in the Anytown Evening News on 17 September 1999. Write a suitable letter requesting further details for the post.

Imagine you have received details about the vacancy. You have been asked to apply in writing, giving personal details and qualifications gained. Write a suitable letter in support of your application.

You may wish to refer to figure A.4 on the previous page to help get you started.

Faraway Travel Agency

Trainee Travel Consultant

Energetic, enthusiastic young person wanted to train as travel consultant with this family run travel agency. Involves working with a variety of customers and some evening and weekend work.

Good pay for the right applicant, plus staff travel discounts and a two-year on-the-job or college day release training programme leading to an NVQ in Travel Services.

For further details please contact:
Mr Milton, Manager, Faraway Travel, High Street, Anytown, AL5 9PQ.

Filling in application forms

Some employers ask you to fill in an application form. Here are some useful tips.

- Photocopy the form and complete the copy before filling in the original. Alternatively, you could complete the original form in pencil before using ink.
- Read through the whole form before you start to fill it in, and make sure you put all the information in the correct places and try to answer all the questions.
- Always use dark ink, preferably black, as the firm may wish to photocopy the form.
- Write clearly and neatly and check your spelling.
- Keep a copy of the form so that you can refer to it if you get an interview.
- Obtain permission from the people you are nominating as referees.
- Write a brief covering letter, to send with the completed form.

Read these tips carefully. Now copy and complete the application form on the opposite page.

Application for Employment

Strictly Confidential

Position for which you are applying _____

Where did you learn of the vacancy?_____

Personal details

Surname _____ Mr/Mrs/Miss/Ms
(delete as applicable)

First name(s)_____

Address _____

_____

_____

Telephone _____

Date of birth _____

Age _____

Nationality _____

Marital status _____

Full and part-time education (Please continue on a separate sheet if necessary.)

School, College, University	From	To	Qualifications obtained

Present and previous employment (Please continue on a separate sheet if necessary.)

Name and address of employer	From	To	Job title, duties and responsibilities

Telephoning about jobs

If you have to ring up about a job vacancy, make sure you have the job details and the name of the person or department (usually personnel) receiving enquiries about the job. If no name is given say 'I'm ringing about the job advertised for...' and let the person taking your call put you through to the right person. It is also a good idea to have a pen and paper and your diary handy so that you can write down details if you are offered an interview.

Curriculum vitae

Sometimes employers ask you to send a copy of your curriculum vitae (CV) in support of your application, although this request is usually made for jobs suitable for more experienced people rather than school leavers. Nonetheless, it is important to understand what information to include in a CV, and how best to present it.

Curriculum vitae is Latin and translates as an outline of your qualifications and career to date. There are several acceptable layouts for producing a CV. Whichever you choose, here are some general points to guide you.

- A CV should usually be presented on one or two sheets of A4 paper (not more), preferably typed.
- Continually update your CV to take into account changes in your circumstances such as a change of address or a newly-gained qualification.
- Enhance the presentation by using clear, bold headings which are neatly arranged.
- Obtain several good quality copies of your CV so that you can use it in approaching other employers.
- Always write a covering letter with a CV explaining your reasons for applying for the particular job and outlining why you think you are suitable.
- If possible, produce your CV using a word processing package so you can easily amend details. Using a computer should also enhance the quality of presentation, particularly if you can use a good quality laser printer.
- Always check spelling and grammar.

The CV opposite provides an example of a layout, presentation style and range of content which would be suitable for sending to prospective employers. Before you send out your CV, make sure someone checks it for you. Teachers and careers advisers will usually give you advice and help.

Curriculum Vitae

NAME
Stephen Wallis

ADDRESS
15 West Park Avenue, Bisham, Woldshire, WD1 7PQ

DATE OF BIRTH
May 28 1982

EDUCATION

Bisham College of Further Education 1998–99

GNVQ Intermediate level (1999)	Leisure and Tourism	Merit

Bisham Comprehensive School 1993–1998

GCSEs (1998)	English Language	B
	Geography	C
	History	D
	French	D
	Mathematics	D
	Biology	E

EMPLOYMENT/WORK EXPERIENCE

1996 to present	Banton's newsagents, part-time sales assistant, Saturdays and Sundays. Duties include handling sales and using electronic cash register.
1998	College work placement (four weeks) at Woldshire Tennis Centre, Rudston. I was involved in supervising and instructing children aged 10–12 during tennis coaching courses.
1997	Trident project: completed three weeks full-time work experience at Bisham Sports Centre. Duties included assisting with children's coaching sessions and facility maintenance.

Interests

Wide variety of sports, including tennis, football, cricket and squash. I have represented Woldshire County Tennis Association at under-15 and under-19 levels and am currently the Bisham under-19 district champion. I am also interested in tennis coaching and have gained the Lawn Tennis Association (LTA) Leader's Coaching Award. Outside of sport, my main interests include visiting foreign places and pop music.

OTHER QUALIFICATIONS/ AWARDS

Clean driving licence; St John Ambulance First Aid Certificate; LTA Leader's Coaching Award; Community Sports Leader's Award.

REFEREES

Mrs S Jameson
Head of Leisure and Tourism
Bisham College of Further Education
Bisham
W10 7LD

Mr J Tate
Head Coach
Woldshire Tennis Centre
17 Parkland Road
Rudston

Note that you should always include the following information on your CV.

- **Personal details** – Age, marital status, address and telephone number.
- **Academic and vocational qualifications** – Details of schools and colleges attended, dates, subjects studied and grades obtained, plus details of qualifications you are currently pursuing.
- **Employment/work experience** – Details of previous employment, including part-time, full-time and voluntary work. Give brief details of your duties and responsibilities and any specialist skills used.
- **Achievements and other qualifications** – For example, driving licence, first aid certificate, lifesaving awards.
- **Personal interests** – Leisure activities, pastimes, membership of clubs or societies. Highlight activities that show initiative and responsibilities.
- **References** – The names of two referees with addresses, identifying in what capacity they know you, for example, youth leader, manager of office during work experience placement.

Interview skills

When you are invited for an interview, there are some useful things to remember. Before the interview you should think positively, you have already done well to get this far! Think carefully about why you want the job, and why you believe you are the best person to do it. Be prepared for anything: interviews can vary tremendously, from a very formal interview with several interviewers combined with a written test, to a more casual approach. Organise yourself: make sure you know where the interview is to be held, and how you are going to get there. Learn as much about the company as you can, and, if possible, find out more about the type of work for which you are applying. Dress smartly: all employers will appreciate that you have made an effort to look good.

During the interview you should put forward a positive image, smile and look interested. Avoid simple 'yes' and 'no' answers, as they stop conversation. When you answer each question give as much relevant information as you can and always tell the truth. Untruths often come to light either during or after the interview. When you have a chance to ask questions, ask one that shows enthusiasm for the job. Your last question might be about clarifying pay and conditions.

Internet directory

During your GNVQ course, you will gather a wide range of information about leisure and tourism organisations, facilities, products, services and events. This textbook provides much of the information that you need to complete your coursework. However, if you have access to the internet you can quickly obtain a wide range of material that will help you in your studies.

The internet is an excellent source of information. Many leisure and tourism organisations now provide information on the worldwide web (www). Their websites provide up-to-date information that you can use for your coursework and assignments. To access the internet, you need a computer with a modem and a browser, such as internet Explorer or Netscape. You may be able to access the internet at your school or college – check with your teacher whether this is possible. When you use the internet, you will quickly find out that there is an enormous amount of information about leisure and tourism.

We have provided a list of websites to help you save time. However, this list does not cover everything and you may need to search further for information on a particular topic, organisation or locality. Happy surfing!

Useful websites

Airlines

Most airlines now have a website. Here are four useful sites.

- British Airways
  http://www.british-airways.com
- easyJet
  http://www.easyjet.com
- British Midland
  http://www.iflybritishmidland.com
- Virgin Atlantic
  http://www.virgin.com

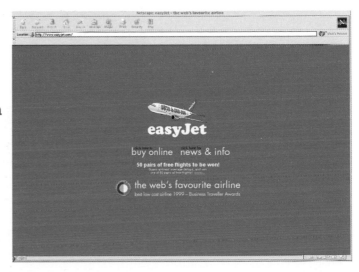

Airports

The British Airports Authority operates several UK airports including Heathrow, Gatwick, Stanstead, Edinburgh and Glasgow. Other airports are operated indepedently.

- British Airports Authority (BAA)
  http://www.baa.co.uk
- Manchester Airport
  http://www.manairport.co.uk
- Birmingham International Airport
  http://www.bhx.co.uk

Arts Council

The Arts Council site provides information about the arts in the UK and their funding. Online regional arts pages provide information about the English regional arts boards. There are also links to other arts-related sites.

- Arts Council
  http://www.artscouncil.org.uk
- Regional arts organisations
  http://www.arts.org.uk

Association of British Travel Agents

The Association of British Travel Agents (ABTA) is the premier trade association for UK tour operators and travel agents. ABTA represents more than 600 tour operators and 2,300 travel agency companies, with over 7,000 offices. It is responsible for the sale of more than 90 per cent of UK-sold package holidays. ABTA's site provides information about tourist destinations, tour operators, travel agents, types of holidays, careers guidance and qualifications offered in the travel services sector.

- Association of British Travel Agents
  http://www.abtanet.com

British Tourist Authority

The British Tourist Authority website provides an extensive range of information about tourism in Britain including tourist destinations, environments to explore, places to stay, activities and attractions, travel information, tourist boards, interactive images and maps of Britain. The site also contains information about careers in the travel and tourism industry and qualifications.

- British Tourist Authority
  http://www.visitbritain.com

Children's play

The Families site has a database of 500 indoor children's play areas, children's party venues and family pubs. The Kids' Clubs Network provides information about children's after-school clubs and guidance for playworkers.

- Families site
  http://www.families.co.uk
- Kids' Clubs Network
  http://www.kidsclubs.com

Department for Culture, Media and Sport

The Department for Culture, Media and Sport is responsible for government policy on the arts, sport and recreation, tourism, the national lottery, libraries, museums and galleries and film.

- Department for Culture, Media and Sport
  http://www.culture.gov.uk

English Heritage

The places to visit site provides information about historic houses, sites and monuments in England. This includes opening times, admission charges, group/school visits, visitor facilities, special events and concerts.

English Heritage
  http://www.english-heritage.org.uk

English and Regional Tourist Boards

The English Tourism Council shares the British Tourist Authority site. For further information about a particular region try the regional tourist boards.

- English Tourism Council
  http://www.englishtourism.org.uk
- Cumbria
  http://www.cumbria-the-lake-district.co.uk
- Northumbria
  http://www.northumbria-tourist-board.org.uk
- Yorkshire
  http://www.ytb.org.uk
- East of England
  http://www.eetb.org.uk
- West Country
  http://www.wctb.co.uk
- South East England
  http://www.se-eng-tourist-board.org.uk

Holiday parks

These are the sites of three major organisations running holiday parks in the UK.

- Butlins
  http://www.butlins.co.uk
- Center Parcs
  http://www.centerparcs.com
- Oasis
  http://www. oasishols.co.uk

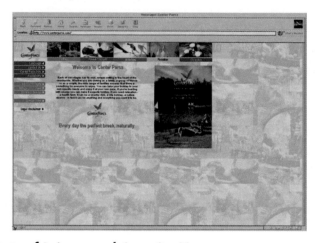

Institute of Leisure and Amenity Management

The Institute of Leisure and Amenity Management site provides the latest news and initiatives in the leisure and recreation industry. There is also useful careers and jobs information.

- Institute of Leisure and Amenity Management (ILAM)
  http://www.ilam.co.uk

Leisure opportunities

The leisure opportunities site provides information about job vacancies in the sport and recreation/leisure industries.

- Leisure opportunities
  http://www.leisureopportunities.co.uk

LeisureHunt

The LeisureHunt site is an extensive database providing information about leisure and tourism facilities throughout the UK, mainland Europe, North America and Australia. It has information on hotels, guest houses, hostels, campsites, art galleries, museums, historic places, restaurants, parks and gardens, golf courses, leisure centres, swimming pools, airports, industrial heritage, libraries, wildlife attractions and tourist information centres. This database can be used to investigate leisure and tourism facilities in a chosen locality.

- LeisureHunt
  http://www.leisurehunt.com

Museums

There are many museums in the UK with websites. A good starting point is the 24 Hour Museum, which provides comprehensive information about a wide range of museums. You will find this site useful when researching museums in a chosen locality. The National Museum of Science and Industry website has information on the Science Museum, London, the National Railway Museum, York and the National Museum of Photography, Film and Television.

- 24 Hour Museum
  http://www.24hourmuseum.org.uk
- National Museum of Science and Industry
  http://www.nmsi.ac.uk
- Royal Armouries
  http://www.armouries.org.uk

National Parks

Many national parks in England and Wales have a website where you can access information about tourism in the parks. This information may be useful when you investigate the impact of tourism on the countryside. Here is a selection of national park websites.

- Dartmoor National Park
  http://www.dartmoor.npa.gov.uk
- Lake District
  http://www.lake-district.gov.uk
- North Yorks Moors
  http://www.northyorkmoors-npa.gov.uk
- Peak District
  http://www.peakdistrict.org
- Pembrokeshire Coast
  http://www.pembrokeshirecoast.org

National Trust

The National Trust's site provides information about more than 300 historic buildings and sites. Every week the National Trust receives hundreds of enquiries about its work as the UK's largest land-owning conservation charity. As a major heritage organisation in the voluntary sector, the Trust provides an excellent case study for leisure and tourism students.

The Trust has a designated site for students aged 14+ which provides information about the history of the National Trust, its funding, marketing, access to its properties for disabled visitors and a range of case studies about issues such as nature conservation and the impacts of tourism.

- National Trust
  http://www.nationaltrust.org.uk
- National Trust's site for students
  http://www.nt-education.org

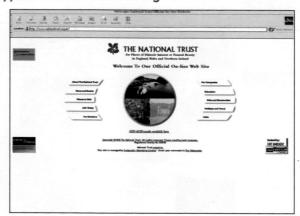

Northern Ireland Tourist Board

Information about tourism in Northern Ireland.

- Northern Ireland Tourist Board
  http://www.ni-tourism.com

Rank Group

The Rank Group is one of the leading leisure, tourism and entertainment companies in the UK. The site provides information about the company and its many businesses which include Mecca Bingo, Grosvenor Casinos, Odeon Cinemas, Rank Entertainment, Tom Cobleigh, Haven, Warner, Butlins, Oasis and Hard Rock Café.

- Rank Group
  http://www.rank.com

Sport England

Sport England (formerly the English Sports Council) promotes and represents sport in England. The site provides a wealth of useful information about sports development and coaching schemes, sports facilities, the national sports centres, voluntary sports clubs and the National Lottery Sports Fund.

The site also has an excellent information service for those studying sport and recreation where you can access the basic facts about sport, participation statistics, the history of the sports council, employment in sport and details of the Sport for All campaigns.

- Sport England
  http://www.english.sports.gov.uk

Staruk

This is the official website of the tourism liaison group of the UK. The group is made up of representatives of the national tourist boards of Britain, England, Scotland, Wales and Northern Ireland and the Department for Media, Culture and Sport. You can find a wide range of statistics and market research on inbound and domestic tourism in the UK. You can also obtain information about tourism publications in the library section.

- Staruk
  http://www.staruk.org.uk

Theme parks

There are many theme parks in the UK and the majority have websites. Here are four examples.

- Blackpool Pleasure Beach
  http://www.bpbltd.com
- Alton Towers
  http://www.alton-towers.co.uk
- Legoland, Windsor
  http://www.lego.com/legoland/windsor
- Thorpe Park
  http://www.thorpepark.co.uk

Tour operators

There are hundreds of tour operators in the UK. Two of the largest are Thomson and First Choice. You can access information on their websites about company history, careers and job opportunities and find out about the holiday products they offer.

- Thomson Holidays
  http://www.thomson-holidays.com
- First Choice
  http://www.firstchoice.co.uk

Travel agencies

Many of the larger travel agencies, such as Lunn Poly and Thomas Cook, have websites.

- Lunn Poly
  http://www.lunn-poly.co.uk
- Thomas Cook
  http://www.thomascook.co.uk

Travel and tourism jobs

This website provides information about jobs, type of work in the industry, qualifications needed and career choices.

- Travel and tourism jobs
  http://www.careercompass.co.uk

Virgin Group

Richard Branson's Virgin Group is one of the largest leisure and tourism operators in the UK. The site provides a company history, details of latest developments, career opportunities and information on the various Virgin businesses. These include Virgin Atlantic, Virgin Express, Virgin Trains, Virgin Holidays, Virgin Cinemas and Virgin Hotels.

- Virgin Group
  http://www.virgin.com

Wales Tourist Board

The Wales Tourist Board site has extensive information about tourism in Wales including holiday destinations, tours, places to stay and things to do. There is also information about the Rugby World Cup, 1999.

- Wales Tourist Board
  http://www.tourism.wales.gov.uk

What's On

Britain's national performing arts information and ticketing service. At any one time, the database has information about more than 2,000 performances around the country. What's On provides information about events in the UK, including theatre, opera, music, dance, ballet, and comedy.

- What's On
  http://www.whatson.com

Yellow Pages

UK Web is a directory listing of websites in the UK. Organisations are grouped by category, such as travel and tourism, sports and leisure, entertainment and music, education and training.

- Yellow Pages
  http://www.yell.co.uk

Answers to activities

Page 5

```
V J E A T N G O T T R E L P W L
L R O S T E N I N G E A E M A I
E I R E S T A U R A N T I E T T
I L S H C P B R C R D I S E C C
$ G C T A I U A E E L N U T H O
U L E I F S N D N S S G R I I M
R E A D I N G G T T G O T N N P
E D I Q E S L T R A F U W G G U
C Q R L B L O N M U T A F T T T
E V O U U N I N K I N G T R E E
N P U X B V R N Z T M A C I L R
T C E N T R A H P X O M H E E G
R L I S T Y L C I N E M A N V A
E K H M A L T C H I N T U D I M
P F N L I B R A R Y O Y C S S E
U O R C I N E L A R Y Y E E X $
E P D X L Y J T I O L E V V O C
G R E G A M E V S I N G E A N O
```

1 Leisure centre
2 Restaurant
3 Reading
4 Eating out
5 Watching television
6 Meeting friends
7 Computer games
8 Library
9 Playing sport
10 Listening to music
11 Cinema
12 Pub

Page 18

```
S R U N N R B S S S Q A B F
O E A S H U F H W K S A E
O E L T E N O S I E O L N
P T I E S N O O M E E H S
K E E P F I T T M F T K Q
C K H A O N B E I G T B N
Y K E E O G A Q K I N O G
C D A R T S L I G N K W O
A S H O S S L E E W I L O
N H C B C O K S Q U A S H
N C Y I Y S N O O K E R L
G N I C A N O E I N G N L
S O L S I N G S S L A W B
```

1 Running
2 Swimming
3 Step aerobics
4 Football
5 Keep fit
6 Bowls
7 Darts
8 Squash
9 Snooker
10 Canoeing
11 Cycling

Page 24

1G, 2E, 3F, 4A, 5B or L, 6C, 7J, 8K, 9B or L, 10H, 11I, 12D

Page 175

1   Variety of goods
2   Amount of car parking
3   Range of services
4   Leisure facilities
5   Ease of public transport
6   Cleanliness
7   Restaurants
8   Floral displays
9   Location of car parking
10 Presence of independent retailers

Index

Numbers in red show the page on which the word is defined or used as a key word.

Useful websites

Company/organisation	Web address	Comments

Useful websites

Company/organisation	Web address	Comments

Useful addresses

Company/organisation	Address	Telephone and fax

Useful addresses

Company/organisation	Address	Telephone and fax

Notes

Notes

Notes

Notes